Ranade IBM Series

K. BOSLER • *CLIST Programming*, 0-07-006551-9

H. MURPHY • *Assembler for Cobol Programmers: MVS, VM*, 0-07-044129-4

H. BOOKMAN • *Cobol II*, 0-07-006533-0

P. McGREW, W. McDANIEL • *In-House Publishing in a Mainframe Environment*, Second Edition, 0-07-046271-2

J. RANADE • *DB2: Concepts, Programming, and Design*, 0-07-051265-5

J. SANCHEZ • *IBM Microcomputers Handbook*, 0-07-054594-4

M. ARONSON • *SAS: A Programmer's Guide*, 0-07-002467-7

J. AZEVEDO • *ISPF: The Strategic Dialog Manager*, 0-07-002673-4

K. BRATHWAITE • *System Design in a Database Environment*, 0-07-007250-7

M. CARATHANASSIS • *Expert MVS/XA JCL: A Complete Guide to Advanced Techniques*, 0-07-009816-6

M. D'ALLEYRAND • *Image Storage and Retrieval Systems*, 0-07-015231-4

R. DAYTON • *Integrating Digital Services*, 0-07-016188-7

P. DONOFRIO • *CICS: Debugging, Dump Reading and Problem Determination*, 0-07-017606-X

T. EDDOLLS • *VM Performance Management*, 0-07-018966-8

P. KAVANAGH • *VS Cobol II for Cobol Programmers*, 0-07-033571-0

T. MARTYN • *DB2/SQL: A Professional Programmer's Guide*, 0-07-040666-9

S. PIGGOTT • *CICS: A Practical Guide to System Fine Tuning*, 0-07-050054-1

N. PRASAD • *IBM Mainframes: Architecture and Design*, 0-07-050686-8

J. RANADE • *Introduction to SNA Networking: A Guide to VTAM/NCP*, 0-07-051144-6

J. RANADE • *Advanced SNA Networking: A Professional's Guide for Using VTAM/NCP*, 0-07-051143-8

J. TOWNER • *CASE*, 0-07-065086-1

S. SAMSON • *MVS: Performance Management*, 0-07-054528-6

B. JOHNSON • *MVS Concepts and Facilities*, 0-07-032673-8

P. McGREW • *On-Line Text Management: Hypertext*, 0-07-046263-1

L. TOWNER • *IDMS/R*, 0-07-065087-X

A. WIPFLER • *Distributed Processing in the CICS Environment*, 0-07-071136-4

A. WIPFLER • *CICS Application Development Programming*, 0-07-071139-9

J. RANADE • *VSAM: Concepts, Programming, and Design*, Second Edition, 0-07-051244-2

J. RANADE • *VSAM Performance, Design, and Fine Tuning*, Second Edition, 0-07-051245-0

J. SANCHEZ • *Programming Solutions Handbook for IBM Microcomputers*, 0-07-054597-9

P. DONOFRIO • *CICS Programmer's Reference*, 0-07-017607-8

M. CARATHANASSIS • *Expert MVS/ESA JCL: A Guide to Advanced Techniques*, 0-07-009820-4

J. RANADE • *DOS to OS/2: Conversion, Migration, and Application Design*, 0-07-051264-7

Relational Databases

Concepts, Design, and Administration

Dr. Kenmore S. Brathwaite

AKI Group, Inc.
Brooklyn, New York

McGraw-Hill, Inc.

New York   St. Louis   San Francisco   Auckland   Bogotá
Caracas   Hamburg   Lisbon   London   Madrid
Mexico   Milan   Montreal   New Delhi   Paris
San Juan   São Paulo   Singapore
Sydney   Tokyo   Toronto

Library of Congress Cataloging-in-Publication Data

Brathwaite, Ken S.
    Relational databases : concepts, design, and administration /
Kenmore S. Brathwaite.
        p.   cm.   — (J. Ranade IBM series)
    Includes bibliographical references and index.
    ISBN 0-07-007252-3
    1. Relational data bases. 2. Data base design. I. Title.
II. Series.
QA76.9.D3B695   1991
005.75′6—dc20   91-16903
                                                        CIP

    2 3 4 5 6 7 8 9 0   DOC/DOC   9 7 6 5 4 3 2 1

ISBN   0-07-007252-3

The sponsoring editor for this book was Jerry Papke, the editing
supervisor was Nancy Young, and the production supervisor was
Suzanne W. Babeuf. This book was set in Century Schoolbook. It was
composed by McGraw-Hill's Professional Book Group composition unit.

Printed and bound by R. R. Donnelley & Sons Company.

Subscription information to BYTE Magazine:
Call 1-800-257-9402 or write Circulation Dept.,
One Phoenix Mill Lane, Peterborough, NH 03458.

To Monica Sanchez whose friendship has been a constant source of inspiration

Contents

Part 2   Relational Database Issues   145

Chapter 8.   Administration of the Database Environment   147

Preface

The work reported in this book was developed from notes I used in courses at the University of Alberta, from research conducted in relational databases since 1979, and from several consulting assignments at major Fortune 500 companies since 1984.

The main objective of this book is to provide selected readings about some topics that pertain to relational databases. In this volume, I provide readers with information about the traditional topics, data modeling, logical and physical database design, and normalization and about database-specific topics, SQL, DB2, and QMF. The book is intended for data administrators, database administrators, systems designers, and application programmers who want to gain familiarity with the relational database environment. Since the book introduces the topics at the fundamentals level, no prerequisites are required.

As the title suggests, the book provides information on interrelated topics that pertain to relational databases but deals with them independently of each other. Thus, each chapter in the book is intended to stand alone and any continuity between chapters is purely incidental. Therefore, the reader who is interested in normalization does not have to read the chapters on logical and physical database design.

Chapter 1 introduces the database environment and covers topics such as data analysis, functional analysis, data administration, data security, and systems development.

Chapter 2 deals with data models, data structures, and the role they play in corporate data modeling, business systems planning, and database design. Chapter 3 discusses designing database applications. It indicates how the phases fit into the systems development life cycle and discusses the deliverables of the phase. Chapter 4 discusses the normalization process and hot it applies to the design of efficient databases. The term *denormalization* is introduced in this chapter and is applied to physical database design, which is the subject of Chap. 2.

Chapter 6 discusses some of the issues involved in managing and controlling databases. The chapter devotes more space to external control mechanism than to internal or software mechanisms design to control the database.

Chapter 7 is probably the most intriguing chapter of the book. It highlights how the various departmental units of a management information systems department would support a database environment. The chapter details the support expected from data administration, logical and physical designers, operations, data control, and systems designers.

Part II of the book deals with more specific relational database topics such as DB2 and SQL/DS in Chapter 12, SQL in Chap. 13, and QMF in Chap. 14. The major departure in the last part of the book is in Chap. 16 and 17. In Chap. 16, I devote a large section to detailed discussions of performance issues and standards. The approach here is "this is how DB2 interfaces must be designed and coded if it must work efficiently." The standards discussed here are a must for any DB2 installation.

Finally, the book ends with a discussion of auditing DB2. This is the first book to devote any space to the auditing of DB2 and relational databases.

Kenmore S. Brathwaite
Brooklyn, New York
June 1991

Acknowledgments

I am grateful for comments and suggestions I received from Vic Howard, Stanley Locke, Francis Chin, and Jay Louise Weldon. The initial draft of the manuscript was ably typed by Arlene Bowman and Andrea Drayton. Their efforts are appreciated.

Relational Databases

The Relational Database Environment

Introduction
to the
Database Environment

Databases are evident in nearly every aspect of data processing today. Database technology became popular during the 1960s. During that period, the underlying data structures for the databases were hierarchical and network. The relational data structures, the subject which forms the backbone of this book, became popular during the 1970s.

Databases, collections of related data, were first marketed as approaches which would allow the greatest amount of data sharing while reducing data dependency and eliminating data redundancy. However, the advent of the database era also heralded new problems with data security, integrity, and privacy and new requirements for developing applications to take advantage of the new technology.

The database era also introduced new tools and management issues into the data processing environment. The remainder of this chapter discusses these tools and issues in greater detail.

1.1 DATA STRUCTURES AND DATA MODELS

Data structures and data models form the underlying structures for the database management systems (DBMSs). The data model is primarily a diagrammatical representation of entities and their association. The constraints of the DBMS are then superimposed on the data model to form the distinguishing features of each DBMS. The DBMS and its attendant software are the dominant tools in the database environment. These tools and their different features will be discussed in the next chapter.

Data structures and data models are the primary deliverables of logical database design, business systems planning activities or study, corporate data modeling activities, information engineering efforts, and knowledge-based systems design.

During the development of application programs, the data analyst collects information on the user requirements. This information is analyzed on the basis of the entities in which the user has an interest, and the data model is produced.

In business systems planning, the organization seeks to determine what data architecture can be developed to support its long-term data needs and assist it in achieving its goals and objectives. The data architecture is manifested as data models showing all the entities that the corporation will need.

In the information engineering and knowledge-based systems design, the data models become the building blocks. The systems designer uses these blocks to develop rule-based and data-based systems.

1.2   DATA ADMINISTRATION and DATABASE ADMINISTRATION

The database era has witnessed or caused the creation of several new staff positions. Two of these positions are data administration (DA) and database administration (DBA).

Data administration is defined as the establishment and enforcement of policies and procedures for managing the organization's data as a corporate resource. It involves the collection, storage, and dissemination of data as a globally administered and standardized resource.

Database administration is a technical function which performs database design and development, provides education on database technology, provides support to users in operational data management-related activities, and may provide technical support for administration.

Before a DA function can be established, certain conditions must exist:

- The management must be willing to take a long-range view of the cost structure.

- Data processing and line management must be prepared for the database approach with the associated protocols and standards.

- The entire line management must view data as a resource similar to raw materials, equipment, finance, and personnel.

The initiative in establishing a DA function can originate anywhere in the data processing organization. However, the most common starting point for the idea is the data processing professional who becomes concerned about the growing demands for the proper administration and management of the organization's data resources. On the other hand, there are times when top management focuses on the data resource issue before the data processing professionals. This usually occurs when management becomes aware of the need to manage data as a resource or when they experience a lack of information supporting a planning or decision-making process.

The establishment of the DA function is fast becoming a critical decision for most organizations. It is a very important area of database management, and once the decision is made to establish the function, everyone charged with that decision should ensure that top management not only supports the decision but becomes involved in the ongoing functioning of the DA department.

1.2.1 The Functions of Data Administration

Data administration serves to provide custody of the organization's data and coordinate data activities with systems developers and users. The DA functions include:

- Logical design of database systems
- Liaison to systems personnel during the application development process
- Training all relevant personnel in DA concepts and techniques
- Setting and monitoring data management standards
- Designing documentation, including data dictionaries
- Promoting and allowing for interdepartmental data sharing
- Resolution of data sharing conflicts
- Setting up facilities to monitor data usage authorization

The functions defined above are achieved by carrying out certain activities. These activities may or may not exist in all DA departments, but those which are classified as successful must undertake to carry out several or all of them. Among all these activities, the development and enforcing of policies governing data collection must rank as the most important activity conducted by the DA.

1.2.2 The Function of Database Administration

Database administration is concerned with the technical aspects of managing the data resource within the organization rather than the administrative aspects. These aspects require expertise in a particular DBMS and in designing the logical and physical structures of a database.

The DA function includes:

- Physical design of database systems
- Assisting in the negotiation for the acquisition of hardware and software to support the DBMS
- Acting as a contact point for users experiencing problems with the DBMS and associated software
- Monitoring the performance of the DBMS and the individual transactions against the databases
- Assisting in the development of long-term plans to ensure that adequate hardware capacity and facilities are available to meet the requirements of new systems and expansions of existing systems

1.3   THE DATA DICTIONARY

The data dictionary is the second most important tool in the database environment; the most important is the DBMS. The data dictionary is used to record facts about objects or events in the database environment in order to facilitate communication and provide a permanent record.

In a database environment, the data dictionary is based on giving information about the database itself, its contents, and its structure. The data dictionary focuses primarily on data-related components, such as:

- Data elements or attributes
- Data groups, rows, or tables
- Data structures
- Databases

The data dictionary should document the following information for the database environment:

- *Name and meaning:*   A unique identifier and descriptive information that conveys the full meaning of the component. The name is used for reference and retrieval purposes, while the description is valuable to managers and users.
- *Physical description:*   The physical characteristics of the components, such as size of an attribute or the length of a table row.
- *Edit and authorization criteria:*   Criteria to be used to test the va-

lidity of instances of the component, such as acceptable range of values (domain) for attributes or passwords for update of a database.

- *Usage:* Information about where and by whom or by what a component is used, such as the programs that can reference a given attribute.

- *Logical description:* The characteristics and structure of each user view of the database, such as logical relationships among tables or table rows.

- *Procedures:* Guidelines for human interaction with the database, such as for backup, recovery, and system restart.

- *Responsibility:* A record of the individual or organizational unit responsible for the generation and maintenance of the database component.

The data dictionary is a useful tool for ensuring data security, integrity, and privacy. It can be used, in the active mode, to protect attributes stored in the database. In the active mode, the DBMS will interrogate the data dictionary about the security level of the requestor. If the security level is greater than or equal to that of the requested item, the DBMS retrieves the item as requested.

The data dictionary can also be used in a passive mode to offer protection in the database environment. For example, if a user consults the dictionary to determine whether another user can have access to a particular item and denies or authorizes access on that basis, the dictionary is being used in a passive mode.

1.3.1 The Data Dictionary and Change Control

Changes are part of the evolutionary process of any database environment. The control of changes is a critical activity in this environment and is necessary for two reasons:

- To preserve the integrity of the data and maintain existing security standards

- To ensure that changes are communicated to all affected users and determine the impact of those changes

The data dictionary can be used to document how these changes are going to be communicated to the affected users and who the affected users are. This can often be accomplished by keeping an inventory of the occurrence of certain items destined for change, the programs that use these items, the data accessed by these programs, and the various users of the data.

1.3.2   The Data Dictionary and Standards

The data dictionary can be used to document the standards that are established in the database environment. These may include data processing, system, and programming standards.

Data processing standards cover the operation and control of computers, whether they are in a mainframe data center under management control or minicomputers in user locations.

Systems standards cover the various phases of the project life cycle, for the initial business information planning process through the steps of system proposal, functional design, detail design, programming, conversion, and post-audit.

The data dictionary must be able to document detailed guidelines and standards for deliverables from the user requirements collection and analysis phase, project-estimating techniques, evaluation of database programs and software, structured design methodology, and documentation standards.

Programming standards must include standard naming conventions, the languages used, program cataloging procedures, access control methods, JCL standards, and the utilities in use.

Standards that govern the naming of attributes can improve communication among database users and can catch inconsistency before it becomes part of the database.

1.4   DATA ANALYSIS IN THE DATABASE ENVIRONMENT

Data analysis is the process of determining the fundamental data resources of an organization. It deals with the collection of the basic entities and the relationship between the entities.

The primary purpose of data analysis is to organize and document all relevant facts concerning the organization's data resource. Data analysis has been used to:

- Determine the fundamental data resources of an organization
- Provide a disciplined approach toward documenting the existing data in terms of the entities and relationships it represents
- Provide the effective means of communicating with nondata processing users since it deals only with things with which the users are familiar
- Analyze the inherent structure of the data independently from the details of the applications
- Form a basis for data control, security, and auditing systems

- Organize all relevant facts concerning the organization's data
- Produce a point of reference, the entity model, against which a logical database structure for each of the database management systems can be designed
- Provide a sound basis for database design

Data analysis is regarded as consisting of two dependent parts. The first is entity analysis, which provides a means of understanding and documenting a complex environment in terms of its entities, their attributes, and relationships. The second is functional analysis, which is concerned with understanding and documenting the basic activities of the organization.

1.4.1   Functional Analysis

Functional analysis is concerned with an understanding and documentation of the basic business activities with which the organization is concerned. Functional analysis has the following objectives:

- To determine how entities are used so as to increase understanding of the entity model
- To provide a firm basis for transaction design
- To gather estimates of data usage for database design

Functional analysis may reveal attribute types of entities which had not been detected during entity analysis. Similarly, relationships between entities which had not been considered meaningful may be found to be required by certain functions.

The basic functions identified in functional analysis would be expected to be translated into transaction types in the data processing system.

Estimates of data usage provide a means for determining which access paths should be made most efficient.

In functional analysis, the data analyst identifies the events and functions. An event may be defined as a stimulus to the organization and functions as tasks that must be carried out as a direct result of the event.

1.5   STRUCTURED SYSTEMS DESIGN IN THE DATABASE ENVIRONMENT

The database environment has gained tremendously from the introduction of new structured design methodologies. The gains have been enormous in terms of shorter development times for systems and improved documentation of the design effort.

Database design refers to the process of arranging the data fields needed by one or more applications into an organized structure. That structure must foster the required relationships among the fields while conforming to the physical constraints of the particular DBMS in use. There are really two parts to the process. There is logical database design, which is then followed by physical database design.

Logical database design is an implementation—an independent exercise that is performed on the fields and the relationships needed for one or more applications. Physical database design is an implementation—a dependent exercise that takes the results of logical database design and further refines them according to the characteristics of the particular DBMS in use.

A variety of reasons make careful database design essential. These include data redundancy, application performance, data independence, data security, and ease of programming. All are important factors in the data processing environment and all can be adversely affected by a poor database design.

Currently, the structured database design methodology that is used the most is the entity-relationship (E-R) approach. This approach is representative of the class of methods that take entities and relationships as input.

Database design using the E-R model begins with a list of the entity types involved and the relationships among them. The philosophy of assuming that the designer knows what the entity types are at the outset is significantly different from the philosophy behind the other approaches.

The basic components that are necessary to achieve a database design methodology are:

- A structured design process that consists of a series of steps where one alternative among many is chosen
- A design technique to perform the enumeration required and to provide evaluation criteria to select alternatives at each step
- Information requirements for input to the design process as a whole and to each step of the design process
- A descriptive mechanism to represent the information input and the results at each design step

Achieving a design which results in an acceptable level of database performance for all users has become a complex task. The database designer must be ever conscious of the cost/performance trade-offs associated with multiple users of a single integrated database. Potential savings of storage space and expanded applicability of databases into corporate decision-making should be accomplished by a critical analysis of potential degradation of service to some users. Such degradation is to be avoided if possible. Acceptable performance for all users should be the goal.

Another aspect of database design is flexibility. Databases that are too tightly bound to current applications may have too limited a scope for many corporate enterprises.

Rapidly changing requirements and new data elements may result in costly program maintenance, a proliferation of temporary files, and increasingly poor performance.

A meaningful overall database design process should account for both integration and flexibility.

1.5.1 Inputs to the Structured Design Process

The major classes of inputs to the database design process are:

- General information requirements
- Processing requirements
- DBMS specifications
- Operating system and hardware configuration
- Application program specifications

The major results from the database design process are:

- Logical database structure, or user view
- Physical database structure, or storage view

The general information requirements represent various users' descriptions of the organization for which data is to be collected, the objectives of the database, and the users' view of which data should be collected and stored in the database. These requirements are considered to be process-independent because they are not tied to any specific DBMS or application. Database design based on these requirements is considered to be advantageous for long-term databases that must be adaptable to changing processing requirements.

Processing requirements consist of three distinct components: specific data items required for each application, the data volume and expected growth, and processing frequencies in terms of the number of times each application must be run per unit of time. Each of these components is very important to a particular stage or step of the database design process.

Performance measures and performance constraints are also imposed on the database design. Typical constraints include upper bounds on response times to queries, recovery times from system crashes, and specific data needed to support certain security or integrity requirements. Specific performance measures used to evaluate the final structure might include update, storage, and reorganization costs in addition to response requirements.

The three major outputs of the database design process are the logical database structure, the physical design structure, and the specifications for application programs based on these database structures and processing requirements. As a whole, these results may be considered the specification for the final database implementation.

1.6   LOGICAL AND PHYSICAL DESIGN

Database development is conducted in two phases: logical and physical. In logical database design, we take the user requirements, analyze them, and produce a data model. The constructs of the relevant DBMS are then superimposed on the data model to form the input to the physical database design process.

The physical database design process is primarily concerned with storing the data as defined in the logical data model and defining access paths to the stored data.

Logical and physical database design will be discussed at length in a later chapter.

1.7   APPLICATION PROTOTYPING

Prototyping represents a significant departure from traditional development methodologies, which are based on the systems development life-cycle framework.

In this framework, the application software development process consists of the following discrete, sequential phases:

- *Inception:* Identification of a problem requiring an information system solution
- *Feasibility study:* Analysis of the economic, technical, and organizational feasibility of the proposed system
- *Requirements analysis:* Determination of user needs and specifications of the information system output and of the characteristics required to satisfy those needs
- *Systems design:* Specification of software and hardware compo-

nents, including processing logic, files, program requirements, and procedures

- *Systems development and testing:*   Creation of programs and determination that software is correct

- *Conversion and installation:*   Introduction of the system to the user department

- *Operation and maintenance:*   Daily use of changes or updates to the application system

The life-cycle-based methodologies assume that the user requirements can be completely and correctly determined during the early phases of the application development process.

Prototyping helps developers solve problems and enhances development effectiveness by eliciting and clarifying user requirements and providing an early opportunity for users to test and experiment with software design and specifications. It is based on the premise that users understand tangible, functional models better than logical, abstract models and are therefore able to evaluate them more effectively.

1.7.1 Prototyping Procedures

The prototyping effort starts with the identification of an initial set of user requirements and specification for the system. The systems designer derives these initial requirements by interviewing users and reviewing the existing procedures and documentation.

As soon as a concrete set of system specifications is identified, the programming team develops a prototype as quickly as possible to meet these requirements. The prototype system is then implemented and operated in context. The users' hands-on operation of the prototype provides a basis for evaluation and learning.

Next, the systems designer solicits user feedback in terms of modification requests and new requirements. The prototype is then quickly modified in response to this feedback. The users again operate and evaluate the revised prototype. The prototype evaluation and revision cycle is repeated as many times as necessary until a satisfactory prototype is obtained.

1.7.2 Prototyping Software

Application software prototyping has become practical because of technological developments in data processing. The following tools are valuable for developing and modifying the prototype:

- *Data dictionaries, DBMS, and query languages:* These tools provide flexible, interactive, and integrated facilities for data storage and retrieval. A data dictionary provides a single definition, integration, and control point for all system entities. A DBMS facilitates data modeling and the creation and modification of databases and application programs. Query languages support ad hoc queries to databases.

- *Interactive programming languages or interactive nonprocedural modeling languages:* These powerful programming facilities allow rapid creation of the application and models. Nonprocedural languages enable the user to specify what needs to be done and the form the results should take. The software facilities then translate the requirements into procedural steps the developers must follow to produce the results.

- *Graphics and report generators:* These tools provide interactive and flexible data formatting and display capabilities. Graphics generators facilitate the creation of graphics (i.e., pie and bar charts and histograms). Report generators are tools to manipulate and format data for reports.

2

Data Models and
Data Structures

Data models are the basic building blocks for all database design. They provide the underlying structure for the dominant data structures of today's database management systems (DBMS). In addition, data models are used by many large corporations in business systems planning, strategic systems planning, and corporate data modeling.

Data models form the basis for entity-relationship (E-R) diagrams, or entity models as they are called, and are used to define a conceptual view, or real-world view, of data and the data requirements of an organization.

2.1 SOME DEFINING TERMS

A data model is defined as a logical representation of a collection of data elements and the association among these elements. The data model can be used to represent data usage throughout an organization or can represent a single database structure. It is to data what a logical data flow diagram is to a process. There are three types of data models: (1) conceptual, (2) logical, and (3) internal or physical.

The entity diagram is a representation of the relationship between entity classes. The representation allows us to include only those entities that are required to solve the particular data processing problem.

The entity diagram is essentially a real-world view of the organization's data in terms of the entities, attributes, and relationships. It is an example of a conceptual data model (see Fig. 2.1).

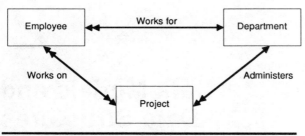

Figure 2.1 Example of a data model.

2.2 ENTITY AND ENTITY CLASSES

The terms *entity* and *entity classes* are used interchangeably in some of the current literature, whereas some researchers define the entity as an occurrence of an entity class. For example, EMPLOYEE is an entity class, whereas P. CAREY, an occurrence of the entity class EMPLOYEE, is an entity.

2.3 SUPERENTITIES AND ENTITY SUBTYPES

An entity may be broken down into smaller subgroups on the basis of the function of each subgroup. These subgroups are often called *entity subtypes*. The original entity is often referred to as a superentity.

The representation of entity subtypes and superentities is shown in Fig. 2.2, where the large boxes, EMPLOYEE and DEDUCTION, represent superentities. The small boxes, PART-TIME EMPLOYEE, etc., represent entity subtypes.

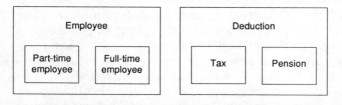

Figure 2.2 Representation of superentity and entity subtype.

2.4 TYPES OF RELATIONSHIPS

A relationship is defined as an association between two or more entities. In this section, we will discuss the types of relationships and how they are represented diagrammatically.

2.4.1 One-to-One Relationship

At a given time, one EMPLOYEE may be assigned to one DEPART-
MENT. The relationship between EMPLOYEE and DEPARTMENT
is termed *one to one*. This relationship is represented diagrammatically in Fig. 2.3, where the arrow denotes the one-to-one relationship.

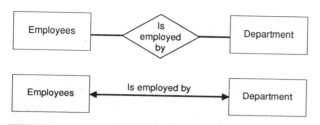

Figure 2.3   Representation of one-to-one relationship.

2.4.2 One-to-Many Relationship

At a given time many EMPLOYEES may be assigned to one
DEPARTMENT. The relationship between EMPLOYEES and
DEPARTMENT is termed *one to many*. This is represented diagram-
matically in Fig. 2.4.

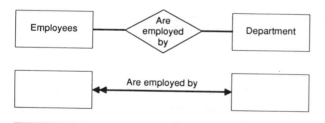

Figure 2.4   Representation of one-to-many relationship.

2.4.3 Many-to-Many Relationship

At a given time many EMPLOYEES may be assigned to many
DEPARTMENTS. The relationship between EMPLOYEES and
DEPARTMENTS is termed *many to many*. This is represented dia-
grammatically in Fig. 2.5.

2.4.4 Mutually Exclusive Relationship

At a given time an EMPLOYEE may be assigned to either DEPART-
MENT A or B but not to both. The relationship between EMPLOYEE

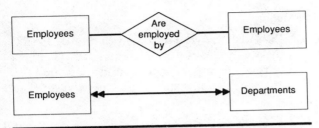

Figure 2.5   Representation of many-to-many relationship.

and either DEPARTMENT is termed *mutually exclusive*. This is represented diagrammatically in Fig. 2.6, where the vertical bar in the direction of DEPARTMENT A must always exist in the relationship. The circle indicates that DEPARTMENT B is optional. We obtain exclusivity by switching the circle and bar around in the relationship.

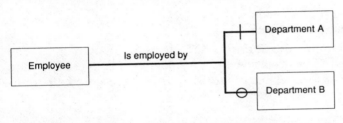

Figure 2.6   Representation of mutually exclusive relationship.

2.4.5   Mutually Inclusive Relationship

At a given time an EMPLOYEE may be assigned to both DEPARTMENT A and B. The relationship between EMPLOYEE and both DEPARTMENTS is termed *mutually inclusive*. This is represented diagrammatically in Fig. 2.7, where the presence of vertical bars in the direction of both departments indicates that both must coexist for the relationship to be completed.

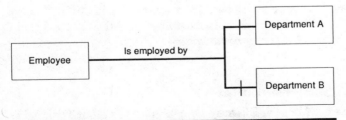

Figure 2.7   Representation of mutually inclusive relationship.

2.4.6 Mandatory Relationship

Sometimes an employer may rule that a DEPARTMENT must exist before the EMPLOYEE is hired. The relationship between EMPLOYEE and DEPARTMENT is termed mandatory. This is represented diagrammatically in Fig. 2.8, where the presence of a vertical bar in the direction of DEPARTMENT indicates that it must exist in the relationship.

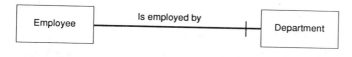

Figure 2.8 Representation of a mandatory relationship.

2.4.7 Optional Relationship

Sometimes an EMPLOYEE may be hired but not assigned to a DEPARTMENT. The relationship between the EMPLOYEE and DEPARTMENT is termed *optional*. This is represented diagrammatically in Fig. 2.9, where the presence of the circle in the direction of DEPARTMENT indicates that DEPARTMENT is not required to exist in the relationship.

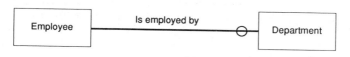

Figure 2.9 Representation of an optional relationship.

2.5 TRANSLATION OF E-R DIAGRAMS TO LOGICAL MODELS

E-R diagrams (models) are sometimes called business entity models since they reflect the business practices of an organization independently of any requirements for the underlying structure of a DBMS. However, in order for these diagrams to be processed by a computer, they must take on the constructs of the chosen DBMS. This section discusses the translation of E-R diagrams to logical data models.

Let's consider the following problem: A company is heavily project-oriented. Each project has one or more employees assigned to it full time, perhaps from different departments. Office space is assigned from time to time. Employees are assigned to an office in the departments in which they work. Several may share an office. Each department has one employee who is a manager. The company needs better information on projects, project costs, utilization of office space, and of employee's time.

2.5.1 Identification of Business Entities

When business entities are identified, careful consideration should be given to:

- A generally acceptable *name* for the entity
- A complete definition that makes clear what is included and what is excluded from the members of the entity
- The identification of a *business-oriented* entity that can be agreed upon across the enterprise

The name, abbreviation, identifier, and description of each business entity in our problem are shown in Table 2.1.

2.5.2 Determination of an Entity-Relationship Diagram for Problems

The determination of the E-R diagram for the problem may be carried out in a variety of ways. The simplest of these is to make the nouns in the problem statement entities and all the significant verbs relationships. The diagram resulting from the problem is Fig. 2.10, in which

TABLE 2.1   Business Entities—Illustrative Example

Entity name	Abbreviation	Identifier	Description
DEPARTMENT	DEPT	Unique ID of DEPT	An organizational unit in the company
PROJECT	PROJ	Unique ID of PROJ	A budgeted project now in progress
EMPLOYEE	EMP	Unique ID of EMP	An active (full- or part-time) employee of the department
OFFICE	OFFICE	Unique ID of OFFICE	A room allocated to a department

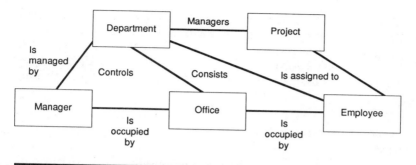

Figure 2.10   Entity-relationship diagram for illustrative problem.

the degree of the relationships between the entities may be denoted by using 1, M, single-headed or double-headed arrows.

2.5.3   Conversion of the Entity-Relationship
Diagram to a logical data model

The following steps are taken to convert E-R diagrams to logical data models:

- Convert business entities to data entities
- Represent the degree of the relationship between entities
- Convert many-to-many relationships to associations
- Look for conditional relationships
- Convert repeating groups to characteristic entities

If we apply the above steps, we can convert the E-R diagram of Fig. 2.10 to a logical data model shown in Fig. 2.11, where the single-headed arrow in the direction of DEPT and the double-headed arrow in the direction of PROJ indicate that one DEPT may administer

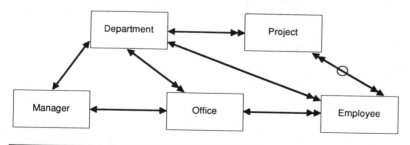

Figure 2.11   Logical data model for problem.

many PROJs. The double-headed arrows in the two directions, PROJ and EMP, indicate that many employees may work on many projects. The circle in the direction of PROJ indicates that there is an optional relationship between PROJ and EMP. In other words, an employee does not have to be assigned to a project in order to become an employee.

2.5.4 Conversion of Many-to-Many Relationship

Many-to-many relationships are common among business entities but awkward to represent in a logical data model by just two entities, since completeness would require much of the same attribute data appearing in each data entity. However, there is often a need to associate two business entities and, further, to store data about that association. Hence, for each many-to-many relationship, we create a new data entity with the following characteristics:

- The new data entity is called an ASSOCIATION data entity.
- It has a many-to-one relationship with each of the original data entities.
- It is a *child* of each of the original data entities.
- The unique identifier of the new data entity contains the unique identifier of both original data entities.

The new data entities form an association with the two original entities as shown in Fig. 2.12.

2.5.5 Handling of Repeating Groups

A repeating group is a group of one or more attributes of a data entity which may have multiple values for a given value of the unique identifier. Repeating groups are undesirable because:

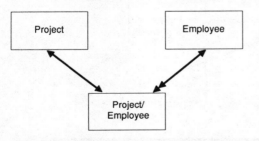

Figure 2.12 Representation of association entity.

- There is no way to pick a single occurrence within the group.
- They either impose limitations or cause more complex processing of the physical structure.

In order to remove repeating groups from the logical model, we must:

- Create a new entity called a CHARACTERISTIC data entity
- Create a one-to-many relationship between the original entity and the new entity
- Use the unique identifier of the original entity as part of the identifier of the new entity

Figure 2.13 illustrates the handling of repeating groups found in the entity PROJ. Let's say that PROJ has the following attributes: proj ID, name, address, cost, type, where cost, address, and type have several values. We can now create a one-to-many relationship with PROJ and a new entity PROJ-TYPE whose attributes are proj-type ID, type name, cost, and address. The relationship is now as shown in the figure.

2.5.6 Translation of Data Models to Logical Schemas

Logical schemas are defined as data models with the underlying structures of particular DBMSs superimposed on them. At the present time, there are the following three main underlying structures for DBMSs:

- Relational
- Hierarchical
- Network

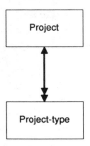

Figure 2.13 Representation of repeating groups.

2.6 OVERVIEW OF DBMS STRUCTURES

The hierarchical and network structures have been used for DBMSs since the 1960s. The relational structure was introduced in the early 1970s.

In the relational model, the entities and their relationships are represented by two-dimensional tables. Every table represents an entity and is made up of rows and columns. Relationships between entities are represented by common columns that contain identical values from a domain or range of possible values. Some of the commercially available relational DBMSs are:

Vendor	DBMS
IBM	SQL/DS, DB2
Tymshare	Magmum
Cincom	Supra
Relational Technology	Ingres

The hierarchical model is made up of a hierarchy of entity types involving a parent entity type at the higher level and one or more dependent entity types at the lower levels. The relationship established between a parent and a child entity type is one to many. At the same time, for a given parent entity occurrence, there can be many occurrences of the child entity type. Some examples of the hierarchical model are:

Vendor	DBMS
IBM	IMS
SAS	System 2000

In the network model, the concept of parent and child is expanded in that any child can be subordinate to many different parent entities or owners. In addition, an entity can function as an owner and/or member at the same time. There are several commercially available systems based on the network model, such as:

Vendor	DBMS
Cullinet	IDMS
Honeywell	IDS
Univac	DMS 1100

DEPARTMENT TABLE		
DEPARTMENT ID	DEPARTMENT NAME	DEPARTMENT ADDRESS
101	Engineering	Building A
102	Computer Science	Building B
103	Biology	Building C
104	Medical Technology	Building D

Figure 2.14 Representation of data in a relational model.

2.7 THE RELATIONAL DATA MODEL

We will use the example discussed in earlier sections of this chapter to illustrate the various relationships between the entities of an organization. The example will also serve to illustrate the various approaches to creating a relational database.

Consider the example shown in Fig. 2.14. This data is represented in a two-dimensional table, which is called a relational model of the data. The data represented in the figure is called a *relation*. Each column in the table is an *attribute*. The values in the column are drawn from a domain or set of all possible values. The rows of the table are called *tuples*.

In Fig. 2.14, the DEPARTMENT ID, 101, is the value of the key that uniquely identifies the first row of the table. This key is called the primary key.

We can now show how the relationship between DEPT and MANAGER in Fig. 2.11 can be represented in the relational model. Let us say that the MANAGER relation is shown as MANAGER ID, TITLE, NAME where MANAGER ID is the primary key of the relation. We can now represent the relationship as shown in Fig. 2.15.

In Fig. 2.15, column MANAGER ID is the primary key and DEPARTMENT ID is the foreign key. We can also have a column or set of columns identifying the rows of the table. This column is called a candidate key.

The creation of a table to represent the many-to-many relationship can be accomplished as follows:

- Create the ASSOCIATION entity as outlined earlier
- Create the ASSOCIATION entity table in a similar manner to the MANAGER table above

MANAGER TABLE			
MANAGER ID	DEPARTMENT ID	TITLE	NAME
MG101	101	Chief Scientist	Mr. Brown
MG102	102	Systems Designer	Mr. Charles
MG103	103	Sr. Biologist	Dr. Green
MG104	104	Sr. Technologist	Mr. Cave

Figure 2.15 Representation of a relationship in a relational model.

2.7.1 Advantages of a Relational Data Model

1. *Simplicity:* The end user is presented with a simple data model. His or her requests are formulated in terms of the information content and do not reflect any complexities caused by system-oriented aspects. A relational data model is what the user sees, but it is not necessarily what will be implemented physically.

2. *Nonprocedural requests:* Because there is no positional dependency between the relations, requests do not have to reflect any preferred structure and therefore can be nonprocedural.

3. *Data independence:* This should be one of the major objectives of any DBMS. The relational data model removes the details of storage structure and access strategy from the user interface. The model provides a relatively higher degree of data independence than do the next two models. To be able to make use of this property of the relational data model, however, the design of the relations must be complete and accurate.

2.7.2 Disadvantages of a Relational Data Model

Although some DBMSs based on the relational data model are commercially available today, the performance of a relational DBMS has not been comparable with the performance of one based on hierarchical or network data models. As a result, the major question yet to be answered concerns performance. Can a relational data model be used for a DBMS that provides a complete set of operational capabilities with required efficiency on a large scale? It appears today that technological improvements in providing faster and more reliable hardware may answer the question positively.

2.8 OPERATORS IN THE RELATIONAL DATA MODEL

The operators described for the relational data model are those that are found in relational algebra. These operators do not operate on individual rows but on entire tables, and they always produce tables as results. The following sections discuss some of these operators.

2.8.1 The Union Operator

The union operator combines the rows from two similar tables to four new tables. The new tables contain the rows that are in either or both of the original tables. Figure 2.16 illustrates the UNION of TABLE A and TABLE B producing TABLE C. In the figure the "noncommon" rows of the two original tables are combined to form a third table.

2.8.2 The Intersection Operator

The intersection operator combines the rows from two similar tables to form a new table that contains the rows that are in both of the orig-

TABLE A

STUDENT ID	STUDENT NAME	FACULTY ID
124	FRENCH	A
256	SMITH	B
301	JONES	C

TABLE B

STUDENT ID	STUDENT NAME	FACULTY ID
124	FRENCH	A
125	HARRIS	D
128	SHARP	E

TABLE C

STUDENT ID	STUDENT NAME	FACULTY ID
124 256	FRENCH SMITH	A B
301 125	JONES HARRIS	C D
128	SHARP	E

Figure 2.16   Example of the union operator.

TABLE A

STUDENT ID	STUDENT NAME	FACULTY ID
124	FRENCH	A
256	SMITH	B
301	JONES	C

TABLE B

STUDENT ID	STUDENT NAME	FACULTY ID
124	FRENCH	A
125	HARRIS	D
128	SHARP	E

TABLE C

STUDENT ID	STUDENT NAME	FACULTY ID
124	FRENCH	A

Figure 2.17   Example of the intersection operator.

TABLE A

STUDENT ID	STUDENT NAME	FACULTY ID
124	FRENCH	A
256	SMITH	B
301	JONES	C

TABLE B

STUDENT ID	STUDENT NAME	FACULTY ID
124	FRENCH	A
125	HARRIS	D
128	SHARP	E

TABLE C

STUDENT ID	STUDENT NAME	FACULTY ID
256	SMITH	B
301	JONES	C

Figure 2.18   Example of the difference operator.

inal tables. Figure 2.17 illustrates the INTERSECTION of TABLE A and TABLE B, which produces TABLE C. In the figure the "common" rows of the two original tables are combined to form a third table.

2.8.3 The Difference Operator

The difference operator combines two tables to produce a third table that contains all rows that are in the first table but not in the second. Figure 2.18 illustrates the difference of TABLE A and TABLE B, which produces TABLE C.

2.8.4 The Product Operator

The product operator combines the rows from two dissimilar tables to form a new table. In this case the third table is formed by concatenating each row of the first table with each row of the second table. Figure 2.19 illustrates the product of TABLE A and TABLE B, which produces TABLE C. In the figure the rows of TABLE A are "multiplied" by each row of TABLE B to form the rows of TABLE C.

2.8.5 The Select Operator

The select operator produces a second table from an original table based on a selection criteria. Figure 2.20 illustrates the select operator working on TABLE A to produce TABLE B. In the figure the select operator (FACULTY ID-A) produced TABLE B with one row as shown.

2.8.6 The Project Operator

The project operator produces a new table that contains all the rows from the original table but only a subset of the columns. Figure 2.21 illustrates the project operator working on TABLE A to produce TABLE B. In the figure the project operator is used to produce TABLE B in which the FACULTY NAME column is PROJECTed off. This operator is useful in the database environment to exclude from a user's view those columns that should not be seen by that particular user.

TABLE A

STUDENT ID	STUDENT NAME	FACULTY ID
124	FRENCH	A
256	SMITH	B
301	JONES	C

TABLE B

CLASS ID	CLASS LOCATION
124	AA
125	AB
128	AC

TABLE C

STUDENT ID	STUDENT NAME	FACULTY ID	CLASS ID	CLASS LOCATION
124	FRENCH	A	101	AA
124	FRENCH	A	102	AB
124	FRENCH	A	103	AC
256	SMITH	B	101	AA
256	SMITH	B	102	AB
256	SMITH	B	103	AC
301	JONES	C	101	AA
301	JONES	C	102	AB
301	JONES	C	103	AC

Figure 2.19 Example of the product operation.

TABLE A

STUDENT ID	STUDENT NAME	FACULTY ID
124	FRENCH	A
256	SMITH	B
301	JONES	C

TABLE B

STUDENT ID	STUDENT NAME	FACULTY ID
124	FRENCH	A

Figure 2.20 Example of the select operator.

TABLE A

STUDENT ID	STUDENT NAME	FACULTY ID	FACULTY NAME
124	FRENCH	A	BIOLOGY
256	SMITH	B	HISTORY
301	JONES	C	ART

TABLE B

STUDENT ID	STUDENT NAME	FACULTY ID
124	FRENCH	A
256	SMITH	B
301	JONES	C

Figure 2.21   Example of the project operator.

2.8.7   The Join Operator

The join operator combines the rows from two tables to form a third. The resulting table is formed in such a way that in each row the data values from the columns on which the join is based have the same data values. Figure 2.22 illustrates the join operator working on TABLES A and B to form TABLE C. The two originals tabled are joined on columns FACULTY ID-A and FACULTY ID-B when the rows of each column have equal values for the joined columns.

2.8.8   The Divide Operator

The divide operator compares the data values in columns from the two tables and produces a third table that eliminates the columns that have equal volumes. For example, the divide operator working on TABLES A and B of Fig. 2.22 will produce TABLE C as shown in Fig. 2.23, in which the empty table is produced since all rows of the two tables had values that matched.

2.9   SUMMARY

This chapter discussed data models and data structures that formed the building blocks of the relational DBMS. It emphasized the fact that relational DBMSs are based on solid algebraic theory. This was brought out in the discussion of relational operators.

TABLE A

STUDENT ID	STUDENT NAME	FACULTY ID-A
124	FRENCH	A
256	SMITH	B
301	JONES	C

TABLE B

FACULTY ID	CLASS ID	CLASS LOCATION
A	101	AA
B	102	AB
C	103	AC

TABLE C

STUDENT ID	STUDENT NAME	FACULTY ID-A	FACULTY ID-B	CLASS ID	CLASS LOCATION
124	FRENCH	A	A	101	AA
256	SMITH	B	B	102	AB
301	JONES	C	C	103	AC

Figure 2.22   Example of the join operator.

TABLE C

STUDENT ID	STUDENT NAME

Figure 2.23   Example of the divide operator.

3

Designing
Database
Applications

IBM's Database 2 (DB2) contains internal tables, called catalog tables, which provide information DB2 needs about the objects it manip-
ulates. This information is recorded automatically and is limited to
data required by DB2. Other information that you need as a database
analyst, designer, administrator, systems analyst, or programmer is
not recorded by DB2 in catalog tables. A full-featured data dictionary
should be used to document descriptive database design detail and related maintenance specifications.

Many CASE tools available today help you model a business enterprise in general and specific applications using some variation of the
entity-relationship (E-R) data model. These tools then allow you to automatically create Structured Query Language (SQL) data definition
language (DDL) statements directly from a data dictionary.

We will assume for most of this chapter that you will build SQL
DDL statements manually, but in reality you can use a tool such as
those available from Index Technology, KnowledgeWare, or Bachman
Information Systems to create SQL DDL statements automatically
from data definitions stored in the repository. Such tools can also help
you create application screens, reports, and process specifications.

Typical information you will want to record in your data dictionary
and repository includes (but is not limited to):

- Database name
- Database description
- Database owner

- Database creator
- Database status (test or production)
- Database copy or version
- Table names
- Table descriptions
- Table owners
- Table creators
- Table and column synonyms
- Data sources
- Table cross-references
- Related columns

The designer of a database should determine how to record information not automatically recorded in the DB2 dictionary. You could extend the DB2 catalog into a comprehensive data dictionary by creating your own tables. If you do this, you will want to be able to define relationships with data already stored in the catalog tables. You need to be able to document entities, relationships, and business rules and relate these to your relational database implementation. You also need to describe how data integrity is maintained, how integrity is audited, what tuning options you have chosen for improved performance, and how you use database utilities.

We now turn to the translation of our data model into the physical database as managed by DB2. Each component of our logical data model will be transformed into a corresponding relational implementation.

3.1 STORAGE GROUPS

A storage group is a set of DASD volumes that DB2 uses to create table spaces and index spaces when physical datasets are allocated for table spaces or index spaces. DB2 refers to volumes defined in the requested storage group and allocates the dataset in one of the designated volumes. You do not have to concern yourself with setting VSAM deletes and defines (unless you choose the option to do so). DB2 will place datasets into the storage group. You can define multiple storage groups in a DB2 system, and a volume can appear in more than one storage group. If you remove a volume from a storage group, you still must delete the datasets on the removed volume.

Here is how you can use SQL to create a storage group:

CREATE STOGROUP PROD0003 VOLUMES
       (VOL010, VOL011, VOL012)
       VCAT (DB2PROD)

PROD0003 is the name of the storage group, VOL0101, VOL011, and VOL012 are volume serial numbers of the DASD volumes included in the storage group. DB2PROD is the name of the VSAM catalog. You can specify a VSAM catalog password with the PASSWORD option, if you wish.

3.2 DATABASES

A DB2 database is a collection of table and index spaces. Each table space can contain one or more physical tables. The database concept is used as an operational unit for starting and stopping all accesses to tables and indexes and for granting and revoking selective access authorizations to tables and indexes. You use a database to refer to a set of tables (representing logical data entities) and their indexes for operations purposes.

Here is how you can use SQL to define a database DSN4FEMP with a default storage group of DSN4F001 and a default buffer pool BP1:

CREATE DATABASE DSN4FEMP
       STOGROUP DSN4F001
       BUFFERPOOL BP1

Buffer pools are virtual storage areas used by DB2 to temporarily store pages of table space and index data during execution of SQL statements. DB2 lets you define four separate buffer pools, one 32K-byte buffer pool (BP32K) and up to three 4K-byte buffer pools (BP0, BP1, and BP2).

You can define a minimum and maximum size for each buffer pool. If a data request needs more than the minimum space, DB2 expands the buffer to the maximum size and then contracts the buffer pool as soon as possible. Buffer pool BP0 is used for accessing DB2 catalog tables and directory data.

Usually, you should use one buffer pool (say, BP0) of the maximum size possible according to the availability of real data storage. For certain critical applications, you can assign accessed table and index spaces to a buffer pool of their own, but overall system performance might suffer. Try to avoid using 32K-byte buffer pool (PB32K) if you can. If you want to use different buffer pools for tables located in the same database, you can specify the buffer pool in the CREATE TABLESPACE statement to override the buffer pool specifications given in the CREATE DATABASE statement (see above).

If you need to destroy the database and start over, you can use this SQL statement:

DROP DATABASE DSN4FEMP:

3.3 TABLE SPACES

DB2 requires that you define the physical location where logical entity information will be stored via relational tables. The DB2 concept of a table space is used to map the logical tables into physical storage locations. You should create a table space to contain one or more DB2 tables and have some options available to you which might affect performance noticeably:

1. You could combine several small tables into a single table space.

2. Large tables, as well as unrelated ones, should probably occupy separate table spaces.

When you create a table space, DB2 stores information about it in the DB2 catalog (one row in SYSIBM.SYSTABLESPACE and one row in SYSIBM.SYSTABLEPART for each table partition). Here is the SQL statement by which you create a simple table space:

```
CREATE TABLESPACE DSN4FEMP.DSN6TDEP
    IN DSN6APP
            FREEPAGE        7
            PCTFREE         10
    USING STOGROUP DSNF  4001
            PRIQTY          100
            SECQTY          20
            LOCKSIZE                ANY
    BUFFERPOOL              BP0
    CLOSE                   NO
    DSETPASS         T410000
```

FREEPAGE and PCTFREE are options you use to control the free space distribution in your table spaces. FREEPAGE defines how a free page will be reserved in the table space. In our example, the value 7 indicates that one in every eight pages in the table space will be left empty during load and reorganization operations. If no pages are free for insertion of new table rows, DB2 will try to insert them in a nearby page (within 64 pages at both sides of the home page). You need to set FREEPAGE so that new rows can be placed in nearby pages and so that, when sequential prefetch of rows is used, rows in nearby pages are read ahead. The default FREEPAGE value is 0.

PCTFREE defines the percentage of space to be left empty in each page. In our example, the value 10 tells DB2 that 10 percent of the page space should be left empty during load and reorganization. The default PCTFREE value is 5 percent.

PCTFREE can affect multiuser accesses because the larger the value the less table data will be locked in any one page. For a low PCTFREE value (less than 10 percent) used on a table with a clustered index, if the rate of row inserts and updates is high, clustering will decrease rapidly. To minimize the need for frequent table space reorganizations, specify a large amount for PCTFREE and a low value for FREEPAGE (less than 10 percent).

The LOCKSIZE option defines the degree of locking you want in a table space when accessing data. Three levels of locking can be used:

1. *TABLESPACE:* The entire table space is locked in shared or exclusive mode, with no page locks. This can reduce concurrency, so try to use it for read-only tables or tables that don't require high concurrency.

2. *PAGE:* Pages are locked individually, and lock escalation will not take place. This option will maximize concurrency, but locking and unlocking at the page level uses more CPU cycles. Use frequent COMMIT WORK statements in applications to free up database resources. With this option, DB2 will not escalate locks to the table space level, even if the number of page locks exceed the NUMLKTS limit. You can manually escalate locks with the LOCK TABLE statement.

3. *ANY:* This option allows DB2 to escalate from page locks to table space locks. If the total number of locks exceeds the maximum for the table space (NUMLKTS), DB2 will escalate locks by changing lock size to TABLESPACE and releasing all PAGE locks. This option gives you some degree of balance in table space concurrency. Use the ANY option and tune the NMLKTS parameter to achieve concurrency without excessive page-locking overhead for most of your applications. The best solution for production databases is to lock pages or tables depending on your processing needs, but ANY will work well for building a prototype.

BUFFERPOOL overrides the buffer pool parameter specified in the CREATE DATABASE statement.

CLOSE NO lets you avoid repeated opening and closing of a table space that is private or accessed only by batch applications.

You have the choice of placing one or multiple tables in a table space. Usually, it is best to have only one table per table space. The reasons for this include:

- You use LOCK TABLE to lock entire tables.
- An index is not used.
- Table space reorganization will rebuild the clustering order of a single table.
- During table space recovery or reorganization, the entire table space is locked.
- If you drop a table, the freed-up space does not become available until a table space reorganization.

You might want to have two or more tables in a table space if:

- Tables are related through primary keys.
- Tables are frequently used together.
- You have many small tables.
- Virtual storage is a constraint.

A table space can be changed using a statement like this:

```
ALTER TABLESPACE DSNF4EMP.DSN6TDEP
      LOCKSIZE              ANY
      BUFFERPOOL            BPO
      CLOSE                 YES
      DSETPASS              T410000
      FREEPAGE              6
      PCTFREE               15
```

You can destroy a table space using this statement:

```
DROP TABLESPACE DSNF4EMP.DSN6TDEP;
```

3.4 TABLES

In our logical data model, an entity is a uniquely identifiable thing such as a person, physical object, business entity, place, or simply a concept about which we desire to record information. In the DB2 relational environment, a TABLE is a collection of rows, with each row representing a specific, identifiable object. A relational table can be said to represent an entity class of unique objects called entities. An entity is a logical object, whereas a table is a relational object that can be mapped by DB2 into physical datasets stored on magnetic disk media.

Our relational database design begins with the translation of each logical entity into a relational table. Each entity should have a business definition, a unique identifier (the primary key), descriptive attributes, and a set of relationships with other entities in your data model. Supertype and subtype entities, for example, should be translated into distinct relational tables. Even though subtypes have the same identifier (primary key) as the corresponding supertype, each subtype entity may have its own attributes. It may participate in relationships other than that of the supertype.

You should assign to each relational table a unique but meaningful name using a consistent naming standard. These standards should include rules for abbreviations and synonyms. Try to be consistent with the names chosen in your logical data model, keeping in mind the naming restrictions imposed by DB2 (18 characters). Try to use intuitive names that are meaningful to users and programmers who will use your database.

The SQL statement for creating a DB2 table begins like this (it will be completed later):

```
CREATE TABLE DSN4FEMP.EMPLOYEE
  (column-name    data-type    NULL/NOT NULL,
```

You can change the structure of existing tables with the ALTER TABLE statement:

```
ALTER TABLE DSNF4EMP.EMPLOYEE   ADD SPOUSE-NAME
                                       CHAR (10);
```

If you want to destroy a table, you can use a statement similar to this:

```
DROP TABLE DSN4EMP.EMPLOYEE;
```

The EMPLOYEE table description will be removed from the DB2 catalog. All indexes and views defined on this table will be automatically removed as well.

3.5 COLUMNS

The attributes of your logical entities will be implemented in DB2 relational tables as columns of the tables. Each column must be identified. One or more columns of the table will consist of the unique identifier, or primary key. Relationships and the corresponding foreign keys will also be implemented as columns of tables. Primary and foreign keys should be the only columns that appear in more than one table because they represent the only attributes that appear in more than on entity. The SQL statement that creates a DB2 table, with the column information added in the outer set of parentheses, is:

CREATE TABLE EMPLOYEE (ID   CHAR (6)   NOT-NULL
                       LAST-NAME   CHAR (20)
                       FIRST-NAME   CHAR (10),
                                •
                                •
                                •
                       BRANCH-CODE   CHAR (6)

The first parameter in each column definition is the column name. The second parameter defines the data type for the column. DB2 lets you define columns to be one of several data types (see Fig. 3.1).

DB2 allows you to define a column to contain NULL values. Any column can contain NULL values unless you define that column as NOT NULL in the CREATE TABLE statement. A NULL value rep-

INTEGER	Fullword binary integer (31 data bits plus sign bit)
SMALLINT	Halfword binary integer (16 data bits plus sign bit)
DECIMAL (p.q)	Packed decimal number (p digits and sign with 0 p 16 and decimal point q digits from the right with q p)
FLOAT	Doubleword floating point number (hexadecimal fraction of 15 digits precision and binary integer exponent)
CHAR(n)	Fixed-length character string of n characters (0 n 255)
VARCHAR(n)	Variable-length character string of n characters (n is the maximum, must be less than the page size for the table space)
LONG VARACHAR	Variable-length string of characters equal to the number of bytes left in a data page
GRAPHIC(n)	Fixed-length string of double byte characters of length $n(1 = n = 27)$
VARGRAPHIC(n)	Varying length string of double byte characters of maximum length n
LONG VARGRAPHIC	Varying length string of double byte characters whose maximum length is equal to the number of bytes left in a data page
DATE	DB2 date format
TIME	DB2 time format
TIMESTAMP	DB2 date and time format

Figure 3.1   DB2 data types.

resents a value that is unknown or not applicable (it is *not* the same as a blank or zero). If an employee's address column is NULL, we know that the address exists but that it is unknown.

In our EMPLOYEE table example, we specified NOT NULL for the ID column only. This is to guarantee that every employee record in the EMPLOYEE table will always contain a genuine (NOT NULL) employee ID value. On the other hand, we allow any or all of the other columns of the EMPLOYEE table to contain NULL values for those columns.

3.6 INDEXES

Indexes are used to create a logical order to rows in a table, based on the value of one or more columns of the table. When you create one or more indexes for a table, DB2 generates an index space dataset in which to place the index. You create indexes on tables for four reasons:

1. *Performance:* An index can be used to avoid scanning an entire table space dataset.

2. *Uniqueness:* An index can be used to ensure that each row in a table is unique.

3. *Physical sequence:* An index can force DB2 to store rows of a table in a certain physical sequence to reduce input-output operations against tables during sequential accesses.

4. *Table space partitioning:* If you want to partition a table space, you must use a clustering index (described below).

When you update a data page of a table, all rows in the page are locked from access by others until your application commits work, terminates, rolls back work, or bends. The operations on indexes are similar except that you can define up to 16 index subpages to manage locking contention. The DB2 optimizer decides whether or not an index will be used for a particular data request, so you should review any index to see how it is being used in practice. Indexes are not copied for recovering tables. Therefore, it is more efficient to create indexes prior to loading tables with data. Here is one way to use SQL to create a nonpartitioned index:

```
CREATE UNIQUE INDEX EMPLOYEE.INDX1-EMPLOYEE ON
                                               EMPLOYEE
   (ID            ASC)
   CLUSTER
   USING VCAT   (DB2PROD)
```

or

```
USING STOGROUP PROD0003
            PRIQTY            20
            SECTY              8
    PCTFREE                   15
    SUBPAGES             BPO
    CLOSE                    NO
```

The UNIQUE keyword indicates that you want values for columns in the index to be unique (rows with identical column values cannot be inserted into the table). CLUSTER tells DB2 to store rows of the table in physical sequence based on the index column(s).

INDX1-EMPLOYEE is the name of the index, EMPLOYEE is the name of the table for which the index is created, and ID is the column upon which indexing should be based (more than one column could have been used for the indexing). DB2PROD is the name of the VSAM catalog if you do not use storage groups.

If you use storage groups, you would use PROD0003 as the storage group for our example. PRIQTY indicates the number of kilobytes of storage to be allocated in the initial allocation of space for the index space dataset. SECQTY defines the number of kilobytes to be allocated if the index space dataset needs more space. Each secondary allocation will use this amount for the allocation. PCTFREE defines the percentage of each index page to be left empty when loading or reorganizing table data.

SUBPAGES tells DB2 to allow 16 subpages for each index page. CLOSE NO indicates that DB2 should leave the index dataset open after each data access.

You can change the attributes of an index like this:

```
ALTER INDEX EMPLOYEE.INDX1-EMPLOYEE
        BUFFERPOOOL          BPO
        CLOSE                   YES
        FREEPAGE                 7
        PCTFREE                 10
```

An index can be removed from the database using a statement like this:

```
DROP INDEX EMPLOYEE.INDX1-EMPLOYEE;
```

3.7 VIEWS

You can use views to restrict access to a table or to simplify the set of data that a user wants access to. Views are derived from tables or other views. If you wish, you can have DB2 check a view definition before allowing inserts and updates to the underlying (base) tables referred to the view. Create a view with a statement like this:

```
CREATE VIEW EMPLOYEE.EMPLOYEE-VIEW1
    (ID, LAST, FIRST, BRANCH)
    AS SELECT ID, LAST-NAME, FIRST-NAME, BRANCH-ID
        FROM DSNF4EMP.EMPLOYEE
        WHERE BRANCH-ID = SALES01
    WITH CHECK OPTION
```

The line beginning with AS SELECT can contain any valid SQL SELECT statement except those with FOR UPDATE OF, ORDER BY, and UNION. A SELECT statement defines rows and columns of data to be retrieved from the base table(s) when accessing the data using the view. SQL SELECT statements will be explored in detail in the next chapter.

EMPLOYEE-VIEW1 is the name of the view being defined. Next is a list of columns to be accessed from the EMPLOYEE table. It must correspond to the columns referenced in the SELECT statement that follows (although the name of a particular column can be different in the view definition than it is in the SELECT statement. If you do not specify column names in the view, the table column names will be used.

The WITH CHECK OPTION forces inserts and updates to be checked by DB2 against the conditions you have specified in the SELECT statement. You can use this option to be sure that a user cannot change the BRANCH-ID number to a value other than that identified in the view definition. A summary of DB2 objects is shown in Fig. 3.2.

3.8 MAINTAINING REFERENTIAL INTEGRITY

Referential integrity of a relational database was discussed briefly in Chap. 2; we now address it more completely in order to ensure that our database design is properly maintained. Domain integrity is also desirable, but it is not supported fully in DB2. Implementing referential integrity without domain support means that integrity of references is maintained, but we then have no way to ensure that all values of a table column involved in a primary or foreign key belong to a valid domain. Thus, domain integrity and referential integrity provide different types of database integrity.

Referential integrity refers to relationships between tables and requires nonnull foreign key values to reference existing key values. We would like our relational DBMS to handle referential integrity en-

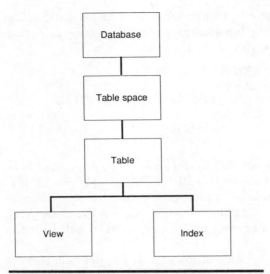

Figure 3.2 Summary of DB2 objects.

forcement for us, avoiding the need for each application program to be coded with referential integrity constraints. DB2 does this for us in Version 2, and we gain several benefits by letting DB2 handle referential integrity enforcement for us:

- Greater application development productivity
- Consistent handling of integrity constraints (coded once in DB2, not numerous times in application programs)
- Probable performance gains
- Possible simplification of applications, resulting in greater ease in maintaining application programs.

3.8.1 Application Development Productivity

Application development productivity can be enhanced as follows if DB2 handles referential integrity:

- Application programmers do not need to code separate SQL statements to enforce integrity—DB2 handles all integrity enforcement.
- Application programs require less debugging during testing and maintenance.

- You may write fewer and shorter programs.

- Ad hoc updates will automatically behave correctly without referential data inconsistencies.

DB2-supported referential integrity is desirable because referential constraints are supported for situations such as transaction program updates, ad hoc updates, and batch updates.

3.8.2 Performance

If you choose to let DB2 handle your referential integrity, you may expect performance equal to or greater than if you enforce integrity in your application code. This is because fewer SQL calls are required in application programs and because DB2 will (usually) choose the most efficient method for integrity enforcement.

Coding referential integrity enforcement yourself can be more flexible and could perform better than the DB2-supported method because you can use knowledge of your application and data to bypass certain checks that DB2 will try to perform. Usually, though, DB2-supported referential integrity will give you at least as good performance as you can get from writing your own enforcement routines.

3.8.3 Application Characteristics

When deciding whether you want to let DB2 handle referential integrity enforcement, you have three options:

1. Don't enforce referential integrity.
2. Check referential integrity at the time that a transaction is committed to the database.
3. Enforce referential integrity in real time.

You might choose option 1 for applications such as read-only applications where referential integrity has already been enforced. Option 2 might be used for application where your data must be consistent only as specific points in time, such as with batch programs. If you absolutely must maintain referential integrity at all times, such as with a debit transaction or credit authorization, option 3 may be the best solution.

In order to have DB2 manage referential integrity, you need to specify primary keys when you build your tables:

```
CREATE TABLE EMPLOYEE
    (ID                  CHAR(6)    NOT NULL,
    FIRSTNAME            CHAR(15)   NOT NULL,
    LASTNAME             CHAR(20)   NOT NULL
    DEPTID               CHAR(5)
    .
    .
    .
    PRIMARY KEY          (ID)
    FOREIGN KEY          (DEPTID)   REFERENCES DEPARTMENT
            ON DELETE SET NULL                              );
```

The primary key is defined to be the ID column. A foreign key is defined for the DEPTID field, referencing the DEPTID field in the DEPARTMENT table. When a department record is deleted from the DEPARTMENT table, all rows in the EMPLOYEE table with DEPTID (foreign key in EMPLOYEE) equal to the deleted DEPTID (primary key in DEPARTMENT) have their DEPTID values set to NULL.

3.8.4 Relationships

Representation of relationships in the relational model were discussed in the last chapter, but a short review will be helpful. Basically, two types of relationships will exist: one to many and many to many (one to one is a special case of the one to many case).

You should implement a one-to-many relationship in your database as a foreign key in one table that frequently references the primary key of the other table. Attributes of the relationship become attributes of the relation containing the foreign key (see Fig. 3.3).

Order-Num + Order-Line is the primary key of the Order Lines table. Order-Num is a foreign key of this table; it references the primary key of the Order table, Order-Num.

Implement many-to-many relationships as two one-to-many relationships. A new table with a primary key consisting of a concatenation of primary keys of the other two tables will be created. If this type of relationship has attributes, they will become attributes (columns) of the newly created table. Each primary key column becomes a foreign key in the new table and references the primary key of the corresponding entity (see Fig. 3.4).

The primary key of the new Order-parts table is Order-Num + Order-Line + Part-Num. The two foreign keys are Order-

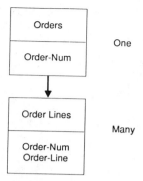

Figure 3.3   A one-to-many relationship.

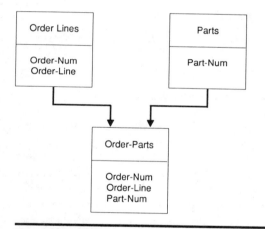

Figure 3.4   DB2 implementation of a many-to-many relationship.

Num + Order-Line, which references the Order table, and Part-Num, which references the Parts table.

3.8.5   Choosing DELETE and UPDATE Options

Absolute dependencies: An entity in our conceptual database model is absolutely dependent on another entity in the model if there exists one and only one occurrence of the second entity for each occurrence in the first entity. For our Order–Order-Line relationship, an order line cannot be inserted unless the corresponding order exists, and an order line must be deleted before, or at the same time as, the corresponding order is inserted. We can use these rules for absolute dependencies:

1. Foreign keys must be defined NOT NULL.
2. DELETE rules should most likely be CASCADE.
3. UPDATE rules should most likely be CASCADE.

Deletes and updates require a more restrictive rule.

Conditional dependencies: This kind of dependency occurs when, for each occurrence of an entity, there is one or no occurrence of the other entity in the relationship. A student can be conditionally dependent upon a course. The student can exist even if he or she is not a member of a class, and a student does not disappear from the database if the class is dropped. These rules apply for conditional dependencies:

1. Foreign keys must be defined NULLable.
2. DELETE rules should most likely be RESTRICT or SET NULL.
3. UPDATE rules should most likely be RESTRICT or SET NULL.

The operations you perform in practice will determine whether RESTRICT or SET NULL options will be chosen.

Although these relationships look identical to each other (see Fig. 3.5), in common usage the business rules are different. An order must have one or more order lines and an order line must appear on one order, but a course does not have to have students (the course appears in the course catalog but is not currently offered), and a student does not have to be taking a course (the student is taking a semester off). This, of course, is just one particular use of the student-course relationship for illustrative purposes. (You could easily find a different situation that does require an absolute dependency, such as a requirement that a student take at least one course in order to be considered a student for registration purposes.)

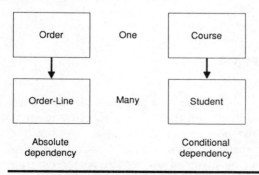

Figure 3.5   Table dependencies.

Depending upon the entity-relationship diagramming technique you use for data modeling, the absolute and conditional relationships will look different. The Bachman technique uses an open circle to indicate a conditional (optional) dependency and a solid circle to indicate that the dependency is absolute (mandatory). Other graphical techniques use similar notations to make the distinctions, such as a 0 (zero) for optional and a 1 for mandatory.

3.8.6 Referential Integrity Design Considerations

You must understand the data modeling semantics of foreign keys when selecting columns to participate in them. Pay careful attention in the following situations:

Multiple columns in a foreign key: Foreign keys are treated by DB2 as NULL if one or more columns of the key contains a NULL. DB2 does not, however, require that all columns participating in the foreign key be defined as NULL. If the DELETE rule is SET NULL and Course-Dept column is defined NOT NULL, a delete of a row in the Course table has a potential foreign key value in Student of NULL (Null Course-Dept and the existing value for Course-Num) (see Fig. 3.6).

Columns shared among multiple foreign keys: If the domain of column(s) participating in a foreign key is different from that of the foreign key, some semantic modeling problems can occur. When a table has foreign keys referencing tables representing mutually exclusive domains of the foreign key, information can be lost if a

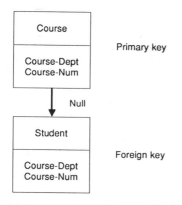

Figure 3.6 Problems with multiple-column foreign keys.

row is deleted in one of the two referenced tables. If a row in one of the product type tables referenced by the Prod-Type-Code foreign key in the Part table is deleted, the information in that record of the Part table becomes invalid (see Fig. 3.7).

Columns shared with the primary key: The SQL data manipulation language restriction that prohibits multiple-row updates of primary key columns can influence your decisions when choosing foreign key columns. Single-row updates of foreign keys become mandatory when a column appears in both a foreign and a primary key (see Fig. 3.8). Cus-Num appears in both the primary and foreign keys of the Invoice table. The only way to change all foreign key values of the Cust-Num column is by using a series of single-row updates.

Referential structures containing cycles: A cycle can exist in a referential structure if a table references itself, either directly or through other intermediate tables (see Fig. 3.9). Cycles prevent insertion of any rows into the involved tables unless rows of at least one of the tables are inserted with NULL foreign key values. In this situation, at least one of the foreign keys must be defined as nullable. Delete operations can be prevented in cycles having delete rules of RESTRICT unless one or more of the foreign keys is defined as nullable. You should not use referential integrity constraints to maintain one-to-one correspondences between rows of two tables.

If a graduate student studies courses in a certain department and also teaches in that department, inserting rows for that student in both the Department and Student tables cannot be done unless one of

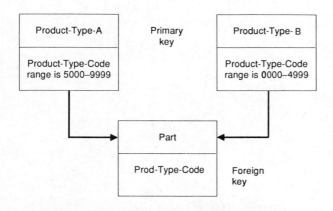

Figure 3.7 Problems with shared columns between foreign keys.

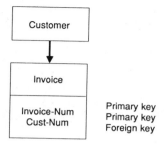

Figure 3.8 Problems with foreign key columns shared with the primary key.

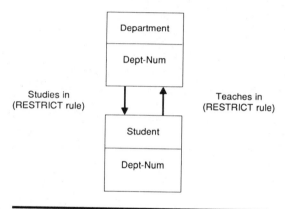

Figure 3.9 Problems with cycles and foreign keys.

the foreign keys is NULL. Thus, the foreign keys cannot both have a RESTRICT rule defined for them.

If we need to maintain two tables containing information about our customers (for performance reasons or because we need to maintain too many columns for one DB2 table), we might create some problems for ourselves (see Fig. 3.10).

For example, if the primary key of each customer table is CUST-ID, this field also becomes a foreign key to the other table in order to maintain one-to-one correspondence between tables. The foreign keys are also primary keys, so they cannot be NULL. This causes insert operations to fail. Also, the delete rule cannot be CASCADE because the tables would be delete-connected. The delete rule cannot be SET

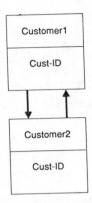

Figure 3.10   Problems with one-to-one correspondence with two-table cycles.

NULL because the foreign keys as part of the primary keys cannot be NULL. The delete rule must be RESTRICT, which will cause delete operations on either table to fail.

For other examples and a more detailed explanation of DB2 referential integrity considerations, refer to the *IBM DATABASE 2 Referential Integrity Usage Guide*. The examples here were structured after those in the guide, which includes some performance considerations and trade-offs that you should consider after your tables and rules have been designed:

1. Whether or not you should use STOGROUP or user-defined pagesets
2. What table space organization you should use
3. How many tables you should include per table space
4. What indexes you must create
5. What lock size parameters you should use

IBM lists these and other referential integrity implementation guidelines:

1. Don't mix different referential structures within a table space set, because of locking considerations.
2. Create indexes on foreign key columns to improve delete and update performance.
3. Keep granularity of locks small and hold locks for the minimum time possible for maximum throughput and performance.

   a. Avoid specifying LOCKSIZE TABLESPACE.
   b. Avoid ISOLATION (RR) on DB2 plans.
   c. Increase the size of NUMLKTS to minimize lock escalations.
   d. Consider using RELEASE (COMMIT) on DB2 plans.
4. For multiple row operations, all qualifying row operations must complete successfully or the operation must be rolled back.
5. Referential integrity constraints must be valid at commit time and can be achieved by one of the following:
   a. Defer integrity checking until the end of each SQL statement.
   b. Defer integrity checking until commit time.
   c. Check integrity in flight.
6. Establish quiesce points frequently when you have a need to re-cover logically related table spaces to a prior point in time.
7. Use the ENFORCE CONSTRAINTS option of the LOAD utility when you load table space sets with data.
8. CHECK primary and foreign key indexes before CHECK DATA. Use the SCOPE PENDING rather than SCOPE ALL option.

3.8.7 User-Enforced Referential Integrity and Locks

When using user-enforced referential integrity, you need to ensure that table locks, as explained below, are taken properly:

Exclusive lock: This type of lock must be taken by our application program so that no concurrent read or update operation is permitted by other tasks until commit time. With DB2, an exclusive lock will be taken when an SQL UPDATE or DELETE statement is used on a table row. Depending upon how you have set the LOCKSIZE parameter for the table space in which the table resides, the exclusive locks might be taken at the table space, table, or page level.

Persistent lock: This lock must be taken so that no concurrent update can occur by other tasks for a time controlled by a user. Concurrent read operations are allowed during the lock time. DB2 takes a persistent lock when one of the following actions is taken on a table row:

1. ISOLATION (RR) is chosen on the rebind of a plan, guaranteeing repeatable reads. Locks are released at commit time.
2. The following occurs: (*a*) A cursor is opened, (*b*) the desired row is fetched, and, (*c*) the cursor is not closed. The lock is released when the ISOLATION(CS) on the rebind of a plan and the next

fetch causes the cursor to move to another table page or when the cursor is closed or at commit time. Depending on the LOCKSIZE parameter on the table space, the persistent lock may be taken at the table space level, the table level, or the page level.

3. VERIFY to check for the existence of rows in a table without concern for the type or duration of a lock. DB2 provides this for single-row SELECT statements and cursor-related SELECT operations.

3.8.8 Implementing User-Enforced Referential Integrity Constraint Rules

Insert rule: The procedure for implementing an insert rule is as follows:

1. Obtain a persistent lock on a row in the Invoice table to prevent the update of the primary key or deletion of the row:

    ```
    DECLARE CURSOR1 CURSOR FOR
    SELECT INVOICE-NUM FROM INVOICE
    WHERE INVOICE-NUM = '00505'
    ```

2. Insert a row in Table B:

    ```
    OPEN CURSOR1
    FETCH CURSOR1 INTO :hostvariable
    ```

    If the FETCH is successful,

    ```
    INSERT INTO INVOICE VALUES
    INVOICE-LNUM, INVOICE-DATE,CUSTOMER-ID
    ```

    Otherwise, print out an error message.

3. Release the lock on the row in Table A:

    ```
    CLOSE CURSOR1
    ```

4. Commit work whenever desired.

Delete rule with restrict: Here we will delete row '00500' in the INVOICE table.

1. Obtain an exclusive lock on row '00500' to prevent insertion of rows with foreign key values of '00500':

    ```
    UPDATE INVOICE
    SET INVOICE-NUM = INVOICE-NUM
    WHERE INVOICE-NUM = '-00500'
    ```

Set INVOICE-NUM equal to itself to guarantee that rollback is not required if dependent rows exist (the value of INVOICE-NUM has not changed).

2. Verify INVOICE-ITEM for dependents with foreign key values equal to '00500':

```
SELECT COUNT(*) INTO :hostvariable
FROM INVOICE-ITEM
WHERE INVOICE-NUM '00500'
```

3. Commit work whenever desired.

Delete rule with cascade—single level: We delete row '00500' in the INVOICE table as follows:

1. Obtain an exclusive lock on row '00500' in the INVOICE table to prevent rows from being inserted into INVOICE-ITEM with foreign key values of INVOICE-NUM = '00500':

```
DELETE FROM INVOICE WHERE INVOICE-NUM = '00500'
```

2. Delete all rows from INVOICE-ITEM that have a foreign key value of INVOICE-NUM = '00500':

```
DELETE FROM INVOICE-ITEM WHERE INVOICE-NUM = '00500'
```

3. Commit work whenever desired.

Delete rule with cascade—multiple levels: Now assume that we have dependent rows in the INVOICE-ITEM table such that the cascading delete of INVOICE-ITEM rows must extend table INV-ITEM-CMTS:

1. Obtain an exclusive lock on row '00500' of INVOICE:

```
DELETE FROM INVOICE
WHERE INVOICE-NUM = '00500'
```

2. Obtain an exclusive lock on row in INVOICE-ITEM with foreign key value of INVOICE-NUM = '00500' and delete:

```
DECLARE CURSOR CURSOR1 FOR
SELECT INVOICE-NUM FROM INVOICE
WHERE INVOICE-NUM = '00500'
OPEN CURSOR1
FETCH CURSOR1 INTO :hostvariable
DELETE FROM INVOICE-ITEM WHERE
CURRENT OF CURSOR1
```

3. Delect a row from INV-ITEM-CMTS table with a foreign key value of INVOICE-NUM = '00500'.

```
DELETE FROM INV-ITEM-CMTS
WHERE INVOICE-NUM =  :hostvariable
```

4. Continue, deleting the next qualifying row in INVOICE-ITEM table with INVOICE-NUM = '00500':

   FETCH CURSOR1 INTO :hostvariable
   DELETE FROM INVOICE-ITEM
   WHERE CURRENT OF CURSOR1

5. Commit whenever desired.

Delete with set null: We delete row '00500' from INVOICE, which may have dependent rows in INVOICE-ITEM:

1. Obtain an exclusive lock and delete row '00500':

   DELETE FROM INVOICE
   WHERE INVOICE-NUM = '00500'

2. Update all rows in INVOICE-ITEM which have foreign key values of INVOICE-NUM = '00500':

   UPDATE INVOICE-ITEM
   SET INVOICE-NUM = NULL
   WHERE INVOICE-NUM = '00500'

3. Commit work whenever desired.

Update foreign key: We would like to update all rows in INVOICE-ITEM which reference INVOICE by having INVOICE-NUM = '00500':

1. Obtain an exclusive lock on '00500' row in INVOICE, if desired.
2. Obtain a persistent lock on row '00640' in INVOICE:

   UPDATE INVOICE SET INVOICE-NUM = '00640' WHERE
   INVOICE-NUM = '00500'

3. Update INVOICE-ITEM foreign key value from '00500' to '00640':

   UPDATE INVOICE-ITEM SET INVOICE-NUM = '00640' WHERE
   INVOICE-NUM = '00500'

4. Release the lock on row '00640' (by closing a cursor if you are using cursor logic).
5. Commit work whenever desired.

Update rule with set null: We would like to update the primary key value of INVOICE-NUM in INVOICE from '00500' to '00640':

1. Update row '00500' to '00640':

   UPDATE INVOICE
   SET INVOICE-NUM = '00640'
   WHERE INVOICE-NUM = '00500'

2. Update all rows in INVOICE-ITEM that have foreign key values of INVOICE-NUM = '00500' to NULL:

```
UPDATE INVOICE-ITEM
    SET INVOICE-NUM = NULL
    WHERE INVOICE-NUM = '00500'
```

3. Commit work whenever desired.

3.8.9 Comments on User-Enforced Referential Integrity

For our examples we assumed only one rule was in force. In reality, you may need to have a mix of these rules. You should always be mindful of the interrelationships of rules in your referential structures. Make sure you take all rules into account when you build SQL statements.

When designing programs to process complex referential structures, you should process from the top to the bottom. For an invoice, process the invoice header first and then proceed to the invoice items. You should check all RESTRICT rules first to avoid extra processing upon violation of a RESTRICT rule.

For your user-enforced referential integrity constraint checking to work, you must ensure that all updates follow the constraint rules. If you do not, your data integrity will probably be compromised.

3.8.10 Altering table structures and referential integrity

You can use the ALTER statement to change the structure of DB2 tables, but if you are using DB2-enforced referential integrity checking, you must take some additional factors into account. You can add a primary key to a table if the table has an existing unique index on the primary key column(s). This index then becomes the primary index. Suppose that the INVOICE table has a unique index defined for the INVOICE-NUM column:

```
ALTER TABLE INVOICE
    PRIMARY KEY (INVOICE-NAME);
```

You can drop the primary key by issuing a statement like this:

```
ALTER TABLE INVOICE
    DROP PRIMARY KEY;
```

This will drop the primary key from the INVOICE table (if you have alter privileges on both the parent and child tables), but the primary index still exists as a unique (but no longer primary) index. The INVOICE table has a dependent table, INVOICE-ITEM, so the relationship between them is dropped when the primary key of the parent table is dropped. This means that you must be careful when you drop the primary key of a table which has dependents. If you enforce referential integrity yourself, your application programs must be coded to manage relationship between tables.

ALTER TABLE can be used to add foreign keys to existing tables as follows:

    ALTER TABLE INVOICE
        FOREIGN KEY CUST (CUSTID) REFERENCES CUSTOMER
        ON DELETE SET NULL;

You can have multiple foreign keys defined for a table as long as two foreign keys in the table do not reference the same parent table. Use a separate statement to define each foreign key. The foreign key of a table for which you are defining foreign keys must have an existing primary key, and the parent table must already exist. Each foreign key should have a delete rule defined for it: ON DELETE RESTRICT, ON DELETE CASCADE, or ON DELETE SET NULL. If you do not define a delete rule, ON DELETE RESTRICT is used as the default.

You can drop a foreign key by naming its relationship in the DROP FOREIGN KEY clause of the ALTER TABLE statement:

    ALTER TABLE INVOICE
        DROP FOREIGN KEY CUST;

You must have ALTER privileges on both parent and child tables. Only the relationship defined by the foreign key is dropped—no key columns or their values are changed. You should carefully consider what effect the dropping of a foreign key will have on your applications if DB2 is managing referential integrity for you.

You can use DROP TABLE to drop a table and all referential constraints in which the table is either a parent or child. The primary index of the table is dropped when the table is dropped. Remember that when you drop a table, you remove its definition from the DB2 catalog, along with all the relationships in which the table participates. Again, this can affect applications that depend upon DB2 to manage referential integrity. The following DROP TABLE STATEMENT drops not only the table INVOICE but also a foreign key relationship CUST, which is defined for the INVOICE-ITEMS table:

    DROP TABLE INVOICE;

3.9 SUMMARY

All of the DB2 logical and physical design issues discussed in this chapter are supported in some way by the Bachman Data Base Analyst tool for DB2. This tool lets you forward engineer data models built in the Bachman Data Analyst tool (or captured from non-DB2 systems) into the Data Analyst tool. The Data Base Analyst tool also supports true DB2 reengineering by generating SQL CREATE and ALTER statements for input to DB2. It also allows you to extract DB2 designs from a DB2 catalog for import into the Data Analyst tool (see Fig. 3.11). Figures 3.12 and 3.13 show typical Bachman Data Base Analyst diagram styles.

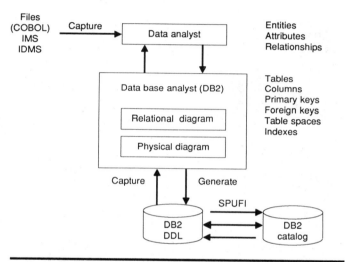

Figure 3.11   Bachman DB2 Database design.

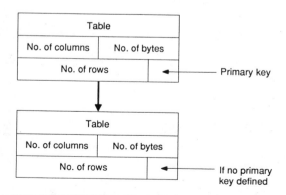

Figure 3.12   Bachman Data Base Analyst design diagram.

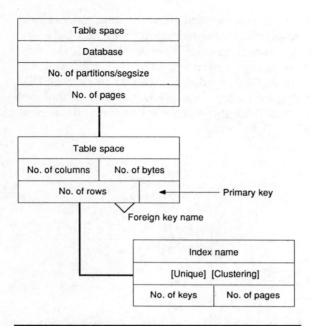

Figure 3.13   Bachman physical design diagram.

Data Normalization

Data normalization is a set of rules and techniques concerned with:

- Identifying relationships among attributes
- Combining attributes to form relations
- Combining relations to form a database

An attribute (also called a field) is a data element. A relation is a group of attributes. For example, a relation called PERSON may contain the attributes NAME, ADDRESS, DATE OF BIRTH, HEIGHT, WEIGHT, SALARY, etc. A human resources database may contain many relations such as PERSON, DEPENDENTS, and DEPART-MENTS.

4.1 MODIFICATION ANOMALIES

A major objective of data normalization is to avoid a modification anomaly, which occurs when facts are lost about two attributes with one deletion. A few examples will help illustrate modification anomalies. Suppose that the following attributes in a marketing database are grouped together in one record:

CUSTOMER NAME
CUSTOMER NUMBER
CUSTOMER ADDRESS
PRODUCT NUMBER
PRODUCT DESCRIPTION
PRODUCT PRICE

In order to insert information regarding a new product, a fictitious "dummy" customer must be created. Information about an existing product will be lost if all customer information corresponding to that product is deleted.

Grouping together the three attributes EMPLOYEE IDENTIFICATION NUMBER, DEPARTMENT NAME, and DEPARTMENT MANAGER provides a second example. If the department changes managers, information for every employee in the department must be modified. This problem can be eliminated by forming two groupings of information:

Group 1	Group 2
EMPLOYEE IDENTIFICATION NUMBER	DEPARTMENT NAME
DEPARTMENT NAME	DEPARTMENT MANAGER

Decomposing a set of attributes into smaller groups is one of the techniques used to reduce or eliminate modification anomalies. Suppose that the following attributes are grouped together:

FOOTBALL PLAYER'S UNION IDENTIFICATION NUMBER
NAME OF TEAM
TEAM COACH
TEAM OWNER

Numerous update problems exist with this grouping. For example, if a team obtains a new coach or new owner, the information for every player belonging in the union must be changed. If all the union players resign from the union, information concerning the coach and owner will be lost. The coach and owner names must be repeated each time a new union player is added. These modification problems are eliminated by forming two groups:

Group 1	Group 2
FOOTBALL PLAYERS' UNION	NAME OF TEAM
IDENTIFICATION NUMBER	TEAM COACH
NAME OF TEAM	TEAM OWNER

A student new to database design may assume that modification anomalies are rare or unusual. An experienced database designer, however, should have no problem relating to fictitious dummy records that are created to support the insertion of new data. Storage devices contain volumes of data that could be deleted except for a few fields that may still contain required information.

4.2 LOGICAL AND PHYSICAL DATABASE DESIGN

Data normalization is an analytical technique that is useful during logical database design. The viewpoints and requirements of the user are considered during the logical database design process. The appropriate attributes, and relationship among these attributes, are identified and defined. The user's view of the data should not be inhibited by technical hardware and software limitations. Thus hardware and software characteristics are not considered during logical database design.

Eventually the logical database design is implemented physically. Physical implementation is the first stage at which the particular characteristics of the database management system (DBMS) are considered. For example, departures from an ideal logical design may be justified by improved system performance. Data normalization will provide a clear understanding of the relevant attributes and the relationships among these attributes. This knowledge will benefit the technicians who are implementing the physical database.

4.3 APPLICATION DATABASES AND SUBJECT DATABASES

Database methodology continues to increase in sophistication. Early data processing applications used a separate file for each application. The design was generally simple and easy to implement. Such a design, however, results in data redundancy and high maintenance costs. Initial database technology was often used to create a separate database for each application. This approach improved data organization and helped reduce data redundancy. Application databases were widely used in the 1970s.

Subject databases provided an additional degree of sophistication. These databases relate to organizational subjects (e.g., products, customers, personnel) rather than to conventional computer applications (e.g., order entry, payroll billing). A subject is data-driven rather than application-driven. This kind of database is independent of any application and is shared by multiple applications. A large initial investment in analysis (including data normalization) is reduced substantially.

Consider the three application databases in Fig. 4.1: a payroll database, an employment history database, and a medical claims database. Each database comprises data common to all the applications. The data must be stored and maintained by all the applications.

Data redundancy increases physical storage requirements and the

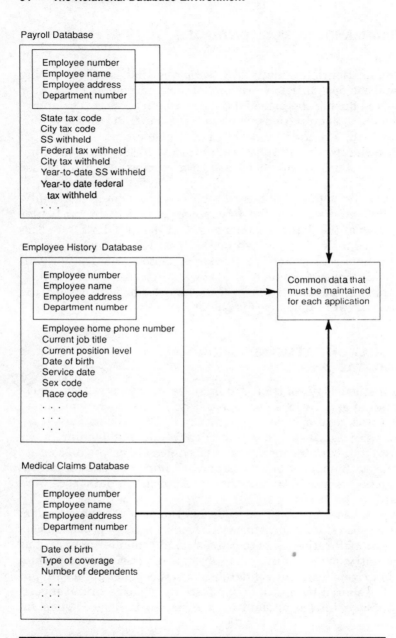

Figure 4.1   Three applications databases.

likelihood of update errors. For example, a change of address must be entered in three different databases. Inconsistencies may result if the definition of an attribute changes within the various application databases. For example, a home address may differ from a mailing address. Multiple application databases may also cause other incompatibilities (e.g., different computer languages or different formats).

The combination of subject databases and application programs is illustrated in Fig. 4.2. Each application program uses data that is stored and maintained in one database. Ad hoc inquiries will use the same data. Thus consistency is maintained among various applications.

Successful design of subject databases and comprehensive information systems usually incorporates both strategic data planning (to identify the required databases) and logical database design (to specify the logical record structure of those databases). Data normalization should be included as an integral part of the logical design process.

4.4 DATABASE MODELS

Databases are often classified as hierarchical, network, or relational. Hierarchical models are also called tree structures (see Fig. 4.3a). A typical corporate organization chart is an example of a hierarchical model. The president of the company is at the top of the structure. Several vice presidents may report to the president. A department head may report to one of the vice presidents. This reporting structure may continue for several additional levels of management.

The terms *parent* and *child* are often used in describing a hierarchical model. The president is the parent of the vice presidents, and each vice president may be the parent of several department heads. A vice president is also a child of the president, while a department head is a child of a vice president.

An important characteristic of the hierarchical model is that a child is associated with only one parent. The relationship between parent and child is one to many. A hierarchical business organization implies that an employee must report to only one supervisor.

A network model allows a child to be associated with more than one parent (see Fig. 4.3b). The relationship between students and classes is an example of a network structure. A student may enroll in more than one class, and most classes contain more than one student. A tree can be considered a special type of network.

The distinction between hierarchical and network models is rapidly becoming obsolete. Software enhancements allow network models to be represented in the major hierarchical database systems. Conse-

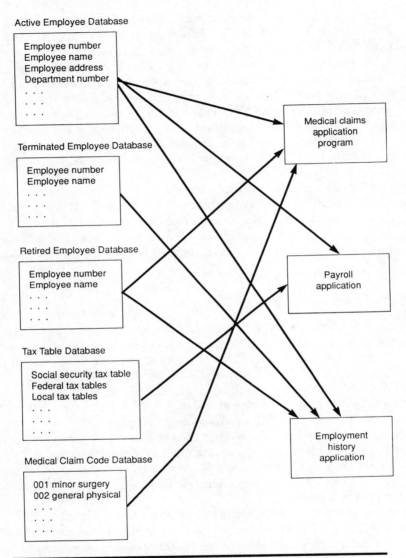

Active Employee Database

Employee number
Employee name
Employee address
Department number
. . .
. . .
. . .

Terminated Employee Database

Employee number
Employee name
. . .
. . .

Retired Employee Database

Employee number
Employee name
. . .
. . .
. . .

Tax Table Database

Social security tax table
Federal tax tables
Local tax tables
. . .
. . .
. . .

Medical Claim Code Database

001 minor surgery
002 general physical
. . .
. . .
. . .

Medical claims
application
program

Payroll
application

Employment
history
application

Figure 4.2   Subject databases and applications programs.

quently the database designer in a hierarchical environment has considerable flexibility.

The relational model is a significant departure from the hierarchical or network models. Relationships among attributes are represented in a tabular format using rows and columns (see Fig. 4.3c). The model is conceptually easier to understand than either the hierarchi-

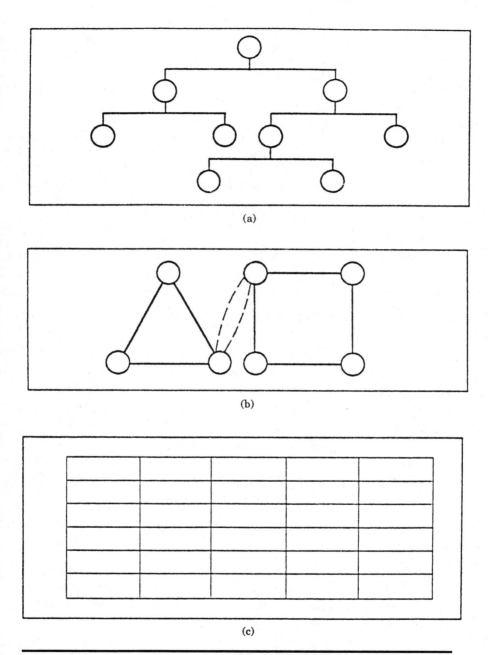

Figure 4.3 Database models. (*a*) A hierarchical database model; (*b*) A network database model; (*c*) A relational database model.

cal or the network model. However, the hardware and software required to implement the relational model efficiently are limited.

Data normalization is a valuable logical design technique in hierarchical, network, and relational database environments, although the normalization process is most often associated with relational databases because it is defined in the context of the relational model. Also, during the initial implementation of hierarchical and network designs, the distinction between logical and physical design was not as prevalent. Techniques used in the logical design process (such as data normalization) were not emphasized in these earlier implementations. Data normalization will increase in importance as the relational structure gains acceptance and as the distinction between logical and physical design is incorporated in the database design process.

4.5   BENEFITS OF DATA NORMALIZATION

The major benefits of a correctly normalized database from the management information systems (MIS) perspective include:

- Development of a strategy for constructing relations and selecting keys
- Improved interfaces with end-user computing activities (e.g., ability to accommodate unplanned inquiries)
- Reduced problems associated with inserting and deleting data
- Reduced enhancement and modification time associated with changing the data structure (e.g., adding or deleting attributes)
- Improved information for decisions relating to physical database design
- Identification of potential problems that may require additional analysis and documentation

From the end user's perspective, a correctly normalized database will translate into improved response time from the MIS organization, as well as improved capabilities for end-user computing activities.

A database contains facts and figures. Information is the knowledge derived from this data. Intelligent planning and decision making require accurate, reliable information. Data normalization is a major component used to transform data into information.

4.6   STRUCTURE OF A RELATION

The definitions and descriptions presented in this section are fundamental to understanding data normalization. Included are a discussion of the basic relational structure, a definition of functional dependence, a discussion of repeating groups, and an introduction to relational operators. This material will be used throughout the text to define, describe, and illustrate the data normalization process.

4.6.1 The Properties of a Relation

A set of two-dimensional tables called relations is required in the normalization process. Relations are developed using the 14 structural properties presented in Fig. 4.4.

4.6.2 Other Definitions

The following definitions are also helpful in discussing data normalization:

- The union of relations R and S is the set of all attributes contained in either R or S or in both. RS is used to denote the union of relations R and S.

- The intersection of relations R and S is the set of all attributes contained in both R and R. R∩S is used to denote the intersection of relations R and S.

- The difference of relations R and S is the set of all attributes contained in relation R but not in relation S. R − S is used to denote the difference of relations R and S.

- A decomposition of a relation R is a set of relations R such that the union of relations R is the relation R.

4.7 FUNCTIONAL DEPENDENCE

The following table represents the annual sales of a corporation over a 16-year period:

YEAR	SALES (billions of dollars)	YEAR	SALES (billions of dollars)
16	3.0	8	2.0
15	3.2	7	1.7
14	3.1	6	1.4
13	3.0	5	1.2
12	2.6	4	1.1
11	2.4	3	1.1
10	2.0	2	1.1
9	1.9	1	0.9

---

1. Columns (also called attributes) represent fields. Each column has a unique name.

2. Each column is homogenous. Thus the entries in any column are all of the same type (e.g., age, name, employee number, etc.).

3. Each column has a domain, the set of possible values that can appear in the column.

4. Rows (also called tuples) represent records. If a relation has n columns, each row is an n-tuple.

5. The order of the row and columns is not important.

6. No duplicate rows are allowed.

7. Repeating groups (collections of logically related attributes that occur multiple times within one record occurrence) are not allowed.

8. A candidate key is an attribute (or set of attributes) that uniquely identifies a row. A candidate key must possess the following properties:

   a. Unique identification: For every row, the value of the key must uniquely identify that row.

   b. Nonredundancy: No attribute in the key can be discarded without destroying the property of unique identification.

9. A primary key is a candidate key selected as the unique identifier. Every relation must contain a primary key. The primary key is usually the key selected to identify a row when the database is physically implemented. For example, a part number is selected instead of a part description.

10. A superkey is any set of attributes that uniquely identifies a row. A superkey differs from a candidate key in that the superkey does not require the nonredundancy property.

11. A foreign key is an attribute that appears as a nonkey attribute in one relation and as a primary key attribute (or part of a primary key) in another relation.

12. A composite key is a key that contains more than one attribute.

13. A relational schema is a set of attributes, dependencies, and other constraints that characterizes a relation. Various types of dependencies and constraints are discussed throughout this book.

14. An instance of a relation is a set of rows that populate the relation. Updates to the database will change the instance of a relation over time. An instance is valid if all the dependencies and other constraints specified in the relational schema are satisfied.

Figure 4.4 The structural properties of a relation.

This data is in relational form. Each row contains two attributes (YEAR and SALES). The primary key attribute is YEAR. This relation (called SALESDATA) is represented using the following notation:

SALESDATA (<u>YEAR</u> SALES)

In this format, the relation is named first. Each attribute is then identified; the primary key attribute(s) are underlined.

Only one sales value exists for a specific year. More than one year, however, may be associated with the same value of sales. For example, the sales value 3.0 is associated with years 16 and 13. Thus YEAR determines SALES but SALES does not determine YEAR. SALES is a function of YEAR (i.e., SALES depends upon YEAR). If SALES is represented as y and YEAR as x, the familiar mathematical expression $y = f(x)$ represents the functional relationship between y and x. Thus a discrete mathematical function may be displayed as a relation.

The 16 values in the SALES attribute are a subset of the domain SALES. Understanding the domain of an attribute is important both in determining the size of the corresponding field and in checking the validity of data. Knowledge of the domain is also used in advanced normalization theory.

Functional dependence in relational terminology can be defined formally as follows: For any R, attribute A is functionally dependent on attribute B if, for every valid instance, the value of B determines the value of A. The phrase "for every valid instance" ensures that the functional dependency is valid irrespective of any insertions or deletions. The functional dependence of A on B is represented by an arrow as follows: B → A. Thus YEAR → SALES. The notation B ↛ A is used to denote that A is not functionally dependent on B.

An instance does not imply a dependency. However, dependencies imply valid instances. An instance cannot be used to show that a dependency is true but can be used to demonstrate that a dependency is false.

An attribute can be functionally dependent on a group of attributes rather than on a single attribute. An attribute (or group of attributes) X is fully functionally dependent on another collection of attributes Y, if X is functionally dependent on the whole of Y but not on any subset of Y.

Functional dependence is limited to numerical data. For example, consider the relation AIRPORT (NAME, CITY) with the following instance:

NAME	CITY
LaGuardia	New York
Hopkins	Cleveland
J. F. Kennedy	New York
Logan	Boston
Burke Lakefront	Cleveland
L.A. International	Los Angeles

Each airport name is unique, but more than one airport can be associated with a given city. Thus CITY is functionally dependent on NAME but NAME is not functionally dependent on CITY. These facts are expressed in the following ways:

CITY = f(NAME)   NAME = f(CITY)
NAME → CITY   CITY → NAME

4.8   INFERENCE AXIOMS FOR FUNCTIONAL DEPENDENCIES

A given set of functional dependencies will usually generate additional, implied functional dependencies. For example, $X \rightarrow Z$ can be inferred from the dependencies $X \rightarrow Y$ and $Y \rightarrow Z$. Sets of inference axioms associated with functional dependencies were developed by W. W. Armstrong ("Dependency Structures of Database Relationship." *Proceedings, IFIP Congress, 1974*) and by C. Berri, R. Fagin, and J. H. Howard ("A Complete Axiomatization for Functional and Multivalued Dependencies in Database Relations," *Proceedings, 1977 ACM SIGMOD International Conference on Management of Data,* Toronto, August 1977). These axioms are presented in Fig. 4.5. All possible functional dependencies implied by a given set can be generated using these axioms.

Suppose that A, B, C, D, and E are attributes with the following dependencies:

A   → B
CD   → A
C   → E
E   → C
BD   → C

Some of the dependencies implied by the inference axioms are:

Let X, Y, Z, and W represent subsets of the attributes that comprise the database; then:

1.	Reflexive rule	$X \to X$
2.	Augmentation rule	if $X \to Y, XZ \to Y$
3.	Union rule	if $X \to Y$ and $X \to Z, X \to YZ$
4.	Decomposition rule	if $X \to Y, X \to Z$ where Z is a subset of Y
5.	Transitivity rule	if $X \to Y$ and $Y \to Z, X \to Z$
6.	Pseudotransitivity rule	if $X \to YZ \to W, XZ \to W$

Figure 4.5 Interence axioms for functional dependencies.

A	$\to$ A	(axiom 1)
AC	$\to$ B	(axiom 2)
CD	$\to$ AE	(axioms 2 and 3)
AD	$\to$ C	(axiom 6)
DE	$\to$ A	(axiom 6)
CD	$\to$ B	(axiom 5)
BD	$\to$ E	(axiom 5)
ED	$\to$ A	(axiom 6)
AD	$\to$ E	(axioms 5 and 6)
DE	$\to$ B	(axioms 5 and 6)

Functional dependencies also exist that are trivially true. Trivial functional dependencies occur when a set of attributes implies a subset of the same set (e.g., $XY \to X$). A trivial dependency is always true for every instance. The dependency is trivial because duplicate rows in XY will also be duplicate rows in X and Y individually.

4.9 REPEATING GROUPS

A repeating group is a collection of logically related attributes that occur multiple times within one row.

Examples of repeating groups include names of employee dependents, products associated with an invoice and employees' career interest designations. A repeating group is often characterized by an OCCURS clause in COBOL, an array in FORTRAN, or a structure in C. For example, consider the following attributes that relate to an employee benefit program:

ESSNUM	Employee number
ENAME	Employee name
PCODE	Code for benefit plan type
DNAME	Dependent name
DBIRTHD	Dependent birth date
DSEX	Dependent sex

The attributes DNAME, DBIRTHD, and DSEX comprise a repeating group that is duplicated for each dependent. The repeating group can be represented in COBOL with an OCCURS clause:

```
01 EMPLOYEE DEPENDENTS RECORD
        03 ESSNUM
        03 ENAME
        03 PCODE
   03 DEPENDENT DATA OCCURS 10 TIMES
        05 DNAME
        05 DBIRTHD
        05 DSEX
```

The repeating group can be represented in FORTRAN using an array, such as:

(ESSNUM(I), ENAME(I), PCODE(I), M(I), (DNAME(I,J), DBIRTHD(I,J), DSEX(I,J), J-1,M(I)))

where M(I) represents the number of dependents associated with the Ith employee and DNAME(I,J) represents the name of the Jth dependent for the Ith employee.

The representation of the repeating group in C can be accomplished with the following structure:

```
struct employee
{
        int essnum;
        char ename [30];
        char pcode;
        struct dep_rec
        {
                char dname [30];
                char dbirthd [6];
                char dsex;
        } emp_deps [10];
};
```

A relational representation begins with a grouping of attributes as follows:

BENEFITS (ESSNUM, ENAME, PCODE, DNAME, DBIRTHD, DSEX)

The repeating group is eliminated by creating two relations:

BENEFITS (<u>ESSNUM</u>, ENAME, PCODE)

DEPENDENTS (<u>ESSNUM</u>, <u>DNAME</u>, DBIRTHD, DSEX)

An employee number, name, and plan code are entered once for each employee. The dependent data is entered in separate relations. DNAME is used to identify a particular dependent. The ESSNUM attribute is used to connect the BENEFITS and DEPENDENTS relations.

4.10 RELATIONAL OPERATORS

Relational operators are used to manipulate relations in a manner similar to the way arithmetic operators (plus, minus, multiply, and divide) are used to manipulate numbers. The relational operators projection and join are especially important in data normalization.

A relation can be decomposed into new relations that consist of subsets of the attributes in the original relation. This is accomplished by using the projection operator. Consider the following instance of the relation EMPLOYEE (<u>NUM</u>, NAME, DEPT, SALARY):

NUM	NAME	DEPT	SALARY
101	Charles Miller	Accounting	35,000
102	Fawaz Ghumrawi	Accounting	40,000
103	Shelly Knight	Marketing	40,000
104	Michael Rodriguez	Human Relations	38,000
105	Clair Schler	Accounting	40,000

The projection of this instance onto the attributes DEPT and SALARY will result in the following instance of a new relation:

DEPT	SALARY
Accounting	35,000
Accounting	40,000
Marketing	40,000
Human Relations	38,000

The new relation contains the two attributes specified (DEPT and SALARY). Note that the number of rows is reduced since the duplicate row (Accounting 40,000) was eliminated from the new instance. This projection answers the question How many unique DEPT and

SALARY combinations exist? but is inappropriate for responding to commands such as List all the salaries for employees in the marketing department.

The projection operator is concerned with the attributes in a relation. A similar operator, selection, is concerned with the rows in a relation.

4.11 FIRST, SECOND, AND THIRD NORMAL FORMS

A major objective of data normalization is to eliminate update anomalies. The first three normal forms progress in a systematic manner toward achieving this objective. More subtle types of anomalies, however, continue to be discovered. Thus the first three normal forms provide an excellent way to begin to learn the normalization process. Advanced normal forms that address more subtle anomalies are introduced in later chapters.

4.11.1 First Normal Form

A relation is in first normal form if it contains no repeating groups. Relations that are only in first normal form suffer serious problems associated with insertions and deletions. For example, the following relation might be used by a university in developing a student and class database:

SCL (SNUM, CNUM, SNAME, SMAJ, TIME, BLDG)

where

SNUM = student number

CNUM = class number

SNAME = student name

SMAJ = student major

TIME = class time

BLDG = class building location

All the data concerning a student will be deleted if the student withdraws from all of his or her classes. Thus data regarding student number, name, and major will be lost. Insertions are also a problem. Data regarding class time and building location cannot be entered until a student enrolls in the class.

A problem with the SCL relation is that nonkey attributes are dependent on various parts of the primary key but not on the entire key. For example:

SNUM → SNAME but CNUM ↛ SNAME
SNUM → SMAJ but CNUM ↛ SMAJ
CNUM ↛ TIME but SNUM ↛ TIME
CNUM → BLDG but SNUM ↛ BLDG

The normalization process must continue beyond first normal form in order to eliminate undesirable insertion and deletion problems.

4.11.2 Second Normal Form

A relation is in second normal form if the relation is in first normal form and every nonkey attribute is fully functionally dependent upon the primary key. Thus no nonkey attribute can be functionally dependent on part of the primary key.

A relation in first normal form will be in second normal form if any one of the following applies:

1. The primary key is composed of only one attribute.

2. No nonkey attributes exist.

3. Every nonkey attribute is dependent on the entire set of primary key attributes.

The SCL relation can be decomposed into three new relations as follows:

SINFO (SNUM, SNAME, SMAJ)
CINFO (CNUM, TIME, BLDG)
STUCLASS (SNUM, CNUM)

The primary keys for both the SINFO and CINFO relations consist of just one attribute. The STUCLASS relation contains no nonkey attributes. Thus the relations are in second normal form.

Student data can be entered into the SINFO relation before the student enrolls in a class. Class data can be entered into the CINFO relation before any student enrolls in the class. Deletion of all students in a particular class in the STUCLASS relation will not result in either class or student data being deleted. Deletion of all classes for a particular student will result in the loss of student data.

Elimination of the insertion and deletion problems is not entirely because of second normal form. Actually the relations are also in third normal form. The differences between second and third normal form can be illustrated by considering another potential relation in the student and class database:

MAJOR (SNUM, MAJDEPT, COLLEGE)

The primary key consists of a single attribute, and thus this relation must be in second normal form. A typical instance is:

SNUM	MAJDEPT	COLLEGE
91001	Statistics	Science
81062	English	Liberal Arts
83719	Music	Liberal Arts
94201	Statistics	Science
86319	Music	Liberal Arts
97001	Statistics	Science

Note the following:

- If student 81062 is deleted, the fact that the english department is in the Liberal Arts College is lost.
- Several rows must be changed if the statistics department moves to the Engineering College.
- The fact that the electrical engineering department is in the Engineering College cannot be entered until a student with that major is added.

These problems appear similar to those encountered with relations only in first normal form. Actually the problems are caused by a different type of dependency. The difficulty is that a dependency exists (MAJDEPT → COLLEGE) that does not involve the primary key. This dependency allows the attribute to determine COLLEGE in two ways:

1. SNUM → COLLEGE

2. SNUM → MAJDEPT → COLLEGE

The second structure creates the insertion and deletion problems. For example, if a student drops all classes, the deletion of SNUM could result in a loss of data regarding the MAJDEPT and COLLEGE relationship. Thus the normalization process must continue in order to eliminate these undesirable dependencies.

4.11.3 Third Normal Form

A relation is in third normal form if, for every nontrivial functional dependency X → A, either attribute X is a superkey, or attribute A is a member of a candidate key.

Third normal form is often described as a situation in which an attribute is "a function of the key, the whole key, and nothing but the key." This description captures the essence of third normal form but is difficult to define precisely and is also partially incorrect.

An attribute is a function of the key, the whole key, and nothing but the key if the following two conditions are true:

1. Every nonkey attribute depends on the entire primary key.
2. No nonkey attribute is functionally dependent on another nonkey attribute.

These conditions, however, are too restrictive. A relation can be in third normal form even if a dependency exists among nonkey attributes. This occurs if all possible values of the implying attribute are unique (e.g., the implying attribute is a candidate key). For example, the relation:

R ($\underline{SSNUM}$, NAME, DEPTNUM)

is in third normal form if NAME $\rightarrow$ DEPTNUM and NAME is guaranteed never to contain duplicate values.

The second condition also becomes somewhat complicated if sets of attributes are considered. The condition should actually be stated as no nonkey attribute is functionally dependent on a set of attributes that does not contain a key.

Third normal form is often described by introducing a concept called transitive dependencies. Consider the relation R (A, B, C). Attribute C is transitively dependent on attribute A if attribute B satisfies:

A $\rightarrow$ B
B $\rightarrow$ C
B $\rightarrow$ A

A relation in second normal form is in third normal form if no transitive dependencies exist.

The dependency B $\rightarrow$ C represents the potential problem in the relation (i.e., functional dependence among nonkey attributes). Attribute B is not a candidate key since B $\rightarrow$ A, and thus the relation is not in third normal form.

Eliminating transitive dependencies will eliminate anomalies of the following nature: If A $\rightarrow$ B $\rightarrow$ C, a B value cannot be associated with an A value unless a C value is also associated with a B value. Thus an A $\rightarrow$ B association cannot be inserted unless a B $\rightarrow$ C association is also inserted. Conversely, if a C value associated with a B value is deleted, corresponding A $\rightarrow$ B association may be lost.

The relation MAJOR ($\underline{SNUM}$, MAJDEPT, COLLEGE), discussed in the previous section, can be decomposed into two new relations that are both in third normal form:

SMAJ (SNUM, MAJDEPT)

MDEPT (MAJDEPT, COLLEGE)

Transitive dependencies may also occur between sets of attributes. For example, consider the following relation:

SHIPMENT (NUM, ORIGIN, DESTINATION, DISTANCE)

This might be used by a transportation company to record shipment order numbers, origin, destination, and distance data. An instance of this relation is:

NUM	ORIGIN	DESTINATION	DISTANCE
101	Atlanta	Boston	1088
102	Atlanta	Boston	1088
103	St. Louis	Chicago	288
104	Cleveland	Dallas	1187
105	Los Angeles	San Francisco	403
106	Kansas City	Memphis	459

Note that ORIGIN, DESTINATION, and DISTANCE are not functionally dependent on each other when the attributes are considered in a pairwise manner. However, the combination of ORIGIN and DESTINATION determines DISTANCE. Since this dependency exists, the rows that contain duplicates of the ORIGIN, DESTINATION combination also contain duplicates of DISTANCE.

The SHIPMENT relation can be decomposed into two relations (each in third normal form) as follows:

SHIPMENT (NUM, ORIGIN, DESTINATION)

DISTANCE (ORIGIN, DESTINATION, DISTANCE)

The fact that the distance between New Orleans and Pittsburgh is 1093 miles can then be added to the database even though a corresponding shipment order does not exist. This flexibility is desirable when analyzing what-if questions. Shipment can also be deleted without loss of the distance data. The distance between reoccurring origin and destination combinations need not be entered with each shipment.

4.11.4 Examples

Three examples are presented in this section to illustrate how relations in third normal form are constructed. The chapter concludes

NAME	Name of person
SNNUM	Social security number of person
ADDRESS	Address where person resides
CITY	City where person resides
STATE	State where person resides
ZIP	Zip code where person resides
AMTL1	Amount of most recent loan
DL1	Date of most recent loan
RL1	Payment rating most recent loan
AMTL2	Amount of second most recent loan
DL2	Date of second most recent loan
RL2	Payment rating for second most recent loan
AMTL3	Amount of third most recent loan
DL3	Date of third most recent loan
RL3	Payment rating for third most recent loan

Figure 4.6   Attributes associated with Example 4.1.

with some general guidelines for developing relations in third normal form.

Example 4.1: Credit history for consumer loans.   This example involves enhancing an existing database used to record consumer loan history by individual. The current database allows space for a maximum of three loans per individual. A major objective is to expand the historical capabilities so that a complete loan record is available for each individual. The attributes associated with this example are illustrated in Fig. 4.6.

A repeating group associated with amount, date, and payment rating must be eliminated. The attributes DL1, DL2, and DL3 can be replaced by the attribute DATE. Similarly, RL1, RL2, and RL3 can be replaced by AMOUNT.

The functional dependencies are:

```
SSNUM, DATE → AMOUNT
SSNUM, DATE → PAYMENT RATING
SSNUM       → NAME
SSNUM       → ADDRESS
```

SSNUM   → CITY
SSNUM   → ZIP
ZIP   → STATE

Three relations, each in third normal form, can be developed:

R1 (SSNUM, DATE, AMOUNT, PAYMENT RATING)
R2 (SSNUM, NAME, ADDRESS, CITY, ZIP)
R3 (ZIP, STATE)

The loan information is no longer restricted to a maximum of three loans per individual. However, relation R1 assumes that at most one loan per day can be granted to any one individual.

Example 4.2: Manufacturing specifications. This example involves the machines, setup times, production times, and name and amount of each ingredient used in manufacturing a specific product. The number of machines and ingredients varies depending on the individual prod-

NUM	Product number
DES	Product description
MACNUM1	Number of first machine used
SETUP1	Setup time for first machine
PRORATE1	Production time for first machine
MACNUM2	Number of second machine used
SETUP2	Setup time for second machine
PRORATE2	Production time for second machine
MACNUM3	Number of third machine used
SETUP3	Setup time for third machine
PRORATE3	Production time for third machine
IGD1	Number of first ingredient used
AMT1	Amount of first ingredient used
IGD2	Number of second ingredient used
AMT2	Amount of second ingredient used

Figure 4.7 Attributes associated with Example 4.2.

uct. However, at most three machines and two ingredients are used in any one product. The attributes identified by a systems analyst are presented in Fig. 4.7.

Two repeating groups must be eliminated:

1. Number, setup time, and production time for each machine
2. Number and amount of each ingredient

The attribute names should be simplified as follows:

1. Replace MACNUM1, MACNUM2, and MACNUM3 with MACNUM.
2. Replace SETUP1, SETUP2, and SETUP3 with SETUP.
3. Replace PRORATE1, PRORATE2, and PRORATE3 with PRO-RATE.
4. Replace IGD1 and IGD2 with IGD.
5. Replace AMT1 and AMT2 with AMT.

The functional dependencies are:

```
NUM, MACNUM → SETUP
NUM, MACNUM → PRORATE
NUM          → DES
NUM, IGD     → AMT
```

The following relations are each in third normal form:

R1 (NUM, MACNUM, SETUP, PRORATE)
R2 (NUM, IGD, AMT)
R3 (NUM, DES)

Note that setup time is dependent on both machine and product but not on the previously produced product on a particular machine. The database also does not capture any information relating to the order in which the machines or ingredients are used.

Example 4.3: An inventory of personal computer hardware and software.
This example involves a database to store information concerning personal computer hardware and software used by employees. An expert "contact" person for each software product is included, along with the expert's rating of the software. The attributes associated with this example are presented in Fig. 4.8. The functional dependencies are as follows:

UFN	User's first name
ULN	User's last name
UDIX	User's work division number
UEXT	User's telephone extension
ULOC	User's work location
CPER	Contact person (individual knowledgeable about the software)
CEXT	Contact person's telephone extension
CLOC	Contact person's work location
HPU	Date hardware was purchased
HTYPE	Type of hardware (e.g., XT, AT, PS/2)
SNAME	Name of software (e.g., Lotus 1-2-3)
SPUR	Date software was purchased
SRATE	Software rating (opinion of contact person)
STYPE	Type of software (e.g., spreadsheet, database)
SVER	Version number of software

Figure 4.8   Attributes associated with Example 4.3.

$$\text{UFN, ULN} \rightarrow \text{ULOC}$$
$$\text{UFN, ULN} \rightarrow \text{UDIV}$$
$$\text{UFN, ULN} \rightarrow \text{UEXT}$$
$$\text{CPER} \rightarrow \text{CEXT}$$
$$\text{CPER} \rightarrow \text{CLOC}$$
$$\text{SNAME} \rightarrow \text{STYPE}$$
$$\text{CPER, SNAME, SVER} \rightarrow \text{STRATE}$$
$$\text{UFN, ULN, HPUR, SNAME, SVER} \rightarrow \text{SPUR}$$
$$\text{SNAME, SVER} \rightarrow \text{CPER}$$

Note that HTYPE was not included in the functional dependencies, and thus it must be included in a relation containing all key attributes.

Two repeating groups must be eliminated:

1. Hardware type and date of purchase
2. Software information (SNAME, SPUR, SRATE, STYPE, and SVER)

Elimination of the repeating groups is accomplished with the following two relations:

R1 (UFN, ULN, HTYPE, HPUR)

R2 (UFN, ULN, HPUR, SNAME, SVER, STYPE, SPUR, SRATE, CPER, CEXT, CLOC)

Relation R1 assumes that an employee purchases no more than one given hardware type on a given day. If HPUR was not included in the primary key, the assumption would be that an individual will purchase at most one given hardware type. R1 also assumes that an individual is uniquely identified by first and last name.

Relation R2 assumes that only one version of a particular software product is installed on any one machine. This relation must be further decomposed since CPER → CEXT and CPER → CLOC. Thus R2 is decomposed into:

R3 (UFN, ULN, HPUR, SNAME, SVER, SPUR, CPER)

R8 (CPER, SNAME, SVER, SRATE)

The contact person provides a software rating independently of any hardware. Thus R7 is further decomposed:

R9 (UFN, ULN, HPUR, SNAME, SVER, SPUR)

R10 (SNAME, SVER, CPER)

Information about the user can be incorporated in the following relation:

R11 (UFN, ULN, ULOC, UDIV, UEXT)

The database now contains seven relations:

R1 (UFN, ULN, HTYPE, HPUR)

R4 (CPER, CEXT, CLOC)

R6 (SNAME, STYPE)

R8 (CPER, SNAME, SVER, SPATE)

R9 (UFN, ULN, HPUR, SNAME, SVER, SPUR)

R10 (SNAME, SVER, CPER)

R11 (UPN, ULN, ULOC, UDIV, UEXT)

Another modification to the database is required. The attribute CPER is not necessary in the key or relation R8, and SNAME and SVER are the only attributes needed since SNAME, SVER → CPER. The original dependency CPER, SNAME, SVER → SRATE should be replaced by SNAME, SVER → SRATE since the inclusion of CPER creates a trivial dependency. Relations R8 and R10 can then be combined. The revised database contains the following six relations:

R1 (UFN, ULN, HTYPE, HPUR)

R4 (CPER, CEXT, CLOC)

R6 (SNAME, STYPE)

R8 (SNAME, SVER, CPER, SRATE)

R9 (UFN, ULN, HPUR, SNAME, SVER, SPUR)

R10 (UFN, ULN, ULOC, UDIV, UEXT)

Suppose that a software vendor introduces a new version of a spreadsheet package. The new version is an integrated package that also contains database, word processing, and graphics capabilities. The dependency SNAME → STYPE is no longer valid since STYPE is determined by both SNAME and SVER. Relation R6 should be modified as follows:

R12 (SNAME, SVER, STYPE)

The database now appears as follows:

R1 (UFN, ULN, HPUR, HTYPE)

R4 (CPER, CLOC, CEXT)

R9 (UFN, ULN, HPUR, SNAME, SVER, SPUR)

R11 (UFN, ULN, ULOC, UDIV, UEXT)

R13 (SNAME, SVER, STYPE, SRATE, CPER)

One other modification may be desirable. To simplify physical implementation, the two key attributes UFN and ULN can be replaced by a single attribute, such as UPER. Key attributes SNAME and SVER can also be replaced by a single attribute SNV. These modifications require the following changes:

Change R11 to R15 (UPER, ULOC, UNDIV, UEXT).

Change R13 to R16 (SNV, STYPE, SRATE, CPER).

Change R1 to R17 (UPER, HPUR, HTYPE).

Change R9 to R18 (UPER, SNV, HPUR, SPUR).

The final database contains R4, R15, R17, and R18. Two additional relations could be created to capture the detailed SNV and HPER information:

R19 (SNV, SNAME, SVER)

R20 (UPER, UFN, ULN)

4.12 GUIDELINES FOR DEVELOPING RELATIONS IN THIRD NORMAL FORM

Relations in third normal form can be developed by following the guidelines presented in Fig. 4.9. Experienced database designers may find that the problems associated with first or second normal form are obvious. Thus the actual design process may not follow a sequential consideration of all three normal forms; an experience designer may develop initial relations in third normal form.

1. Define the attributes.
2. Group logically related attributes into relations.
3. Identify candidate keys for each relation.
4. Select a primary key for each relation.
5. Identify and remove repeating groups.
6. Combine relations with identical keys (first normal form).
7. Identify all functional dependencies.
8. Decompose relations such that each nonkey attribute is dependent on all the attributes in the key.
9. Combine relations with identical primary keys (second normal form).
10. Identify all transitive dependencies.
    a. Check relations for dependencies of one nonkey attribute with another nonkey attribute.
    b. Check for dependencies within each primary key (i.e., dependence of one attribute in the key on other attributes within the key).
11. Decompose relations such that there are no transitive dependencies.
12. Combine relations with identical primary keys (third normal) if no transitive dependencies occur.

Figure 4.9 Guidelines for developing third normal form.

Database
Retrieval
Concepts

All you need to retrieve data from a DB2 table is the key word SELECT and the name of the table from which you want data. The most basic select statement consists of the following:

SELECT * FROM EMPLOYEE;

where the asterisk (*) indicates all columns and EMPLOYEE is the name of the table. The semicolon (;) ends the statement. The SELECT key word is the verb and, combined with the asterisk and table name, will retrieve all rows and all columns of the EMPLOYEE table. This is because the asterisk indicates that you want all columns of the table, and no additional information appears after the table name to indicate any restrictions on the rows to be retrieved.

5.1 LIMITING COLUMNS RETRIEVED FROM A TABLE

We could write out the names of the columns, separated by commas, that we want included in our request as follows:

SELECT ID, LAST_NAME, FIRST_NAME, ADDRESS, CITY
              STATE, ZIP,   BRANCH_ID
   FROM   EMPLOYEE

If this list of fields comprises all of the columns in our EMPLOYEE table, this SELECT statement is equivalent to the one with the asterisk in place of the field names. The asterisk retrieves columns in the order given in the CREATE TABLE statement that built the table, so you might want to spell out the table names and list them individually in the SELECT statement.

With our SELECT statement so far, we can select which columns to include in our data request, but we cannot limit the number of rows to include. The next section shows how to limit rows in the query.

5.1.1 Limiting Rows in Queries—The WHERE Clause

Now that we know how to select some or all of the columns in a table, we will see how to select only certain rows. The SQL WHERE clause of the SELECT statement will accomplish this for us:

```
SELECT ID, LAST_NAME, FIRST_NAME, BRANCH_ID
FROM    EMPLOYEE
WHERE BRANCH_ID = 'SALES01';
```

Only those employee records containing a BRANCH_ID column value of 'SALES01' will be included in the results of our request. If no records are found which meet our requirements, no records will be returned from the table.

We can include in our WHERE clause a variety of conditions to be met in answering our requests. Conditions may be applied to character and numeric fields.

5.2 RETRIEVAL CONDITIONS— INEQUALITY

We have just seen how we can tell DB2 to match the column value(s) of each table row with a test value in order to filter out records we do not want to see. This is done with the equal sign (=) operator. Now we will see how to test for records that do not meet certain filtering criteria. First, we check for records with a BRANCH_ID that is not equal to 'SALES01':

```
SELECT * FROM EMPLOYEE
WHERE BRANCH_ID < > 'SALES01';
```

A not equal to condition is indicated by a less-than and a greater-than sign (< >). As you might guess, we can use the less-than or greater-than signs alone or in combination with the equal sign to form other filter conditions for our WHERE clauses as follows:

```
SELECT * FROM EMPLOYEE
WHERE    SALARY < 65000;
```

```
SELECT * FROM EMPLOYEE
WHERE SALARY > 60000;

SELECT * FROM EMPLOYEE
WHERE SALARY > = 18000
  AND   SALARY < = 65000;
```

The last example includes the word AND, which is a boolean operator. You may use AND, OR, and NOT to form rather complex queries. If your queries do get complex, place parentheses around the phrases you are stringing together with the AND, OR, and NOT boolean operators.

The WHERE clause operators in the examples above work with character fields as well as numeric fields, but be careful of case sensitivity. An uppercase A is different from a lowercase a, so you might get some unexpected results if your fields contain a mix of upper- and lowercase letters. With character fields, the greater-than and less-than conditions are determined by the alphabetic order of the characters in a field. An employee LAST_NAME of 'Anderson' would be less than 'Jones', as you would expect. Likewise, 'Andersen' would be less than 'Anderson' and would *not* appear in the results of the last query listed below:

```
SELECT * FROM EMPLOYEE
WHERE LAST_NAME > = 'Anderson';
```

If two character fields of different length are being compared, the shorter character string is padded at the right with blank characters before the WHERE clause condition check is made.

5.2.1 Ranges—BETWEEN

A numeric or character range can be built using inequality and equality operators, but DB2 allows us to use the keyword BETWEEN combined with AND to simplify our queries a bit like this:

```
SELECT * FROM EMPLOYEE
WHERE LAST_NAME BETWEEN 'JONES' AND 'SMITH';

SELECT * FROM EMPLOYEE
WHERE SALARY BETWEEN 18000 AND 65000;
```

These are equivalent to:

```
SELECT * FROM EMPLOYEE
WHERE LAST_NAME > = 'JONES'
AND LAST_NAME < = 'SMITH'
```

```
SELECT * FROM EMPLOYEE
WHERE SALARY > = 18000
AND SALARY < = 65000;
```

5.2.2 Pattern Matching—LIKE

This condition is available only for character fields. Such a condition may be expressed using the LIKE keyword and a pattern-matching template as follows:

```
SELECT * FROM EMPLOYEE
WHERE LAST_NAME LIKE 'A%';
```

or

```
SELECT * FROM EMPLOYEE
WHERE LAST_NAME LIKE 'J__s';
```

The first example uses the percent sign (%) "wild card" character to match one or more characters after the literal 'A', causing the query to retrieve all employee records with a last name beginning with A.

The second example uses the underscore (_) wild card character to match any one character, causing the query to retrieve all employee records with a last name beginning with J and having any other three characters followed by S. This will match, for instance, a last name of JONES or JAMES.

5.2.3 Lists—IN

The IN key word allows us to search a list of values delimited by parentheses and separated by commas like this:

```
SELECT * FROM EMPLOYEE
WHERE LAST_NAME IN ('ANDERSON', 'JONES', 'SMITH');

SELECT * FROM EMPLOYEE
WHERE SALARY IN (20000, 30000, 40000);
```

These examples are equivalent to the following much longer ones that use equality comparisons:

```
SELECT * FROM EMPLOYEE
WHERE LAST_NAME = 'ANDERSON'
    OR LAST_NAME  = 'JONES'
    OR LAST_NAME  = 'SMITH';
SELECT * FROM EMPLOYEE
WHERE SALARY = 20000
    OR SALARY  = 30000
    OR SALARY  = 40000;
```

5.2.4 Negation—NOT

For those times when you want to retrieve all records *except* ones that meet certain conditions, use the NOT operator, as follows:

SELECT * FROM EMPLOYEE
WHERE LAST_NAME NOT IN ('ANDERSON', 'JONES', 'SMITH');

This example will retrieve all employee records with a last name other than Anderson, Jones, or Smith. Another example is:

SELECT * FROM EMPLOYEE
WHERE SALARY NOT 65000;

Here all employees in the EMPLOYEE table except those with a salary of $65,000 will be retrieved.

5.2.5 Handling NULL Conditions

You may wish to retrieve all records that have no value defined for a certain field. If so, build a query like this:

SELECT * FROM EMPLOYEE
WHERE JOB_TITLE IS NULL;

This is a handy way to go back and enter job titles after the basic employee information has already been entered. If you want to retrieve all employee records which *do* have a job title defined for them, use this query:

SELECT * FROM EMPLOYEE
WHERE JOB_TITLE IS NOT NULL;

5.3 CALCULATED FIELDS—SQL OPERATORS

We would like to do more with numeric fields than simply store a single value in a numeric column of a particular table row. SQL provides us with several mathematical operators and functions for manipulating numeric fields in our SQL queries (see Fig. 5.1). The result of each of these mathematical operations is, in effect, a new numeric field not stored in the database but created at retrieval time. This means that we do not need to store information such as employee age or days that a customer account or customer order is overdue. We instead store the starting date and calculate the age or other time interval from the difference of the current date and the starting date.

5.3.1 Addition and Subtraction

SQL provides us with the plus symbol ($+$) and subtraction symbol ($-$) for applying addition and subtraction operations to numeric database

Symbol	Operation
+	Addition
−	Subtraction
*	Multiplication
/	Division
COUNT	COUNT
MAX	Maximum
MIN	Minimum
AVG	Average
SUM	Summation

Figure 5.1   SQL Operators.

fields. Using these symbols, we can add (or subtract) constants or other database numeric fields to (from) numeric fields. For instance, if we want to see how much money, in total, our hourly employees would earn with a $1.00-per-hour raise, we would code something like this:

```
SELECT LAST_NAME, (PAY_RATE + 1.00) FROM EMPLOYEE
WHERE PAY_TYPE = 'HOURLY';
```

Another query with the last name, original pay rate, and the new pay rate with a $0.35 per hour deduction is:

```
SELECT LAST_NAME, PAY_RATE, ( ( PAY_RATE + 1.00) ) − .35)
FROM EMPLOYEE
WHERE PAY_TYPE = 'HOURLY';
```

5.3.2 Multiplication and Division

As with algebra, we can also multiply and divide using SQL mathematical operators for multiplication (∗) and division (/). Again, these operators can only be applied to numeric fields and constants. To calculate sales tax on invoice cost, at 5.00 percent, for a particular invoice line item, use this query:

```
SELECT   (INVOICE_COST * .05)
FROM     INVOICE_ITEMS
WHERE    INVOICE_ID   = '00500'
  AND    INVOICE_ITEM = 2;
```

Calculate shipping cost as a percentage of the total cost to the customer from us (ignoring sales taxes) this way:

```
SELECT ((SHIPPING_COST / (INVOICE_COST + SHIPPING_COST))
                                                      * 100)
FROM   INVOICE
WHERE INVOICE_ID = '00500';
```

Notice that I have placed parentheses around not only the entire calculation but around INVOICE_COST + SHIPPING COST and around SHIPPING_COST / (INVOICE_COST + SHIPPING_COST). This is to ensure that the addition operation is performed first, division next, and multiplication last. It is usually a good idea to use parentheses in mathematical calculations to increase readability and to ensure that SQL calculates things in the order you want. As you can imagine, the four mathematical operators can be combined to create some rather complex queries, so use parentheses liberally.

5.3.3 Maximum and Minimum

We can use the basic mathematical operators discussed thus far to find the maximum and minimum values in a list of numeric fields and constants, but there is an easier way. SQL provides the MAX () and MIN () operators (or functions) for this purpose. Select the highest- and lowest-priced items in our parts table as follows:

```
SELECT MAX (COST), MIN (COST) FROM PARTS;
```

Find the part representing the highest inventory value at the current time this way:

```
SELECT MAX (COST * QTY_OF) FROM PARTS;
```

We can also use these functions for characteristic fields like this:

```
SELECT MAX (LAST_NAME), MIN (LAST_NAME) FROM EMPLOYEE
```

5.3.4 Counts

If we want to get the count of the occurrences of a certain field in a table (a count of rows), we can use the SQL COUNT () operator as follows:

```
SELECT COUNT (NAME) FROM EMPLOYEE;
```

or

```
SELECT COUNT (*) FROM EMPLOYEE;
```

Find the number of hourly employees like this:

```
SELECT COUNT (NAME) FROM EMPLOYEE
WHERE PAY_TYPE = 'HOURLY';
```

5.3.5 Sums

When we want to add up all the values in certain numeric fields (but not character fields), we can use the SQL SUM () operator. To find the total invoice revenue for a particular date, use this query:

SELECT SUM (INVOICE_COST) FROM INVOICE_ITEMS
WHERE INVOICE_DATE = '07-JUL-89';

Retrieve the total value of our parts inventory this way:

SELECT SUM (COST * QTY_OH) FROM PARTS;

5.3.6 Averages

The SQL AVG () operator lets us find the sum of a numeric field and divide that sum by the count of the rows in the table. This is much easier than adding up the field values, counting the rows, and dividing. Find the average cost of parts in our parts inventory as follows:

SELECT AVG (COST) FROM PARTS;

This is the same as:

SELECT (SUM (COST) / COUNT (COST)) FROM PARTS;

5.3.7 Distinct Values

SQL provides us with the key word DISTINCT to eliminate duplicate values from the results of our queries. We can use DISTINCT with other SQL operators. To find the number of part types we can use the following query:

SELECT DISTINCT TYPE FROM PARTS;

The DISTINCT key word tells SQL to count the number of different part types occurring in our part table. To find the number of employee pay classifications, we can use the following:

SELECT DISTINCT PAY_TYPE FROM EMPLOYEE;

Find the number of different cities our customers are in this way:

SELECT DISTINCT CITY FROM CUSTOMERS;

5.3.8 Handling NULL Values

If any numeric values in a field are unknown, we can find either a NULL or a blank zero (character or numeric). NULL values, as we learned earlier, represent unknown or not applicable values for fields. We must be careful when we perform some SQL operations on NULL fields, because when SQL performs an arithmetic operation on a NULL value, a NULL result is always returned.

The MAX (), MIN (), COUNT (), SUM (), and AVG () SQL operators all ignore NULL values in table columns. MAX () and MIN () return the maximum or minimum value of fields that are NOT NULL. COUNT () ignores NULL values, so the following queries are not necessarily equivalent:

```
SELECT COUNT (COST) FROM PARTS
WHERE TYPE = 'B';

SELECT COUNT (*) FROM PARTS
WHERE TYPE = 'B';
```

The first query will return the same result only if all COST values are NOT NULL. If some of the COST values in the PARTS table are NULL, the first query result will be less than the result of the second query. Likewise, the SUM () operator used with the COST column returns the sum of NOT NULL values, and AVG () averages only values which are NOT NULL.

To find the number of parts that have no cost entered for them, use this query:

```
SELECT COUNT (*) FROM PARTS
WHERE COST IS NULL;
```

Based on the result of the above query, we could have an application program display a screen of parts that need cost values entered by using the following:

```
SELECT ID, TYPE, DESCRIPTION FROM PARTS
WHERE   COST IS NULL;
```

5.4   ORDERING AND GROUPING ROWS

There are many times when we would like to gather records into logical groups and display them in a certain order. SQL gives us this ability.

5.4.1   Ordering Rows

We can determine the order of selection by using the SQL ORDER BY phrase in our SELECT statements. ORDER BY must follow the WHERE clause or immediately follow the table name (if no WHERE clause is used) as shown below:

```
SELECT LAST_NAME, FIRST_NAME FROM EMPLOYEE
WHERE CITY = 'CHICAGO'
ORDER BY LAST_NAME;
```

```
SELECT    LAST_NAME, FIRST_NAME FROM EMPLOYEE
ORDER BY LAST_NAME;
```

Selected records can be ordered by any field, character, or numeric in a particular table. The display order can be ascending or descending by using the ASC or DESC designation after the ORDER BY value as follows:

```
SELECT    * FROM EMPLOYEE
ORDER BY LAST_NAME ASC;
```

```
SELECT    * FROM EMPLOYEE
ORDER BY PAY_RATE DESC;
```

The default order is ascending, so you do not need to code ASC for ascending order. You can order records by a combination of fields like this:

```
SELECT    * FROM EMPLOYEE
ORDER BY LAST_NAME, FIRST_NAME;
```

5.4.2 Grouping Rows

SQL lets you group records from a table into logical subsets of the entire table. To make SQL do this for you, use the GROUP BY phrase following the WHERE clause in your SELECT statement or immediately after the table name if you do need a where clause as follows:

```
SELECT  * FROM EMPLOYEE
WHERE CITY = 'CHICAGO'
GROUP BY ZIP;
```

```
SELECT  * FROM EMPLOYEE
GROUP BY PAY_TYPE;
```

The first query returns employees living in Chicago grouped by ZIP code. The second example returns all employees, grouped by PAY_TYPE. You can combine the GROUP BY with the ORDER BY phrase if you place the ORDER BY last in the SELECT statement as follows:

```
SELECT    * FROM PARTS
GROUP BY TYPE
ORDER BY ID;
```

You can also group by more than one field this way:

```
SELECT    * FROM PARTS
GROUP BY TYPE, SUBTYPE
```

5.4.3 Obtaining Summary Information about Groups

The GROUP BY phrase can give us summary information about certain groups in a table, but we cannot use a simple WHERE clause as shown below to select the groups:

```
SELECT  TYPE, COUNT (ID) FROM PARTS
WHERE COUNT (ID) > 1
GROUP BY TYPE;
```

We cannot do this because the WHERE clause is used by SQL to test records (select or reject). The WHERE clause above refers to summary information produced by the GROUP BY clause and is illegal as written. Conditions and boundaries to be used with GROUP BY must be constructed using the HAVING key word as follows:

```
SELECT TYPE, COUNT (ID) FROM PARTS
GROUP BY TYPE HAVING COUNT (ID) > 1;
```

HAVING specifies conditions that groups of records must match in order to be included in the result. WHERE specifies conditions that individual records must match in order to be included in the result.

5.5 JOINING TABLES TOGETHER

There will be times when you will want to combine data in two or more tables in a single retrieval operation. DB2 offers you the ability to do this rather easily. This can greatly simplify many types of retrievals in application programs.

5.5.1 Simple Joins

Suppose that you want a list of all customers by territory who have purchased from you, perhaps to announce that you are offering a special price on your products. Here is one way to retrieve these customers:

```
SELECT CUSTOMER.CUST_ID, CUSTOMER.NAME,
       CUSTOMER.ADDRESS
FROM   CUSTOMER, INVOICE
WHERE CUSTOMER.CUST_ID = INVOICE.CUST_ID;
```

This statement joins the customer and invoice tables based on the customer identification code. The two tables are referenced in the FROM clause and the match conditions are listed in the WHERE clause. The result is one logical table with rows containing only CUST_ID codes common to both the CUSTOMER and INVOICE tables.

5.5.2 Joins with Inequality Conditions

We are not limited to joining data in two or more tables based on the simple equality condition. DB2 offers us the ability to combine data from two or more tables based on inequality conditions as well (see Fig. 5.2). Suppose that we want a list of all those who have not purchased from us:

```
SELECT CUSTOMER.CUST_ID, CUSTOMER.NAME
FROM    CUSTOMER, INVOICE
WHERE CUSTOMER.CUST_ID < > INVOICE.CUST_ID
```

This example is similar to the equality example above, but now only those with no invoices are retrieved.

5.5.3 Joins with Multiple Conditions

SQL allows us to specify more than one condition in a join predicate (the WHERE clause conditions), thus giving us added flexibility. Here is how we can get a list of all customers who have purchased a batch worth more than $1000 of part 'A312' from us (a single line item totaling more than $1000 of the part):

```
SELECT CUSTOMER.CUST_ID, CUSTOMER.NAME
FROM    CUSTOMER, INVOICE_ITEM
WHERE CUSTOMER.CUST_ID       = INVOICE_ITEM.CUST_ID
  AND INVOICE_ITEM.PART_NUM = 'A312'
  AND INVOICE.AMOUNT >          1000;
```

Symbol	Condition
=	Equal
>	Greater than
<	Less than
<=	Less than or equal
>=	Greater than or equal
< >	Not equal
BETWEEN	Between two values
LIKE	Character pattern match
IN	Equal to an item in a list
NOT	Negation of a condition

Figure 5.2 SQL search conditions.

5.5.4 Joining Three Tables

We have mentioned in this chapter that you can use SQL to join more than two tables together. What is needed in this situation is a set of two join predicates, one to link the first and second tables and one to link the second and third tables. We can list parts purchased from us by IBM this way:

```
SELECT   INVOICE.INVOICE_NUM, INVOICE_ITEMS.PART_NUM,
         PARTS.PART_DESC, INVOICE_ITEMS.AMOUNT
FROM    INVOICE, INVOICE_ITEMS, PARTS
WHERE   INVOICE_ITEMS.INVOICE_ID = INVOICE.INVOICE_ID
 AND    PARTS.PART_NUM = INVOICE_ITEMS.PARTS_NUM
 AND    INVOICE.CUST_ID   = 'IBM'
```

The above query will list the invoice number, part number, part description, and line item amount for all parts purchased by IBM. The first line in the WHERE clause joins the INVOICE table to the INVOICE_ITEMS table. The second line in the WHERE clause joins the PARTS table with the INVOICE_ITEMS table. Finally, the third line of the WHERE clause selects only invoices for IBM.

5.5.5 Joining Tables to Themselves

Why would we ever want to join a table to itself? If we wanted to retrieve a list of customers located in the same city, we could do so by joining the CUSTOMER table to itself by pretending that we really have two identical tables:

```
SELECT  A.CUST_ID, B.CUST_ID
FROM    CUSTOMER.A CUSTOMER.B
WHERE  A.CITY     = B.CITY
  AND  A.CUST_ID < B.CUST_ID;
```

We have joined the CUSTOMER table to itself over matching CITY values. Note that we use table alias names A and B to accomplish the join. The second line of the WHERE clause is used to eliminate rows in the resulting table where a customer appears twice (a,a and b,b) and pairs of customers with the names reversed (a,b and b,a).

5.6 SUBQUERIES—QUERIES WITHIN QUERIES

After gaining some experience with SQL SELECT statements, you will eventually find it useful to nest one SELECT query within another SELECT query.

5.6.1 Simple Subqueries

Here is how we could list the names and addresses of customers who purchased over $1000 of parts from us on a single invoice:

```
SELECT CUSTOMER.NAME, CUSTOMER.ADDRESS
FROM    CUSTOMER
WHERE CUSTOMER.CUST_ID IN
        (SELECT INVOICE.CUST_ID
        FROM    INVOICE
        WHERE   INVOICE.AMOUNT > = 1000);
```

The nested query (the SELECT statement in parentheses) is evaluated first to retrieve all invoices with amounts over $1000. Then the customer names and addresses are retrieved from the CUSTOMER table based on the CUST_ID value found in each INVOICE row returned from the nested query.

5.6.2 Multiple-Level Subqueries

We can nest more than one level of subquery. Here is how we would retrieve the names and addresses of all customers who purchased from us a part with description 'LYNCH PIN':

```
SELECT    CUSTOMER.NAME, CUSTOMER.ADDRESS
FROM      CUSTOMER
WHERE     CUSTOMER.CUST_ID IN
          (SELECT INVOICE.CUST_ID
          FROM    INVOICE
          WHERE   INVOICE.INVOICE_NUM IN
                  (SELECT    INVOICE_ITEMS.INVOICE_NUM
                  FROM       INVOICE_ITEMS
                  WHERE      INVOICE_ITEMS.PART_NUM IN
                  (SELECT PARTS.PART_NUM
                  FROM    PARTS
          WHERE       PARTS.PART_DESC =
                      'LYNCH PIN')));
```

First, the PART_NUM for 'LYNCH PIN' is retrieved from the PARTS table. Second, the invoices containing that PART_NUM are retrieved from the INVOICE_ITEMS table. Third, invoices containing the INVOICE_NUM values are retrieved from INVOICE. Last, the customer names and addresses are retrieved from CUSTOMER based on the CUST_ID value in each invoice. This example might seem a bit contrived, but this author has actually had to build such a query for a client.

As you can see, SQL offers you much power in building queries to retrieve database information. With enough creativity, you could build complex queries to retrieve database information or put complex queries into your application programs, using host variable substitution to gather desired search values from users and passing these values to DB2 in nested SELECT statements. This way, you could build powerful decision support systems for your end users.

5.6.3 Correlated Subquery

We can create subqueries that are evaluated with respect to certain values selected by the main query. The inner query runs in correlation with the test value of the main query. To get the names of all suppliers of part 'A212' we can build this correlated subquery:

```
SELECT   SUPPLIER.NAME FROM SUPPLIER
WHERE    'A212' IN (SELECT PARTS.PART_NUM FROM PARTS
                    WHERE PARTS.SUPPLIER_ID =
                    SUPPLIER.SUPPLIER_ID);
```

The main query goes through each supplier record in the SUPPLIER table, and the SUPPLIER_ID field of each record becomes a test value that will be sent to the subquery. The subquery will then find the PART_NUM from the PARTS table that correlates to the test SUPPLIER_ID. The subquery must be evaluated repeatedly, once for each value of the test available. We could use an alias (CV, for correlation value) as follows for the SUPPLIER table to make this a bit clearer:

```
SELECT   CV.NAME FROM SUPPLIER CV
WHERE    'A212' IN (SELECT PARTS.PART_NUM
                    FROM    PARTS
                    WHERE   PARTS.SUPPLIER_ID =
                    CV.SUPPLIER_ID);
```

The alias CV is placed in the FROM clause as an alternate name for the SUPPLIER table and then is used to qualify the WHERE clause in the subquery and in the outer query SELECT. The CV variable, at any given time, represents some record in the SUPPLIER table. For each value of CV, evaluate the subquery to retrieve a set of PART_NUM values and add the current value of CV.NAME to this set if (and only if) 'A212' is in the set of PART_NUM values.

5.6.4 Union of Two Tables

Two or more SQL queries can be combined with the UNION operation. The UNION key word is placed, as follows, between any two SELECT statements to indicate that the result table should contain all records selected from the first table and all records selected from the second table (duplicate records will be discarded):

```
SELECT    LASTNAME, FIRSTNAME, SALES_AMOUNT
FROM      JAN90_SALES

UNION

SELECT    LASTNAME, FIRSTNAME, SALES_AMOUNT
FROM      FEB90_SALES;
```

In order for this kind of operation to work, each column selected from the first table must exactly match the data type and length of the columns selected from the second table.

5.6.5 Unions of Unions

We are not limited to combining just two SELECT queries together. We can combine more than two queries together using a UNION operation in order, for example, to report on our sales force results during the last four months:

```
SELECT    LASTNAME, FIRSTNAME, SALES_AMOUNT
FROM      JAN90_SALES
UNION
(SELECT   LASTNAME, FIRSTNAME, SALES_AMOUNT
FROM      FEB90_SALES
UNION
(SELECT   LASTNAME, FIRSTNAME, SALES_AMOUNT
FROM      MAR_SALES
UNION
(SELECT   LASTNAME, FIRSTNAME, SALES_AMOUNT
FROM      APR90_SALES)));
```

Notice that the UNION groupings are nested one within another by separating each UNION grouping by a set of parentheses. The names of the columns do not necessarily have to be the same, but they often will be if you are maintaining several versions of a file, as in our example.

5.7 THE INSERT STATEMENT

Suppose we want to insert an employee row into our EMPLOYEE table. A simple example of the command to do this is:

```
INSERT INTO EMPLOYEE (LASTNAME, FIRSTNAME, SALARY)
VALUES ('JONES', 'JOE', 35000);
```

We are specifying here the employee last name, first name, and salary with the values 'JONES', 'JOE', and 35000. This list of field names (in parentheses) to be assigned values follows the table name in the order indicated in the column name list. Values must be separated by commas, and dates and alphabetic data must be enclosed in single quotation marks (numeric data must not be enclosed in quote marks).

Columns that are not assigned data will be set to null values. Null values can be specified for individual columns by placing the key word NULL in the value list where the value would normally go. If all columns are being assigned values, you need not list the column names after the table name, but specifying the column names in the INSERT command allows you to insert values in an order that is different from those listed in the CREATE TABLE command that built the table.

When you insert a row into a table, the data type of each column being assigned a value must match the defined data type of the table column. If you define a column as NOT NULL at table creation time, you will have to specify a value for the column at the time you insert a new table row. Otherwise, nullable or NULL WITH DEFAULT columns will be assigned a null or default value for the new row.

5.7.1 Multiple-Row Insert from Another Table

We need not use the VALUES clause of the INSERT statement to insert a single row into a table. We could instead create multiple records in a table by copying the data from another table via a SELECT statement embedded in the INSERT statement like this:

```
INSERT    INTO MANAGER
(SELECT    ID, LASTNAME, FIRSTNAME, PHONE
FROM      EMPLOYEE
WHERE TYPE = 'MANAGER');
```

Now the INSERT statement loads rows into the MANAGER table using data found in the EMPLOYEE table. The SELECT statement retrieves certain rows from the EMPLOYEE table (those for managers) and feeds these rows to the INSERT statement. Any columns from EMPLOYEE can be chosen for insertion into the MANAGER table as long as the columns are defined in the MANAGER table.

In general, any valid SELECT statement can be used as a subquery in the INSERT command as long as the column data types match and the table name listed in the SELECT subquery is not the same table as the one listed in the main INSERT statement. You can gather data from more than one table using a SELECT subquery in an INSERT statement if you wish.

5.7.2 Using the INSERT Statement in an Application Program

There will probably be times when you want to use an application program written in a language such as COBOL or PL/I to load data into your tables (in fact, you may use this method exclusively). Some additional programming considerations must be taken into account in order to do this. First, you will need to check the status of the INSERT command return code, referred to as the SQLCODE field of the SQLCA (SQL communications area).

If DB2 detects an error while inserting a row into a table, the insertion process ceases. No data is inserted into the table and the SQLCODE field is set to an error value. The number of rows actually inserted during the INSERT command execution is reflected in the SQLERRD (3) value.

5.7.3 INSERT with Referential Constraints

When you insert rows into a table that has referential constraints defined for it, you must take some additional processing factors into account. For parent tables containing a primary key, define a unique index on the primary key. Do not insert duplicate values for the primary key, and do not insert null values for any column of the primary key.

When you insert rows into a dependent (or child) table that contains foreign keys, remember that each nonnull value inserted into a foreign key column must be equal to the value in the primary key of the parent table. If any value for the foreign key is null, the entire foreign key is null. Dropping indexes that enforce the primary key rules of the parent table will cause subsequent row inserts into either the parent or dependent table to fail. For example:

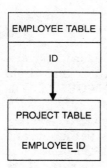

In this example, every row inserted into the PROJECT table must have a value of EMPLOYEE_ID which is either equal to an employee ID value (the primary key) in the EMPLOYEE table or is null. If an index on ID for the EMPLOYEE table is dropped, the INSERT of that employee ID into the EMPLOYEE or PROJECT tables will fail. Any

EMPLOYEE_ID in the PROJECT table must exist in the EMPLOYEE table for an INSERT operation with referential constraints to succeed.

5.8 THE UPDATE STATEMENT

The UPDATE statement is the one to use to change the values of data in a table. It lets you change the value of one or more columns in each row indicated in the WHERE clause. If we want to update the phone extension for Jim Smith, we would use a statement similar to this:

```
UPDATE    EMPLOYEE
SET  PHONE = '2955'
WHERE LASTNAME = 'SMITH'
AND  FIRSTNAME = 'JIM';
```

Actually, you would probably use the employee ID number to locate a particular employee record, but this example shows you the AND option in the WHERE clause. The table name is indicated after the UPDATE key word, and the SET key word lets you specify the column name and update value. The WHERE clause indicates which row(s) should have this column value updated.

The update value you specify after the SET key word can be a constant, a host variable (for using embedded SQL in application programs), a special register value (USER, NULL, CURRENT DATE, CURRENT TIME, CURRENT TIMESTAMP, or CURRENT TIMEZONE), or an arithmetic expression. If you omit the WHERE clause, use the ALL ROWS UPDATE statement to indicate only those rows that should really be updated.

If DB2 detects an error when executing an UPDATE statement, the UPDATE process stops and an error code is returned in the SQLCODE field for the SQLCA. No rows are then updated, and any rows already changed have their values restored to the state existing before the UPDATE operation began. If no rows satisfy the WHERE clause conditions, a not-found code of 100 is returned for the SQLCODE field.

5.8.1 Multiple-Row UPDATE

You can update more than one row of a table by specifying certain conditions in the WHERE clause of the UPDATE statement as follows:

```
UPDATE   EMPLOYEE
SET PAY_RATE = PAY_RATE * 1.07
WHERE PAY_TYPE = 'HOURLY';
```

This statement will give all hourly employees a 7 percent raise in their hourly pay rate. We can also build UPDATE statements, as shown below, that copy multiple update values from another table using a SELECT subquery:

```
UPDATE P_SUPPLIERS SET QUANTITY = 0
WHERE 'CHICAGO' = (SELECT CITY
                   FROM SUPPLIERS
                   WHERE SUPPLIERS.ID = P_SUPPLIERS.ID);
```

This statement will set the shipped quantity to zero for all suppliers located in Chicago. The SELECT subquery checks the SUPPLIERS table for supplier records that have corresponding records in the P_SUPPLIERS table. The CITY value is not stored in the P_SUPPLIERS table (it is stored in the SUPPLIERS table). The WHERE clause of the main UPDATE statement indicates the CITY value to search for in the SELECT subquery. This is an example of a correlated subquery, which is similar to a correlated SELECT query within a main SELECT statement.

5.8.2   UPDATE with Referential Constraints

When you update a parent table, you cannot modify a primary key that has corresponding rows existing in a dependent (child) table because this would result in "orphan" rows that have no rows in the parent table. When updating a dependent table, nonnull foreign key values must match a primary key in a parent table. We will again use our referential constraint example, which is:

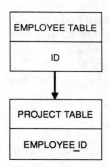

If referential constraints are to be enforced for this relationship, we can assign a project to no employee (NULL EMPLOYEE_ID) in the PROJECT table, but we cannot assign a project to an employee whose ID does not exist in the EMPLOYEE table. If '00900' is not an ID value in the EMPLOYEE table, the following UPDATE statement will fail:

```
UPDATE  PROJECT
SET EMPLOYEE_ID = '00900'
WHERE  EMPLOYEE_ID = '00900';
```

Referential integrity constraint is violated because the ID value of '00900' does not exist in the parent table. All changes made up to the point when this statement executes will be rolled back to their original values.

5.9 The DELETE Statement

We need a way to remove rows from tables, and the SQL DELETE statement lets us do this. The DELETE command will remove an entire row, not just specific columns. Rows to be deleted are specified in a WHERE clause. If you do not specify a WHERE clause in a DELETE statement, *all rows of the table will be deleted*. Therefore, always use a carefully constructed WHERE clause to choose only certain rows, except in cases where you really want to delete all table rows.

Use the following to delete an employee whose ID is '00900':

```
DELETE FROM EMPLOYEE
WHERE ID = '00900';
```

If the ID value of '00900' is unique in the EMPLOYEE table, only one row is deleted.

5.9.1 Multiple-Row DELETE

This is how we would delete rows from our CUSTOMER table for all customers located in Chicago (we have a separate division of our company which now supplies customers in the Chicago area):

```
DELETE FROM CUSTOMER
WHERE CITY = 'CHICAGO';
```

Every row in the CUSTOMER table with a CITY value of 'CHICAGO' will be deleted. If DB2 encounters an error while executing this statement, the DELETE operation ceases and an error code is returned in the SQLCODE field. If no rows satisfy the WHERE clause conditions, SQLCODE is set to 100.

We delete all rows in the TEMP TABLE this way:

```
DELETE FROM TEMP;
```

The TEMP table will still exist but now contains no rows. If you really want to remove the TEMP table, as well as its definition in the DB2 catalog, use this statement:

DROP TABLE TEMP;

5.9.2   DELETE with Referential Constraints

When you have a table with a primary key and a dependent table, DELETE must follow referential constraints rules. This means that all DELETE rules of all the dependent tables must be followed before any rows will be deleted.

The DELETE RESTRICT rule says that a row can only be deleted if no other row depends on the row that is to be deleted. The DELETE will fail if any rows in a dependent table exist with foreign keys equal to the primary key of the row to be deleted. An invoice row in an INVOICE table cannot be deleted if invoice items for that INVOICE_ID exist in the INVOICE_ITEMS table.

The DELETE SET NULL rule indicates that nullable foreign key columns of the foreign key columns of the foreign key in a dependent table row should be set to NULL when a row of the parent table that has a primary key value equal to the foreign key in dependent table rows is deleted. In other words, rows in a dependent table that are children of a row to be deleted in the parent table will have their references to the parent table set to NULL. This means that a child row can exist without a corresponding parent table row.

A DELETE CASCADE rule dictates that parent table rows are deleted first and then dependent table rows are deleted. When you delete an invoice from the parent INVOICE table, all items for that invoice are deleted from the INVOICE_ITEMS table.

A summary of the rules for referential integrity is given in Fig. 5.3.

5.10   BASE TABLES AND VIEWS

DB2 supports the concept of logical views, which are abstractions of physical tables. You can think of a view as a table that does not actually exist but appears to users as a real table that does exist. Data in a physical (base) table actually exists, and for each row of such a table the entire row is physically stored as the user sees it. A view can reference just part of a base table, so more data might exist in the base table than the view allows a user to see.

In Fig. 5.4 you can see that one view can reference more than one base table. View 2 can retrieve (but not update or delete from) Tables 2, 3, and 4, and Views 1 and 3 might reference only some of the rows

INSERT, UPDATE, and DELETE Restrictions with Referential Integrity

- The primary key of a row with dependents cannot be updated.

- Primary key columns updated without cursor cannot operate on more than one row.

- Primary key columns cannot be updated with UPDATE...WHERE CURRENT OF.

- A subquery cannot make deletions if it references another table that is affected by the deletion of rows from the first table.

- Only one row can be inserted via a subquery into a self-referencing table.

- Rows cannot be deleted from self-referencing tables using DELETE.... WHERE CURRENT OF.

Figure 5.3   Summary of referential integrity constraints.

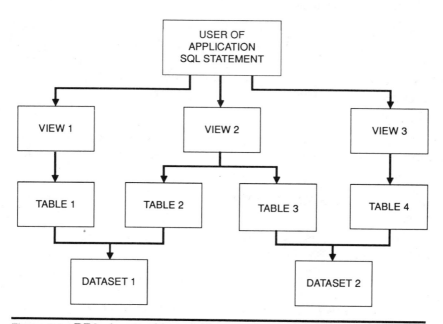

Figure 5.4   DB2 views and base tables.

and some of the columns in the base tables referenced. Views are not actually stored as the user sees them but rather the definitions of the base Tables 1 through 4 are mapped to Datasets 1 and 2, and Views 1, 2, and 3 are mapped to Tables 1 through 4. Data are actually stored only in Datasets 1 and 2.

5.11   THE BENEFITS OF USING VIEWS

Views can provide extra flexibility to your users and application programs as follows:

1. Logical data is independent.
2. The same data can be viewed in different ways.
3. User perception of table data is simplified.
4. There is automatic security for hidden data.

Logical data independence is provided because the underlying base tables of your database can be restructured, but user views may not need to be modified. For instance, you could change the order of columns in the base table and a query like the following against the base table would not return columns in the same order:

SELECT * FROM EMPLOYEE;

On the other hand, the following query using a view would return columns in the same order as before the reordering of base table columns:

SELECT * FROM EMPLOYEE_V1;

This is true if the EMPLOYEE_V1 view was defined using this statement:

CREATE VIEW EMPLOYEE_VI AS
SELECT * FROM EMPLOYEE;

Views also allow users to look at base table data in different ways. One user view could be defined to reference only certain columns and/ or rows. Other views could sequence columns in different orders or list different columns or specify different sets of rows. All of these views could access one base table.

User views can simplify the specification of data that a user needs access to. A user can refer to a view that specifies a complex SELECT statement by using a much simpler statement like this:

SELECT * FROM CUSTOMERS;

This statement might select only certain columns from the CUSTOMER table and specify only certain types of customers, but the user only needs to select all rows and all columns using the simple statement above. Normally, you should not use the SELECT * form of SQL data retrieval; but with a user view that restricts the amount of data returned by a data request, this can allow for easier user and application program data access.

Some degree of security is provided automatically with DB2 views because data which a user must not have access to can be hidden from the user by having the view not reference columns or rows that the user should not see. The hidden data is secure because, assuming the user can only access the table using the view, data not defined through the view simply cannot be accessed by the user. If the user cannot issue a data request directly to the table or with another view, security is maintained.

5.12   CREATING A VIEW

You could store a definition of just your hourly employees by defining a view that selects only hourly employees from your EMPLOYEE table with an SQL statement like this:

```
CREATE VIEW HOURLY_EMP AS
        SELECT      ID, LASTNAME, FIRSTNAME, PHONE
        FROM        EMPLOYEE
        WHERE       TYPE = 'HOURLY';
```

This statement causes the SELECT statement to be stored in the DB2 catalog—the set of actual employees is not stored, but the definition of how to retrieve these employees from the EMPLOYEE base table is stored. Users and application programs will be able to access hourly employees as if these employees were the only ones in an actual table called HOURLY_EMP. Only rows from the EMPLOYEE table which contain a value of 'HOURLY' for the TYPE column are included in the HOURLY_EMP logical view.

By storing a definition of part of a table as a view in the DB2 catalog, users and application programs do not need to supply a new SQL statement to describe this data to DB2 when they need access to the data. The SELECT statement in the CREATE VIEW statement acts just like the same statement used to access the EMPLOYEE base table. If you want to rename the columns in the base table, you can do this by listing the new field names (in the same order as the base table column names in the SELECT statement that follows) just after the CREATE VIEW clause:

```
CREATE VIEW HOURLY_EMP (ID, LAST, FIRST, TEL) AS
SELECT     ID, LASTNAME, FIRSTNAME, PHONE
FROM       EMPLOYEE
WHERE      TYPE = 'HOURLY'
```

5.13   INSERTING TABLE ROWS USING VIEWS

A view can be used to update base table rows only if the view defines a row and column subset of a single base table. Views that define joins between tables cannot be used for insert and update (but can be used for read-only operations). In order for a DB2 view to support INSERT and UPDATE operations, the following must hold true:

1. If a view references multiple tables, the view cannot be updated.
2. Views cannot be defined over other views that cannot be updated.
3. Fields to be inserted or updated cannot be derived from arithmetic expressions or constants.
4. Fields to be updated cannot be derived from an SQL function.
5. Views that include a GROUP BY clause or DISTINCT key word cannot be updated.
6. Views defining a subquery referencing the same base table that the outer query references cannot be updated.
7. You cannot create an index on a view or alter the structure of a view.

When using views to update base tables, be careful to reference only columns and rows defined to the view. Otherwise, your inserted row will be lost. For instance, you could attempt to add a salaried employee to a view defined for only hourly employees as follows:

```
INSERT INTO HOURLY_EMP (ID, LASTNAME, FIRSTNAME, TYPE)
VALUES     ('523440', 'PETERSON', 'NEIL', 'SALARIED');
```

You would not normally attempt to do this; but if a user made a mistake and tried to do this, DB2 would accept the inserted row. However, since the row is not defined to the view, it would instantly disappear from the view. The user would probably try the insert again, this time on the ID column. One way to avoid this is to include the following clause WITH CHECK OPTION after the CREATE VIEW statement:

```
CREATE VIEW HOURLY_EMP AS
SELECT    ID, LASTNAME, FIRSTNAME, TYPE
```

```
FROM      EMPLOYEE
WHERE     TYPE = 'HOURLY'
WITH CHECK OPTION;
```

Now all insert and update operations using this view will be checked to make sure that attempts to insert or update rows satisfy the view definition; if not, the insert will only be used in cases where a view is not updatable and contains no nested subqueried. If updates are allowable on only certain fields (inserts are thus disallowed), WITH CHECK OPTION is used only with updates of these certain fields.

5.14 UPDATING TABLES USING VIEWS

You can use the UPDATE statement to update employee records using the HOURLY_EMP view as follows:

```
UPDATE HOURLY_EMP
SET PAY_RATE = PAY_RATE * 1.05
```

This is the same as using the following statement with the EMPLOYEE base table:

```
UPDATE HOURLY_EMP
SET       PAY_RATE = PAY_RATE * 1.05
WHERE     TYPE = 'HOURLY';
```

Both of these statements will give all hourly employees in the EMPLOYEE table a 5 percent raise in their hourly pay rate. Note that you can only update one table using a view—a DB2 view that references more than one table cannot be used to update a base table. The previous section on insert operations describes which views are updatable.

5.15 DELETING FROM TABLES USING VIEWS

You can also use a view as follows to delete all hourly employees (say, if you wanted to create a separate table for these employees):

```
DELETE HOURLY_EMP;
```

This is the same as using the following statement with just the base table EMPLOYEE:

```
DELETE FROM EMPLOYEE
WHERE TYPE = 'HOURLY';
```

As with the UPDATE statement, you can only delete from one table using a view; DB2 will not allow you to DELETE from joined tables using a view.

5.16 VIEWS OF MULTIPLE TABLES

One very handy use of views is to define joins of multiple tables for read-only operations (inserts and updates are not allowed). A view of this kind can be used to create a single table from portions of other tables (or views). A user will not be able to detect whether the view is one base table or several tables combined.

For reporting purposes, you might want to retrieve and print full customer names on a list of parts sold to customers. You can accomplish this using a view like this:

```
CREATE VIEW PARTS_SOLD (PARTNO, CUSTID, NAME, CITY) AS
SELECT      PARTNO, CUSTID, NAME, CITY
FROM        INVOICE_ITEMS, CUSTOMER
WHERE       INVOICE_ITEMS.CUSTID = CUSTOMER.CUSTID;
```

This would produce a table that contained part number, customer ID number, customer name, and customer city. You could get more elaborate and combine this with the PARTS table in order to get a full description of each part (if the description was not used stored in the INVOICE_ITEMS table when the invoice was created). The nice thing that such views provide for your users is a simple way to retrieve data from views, instead of having to create the SELECT statements each time a report is needed.

5.17 DELETING VIEWS

A DB2 view can be easily removed from the DB2 system by any person (or program) who has the proper access authority. The following drop view statement is all that is required to remove a view:

```
DROP VIEW HOURLY_EMP;
```

Remember, views do not store data. Only the definition of a set of data is removed from the DB2 catalog when you drop a DB2 view.

If you let only a system security administrator create and drop views, data access by users and application programs can be easily and effectively controlled.

6

Management and Control of the Database Environment

The advent of mini- and microcomputers meant that organizations could begin to establish distributed processing database environments. MIS-driven distributed processing usually resulted in a centralized distributed environment, whereas user-driven distributed processing led a decentralized distributed environment. In either situation, an organization may need to share some of the data that has been either distributed across or decentralized to various locations and departments. Sharing data can be difficult, especially in a decentralized distributed environment in which each department is responsible for the systems that automate its functions.

Problems of autonomy, or decentralized control, are particularly acute in a database environment. The architecture of the database management system (DBMS) may dictate its usefulness primarily in one type of control environment. If a DBMS is selected solely on the basis of one application's needs, it may prove inappropriate for the desired control environment. In such cases, management control decisions may unwisely be made on the basis of previous technical decisions.

Unfortunately, many organizations select a DBMS without a long-term objective. When problems arise, the DBMS may be discarded and replaced with another. In some cases, the organization may become dependent on the DBMS because of the amount of data and systems that have been committed to it. The organization may then continue to use the inappropriate DBMS and acquire another for future development. If a new DBMS is acquired, however, problems may occur when data must be shared between the DBMSs. If a desired database environment has not been specified, the MIS manager may want to consider a strategy that will avoid commitment to a specific environment.

This chapter examines several alternative database environments from a management control perspective and explores the impact of the DBMS selection on the ability to achieve the desired management control.

6.1 CENTRALIZED VERSUS DECENTRALIZED CONTROL

The terms *centralized* and *decentralized* refer to the organizational level at which control and decision-making are exercised. Absolute centralization or decentralization cannot be achieved. Absolute centralization would imply that only one person could decide anything, whereas absolute decentralization would imply that a manager delegated all authority.

Figure 6.1 illustrates decentralization and centralization of database authority in an organization. In the decentralized example, each function is responsible for its own database. Function 1 makes all decisions concerning database A, and function 2 makes those concerning database B. Such authority is delegated by the manager to whom the function reports. In a centralized environment, the manager usually delegates authority to one functional area. In this case, it is the database administration function. The manager may choose not to delegate the authority but may elect to retain some authority or delegate

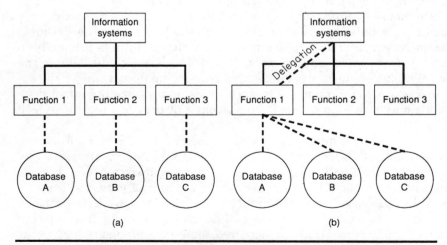

Figure 6.1   (*a*) Decentralized, and (*b*) centralized database authority.

some to the other functional areas. Centralization and decentralization imply tendencies to delegate or not delegate; the two extremes encompass a broad spectrum of possibilities.

6.2 DISTRIBUTED VERSUS NONDISTRIBUTED LOCATION

The terms *distributed* and *nondistributed* refer to location. Distributed and nondistributed database environments are illustrated in Fig. 6.2. In the distributed environment, each location—ABC, DEF, and GHI—has its own processor and databases. The databases are distributed to the location at which they are primarily ruled. The nondistributed environment shows the same three locations. Each has its own processor, but all the databases are concentrated on processor 2 at location DEF—a case of nondistributed data and distributed processing.

6.3 ALTERNATIVE DATABASE ENVIRONMENTS

Centralized or decentralized and distributed or nondistributed can be combined in the same environment. The following sections describe four possible environments: Centralized and nondistributed, centralized and distributed, decentralized and nondistributed, and decentralized and distributed.

6.3.1 Centralized and Nondistributed

In this environment, the data is located in one place and management retains control or delegates it to a single entity. A typical example is a mainframe environment with a string data or database administration function.

6.3.2 Centralized and Distributed

In this environment, management retains control or delegates control to a single entity, and the data is physically located in many places. The metadata, or data about the data, is usually located in one place with the controlling organization unless it is required by the distributed data. A typical example is a bank machine network with customer and account data stored at the owning branch.

6.3.3 Decentralized and Nondistributed

In this environment, the data is located in one place, and management delegates control of the data to many lower-level entities. A typical

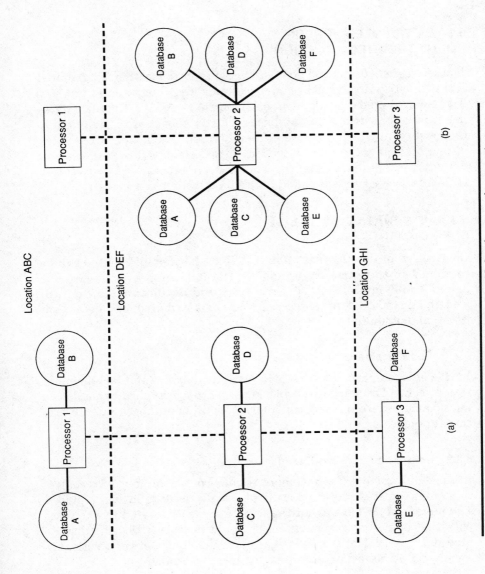

Figure 6.2 (*a*) Distributed and (*b*) nondistributed database environments.

example is a mainframe environment in which each user organization has its own systems and programming staff.

6.3.4 Decentralized Distributed

In this environment, management delegates control of the data to many lower-level entities. The data is physically located in many places, and the metadata is usually distributed with the data. A typical example is an organization with many minicomputers located at and under the control of the using department.

6.4 DBMS CHARACTERISTICS AND CONTROL

The characteristics of a DBMS can affect an organization's ability to establish a particular control environment. With some DBMSs, for example, it is very difficult to relate a diversity of data for the purpose of sharing. If sharing data at the physical level is one of the organization's goals, the manager should beware of selecting a DBMS with characteristics that make this relating of data difficult. Other DBMSs require central management because they can be used economically only if applications share physical facilities.

6.4.1 Characteristics Requiring Central Control

DBMS characteristics that require an organization to adopt centralized operational control of the data include the sharing of physical resources by applications, a large number of optional functions, and any characteristic that requires expertise in a particular area. Many well-known mainframe DBMSs have such characteristics.

Some DBMSs require all applications, or at least major subsets of them, to share physical resource, including databases and files, program libraries, dictionaries, and operating system regions. In some cases, resource limitations, rather than the software, necessitate sharing. For example, an organization with 15 online DB2 database applications would not want 15 copies of the communications handler up and running at the same time. This would require extraordinary machine resources and management. If the organization required all 15 applications to be running simultaneously, they would have to share the physical resources of one or perhaps a few DB2 control regions. Systems such as DB2, IMS, ADABAS, and IDMS were designed to share control regions, as noted in Fig. 6.3.

Another DBMS characteristic that requires an organization to

Programs

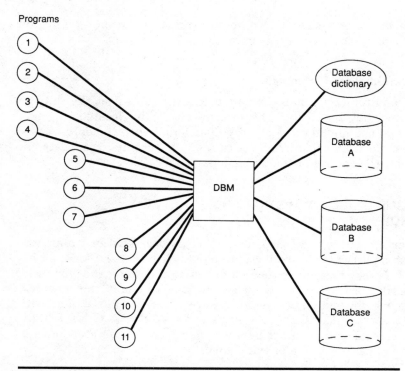

Figure 6.3   Example of sharing of control regions.

adopt central control is a large number of optional functions. The more functions a system has, the more complex it is; many decisions must be made for configuring the systems to meet the organization's needs, and many trade-offs must be evaluated. Because such decisions require scarce expertise, the formation of a central group that can share its expertise with others is recommended.

In fact, any characteristic of a DBMS that requires expertise should make the system a candidate for central control. Many functions and characteristics of a DBMS fall into this category. Unfortunately they are not always discovered during the selection process or with the implementation of the first few applications. One such characteristic is a limit on the number of files or databases that a DBMS will support from one control region. Such a limit may seem unimportant until an organization approaches it. At that time, it may be too late to prevent the purchase of an additional machine and the partitioning of the databases into unrelated systems. Intelligent central control of the physical resources can prevent such a situation.

6.4.2 Characteristics Hindering Central Control

When central physical control is unnecessary, centralized planning and control is often difficult to establish. DBMS characteristics that make central control of the physical facilities unnecessary include ease of use, lack of shared resources, and a limited ability to share and relate data.

If a DBMS is easy to use, justifying the formation of a special group to provide centralized operational control is difficult. When database definitions are embedded within the data, each database is self-contained. In these cases, it is usually unnecessary to share other resources of significance from a control point of view. The lack of shared resources reduces the requirements for central operational control. Figure 6.4 illustrates this type of environment.

Finally, if a DBMS does not allow for logically relating separate physical databases, the ability to share and relate data is significantly diminished, substantially limiting the ability to gain the benefits a centralized control environment can offer.

6.4.3 Characteristics Hindering Decentralized Control

Many DBMSs that are marketed as easy to use may enable end users to easily retrieve and report data in the desired format but require considerable effort on the part of the database administrator. An organization seeking decentralized operational control in the database environment must be assured that no special requirements lurk behind the ease of use offered by the vendor.

6.5 ADMINISTRATIVE CONTROLS IN DATABASE ENVIRONMENT

Administrative controls may be defined as management policies formulated to ensure adequate maintenance of a selective access program, which can be selective authorization to databases or physical areas. The controls may include the development and implementation of security policies, guidelines, standards, and procedures. Effective administrative controls can go a long way in helping to ensure that an organization has a secure operating database environment. These controls certainly will assist in reducing or eliminating both deliberate and accidental threats. Once intruders realize that the chances of being detected are good, they may be deterred from attempting to breach the security. This determination of the probability of being detected

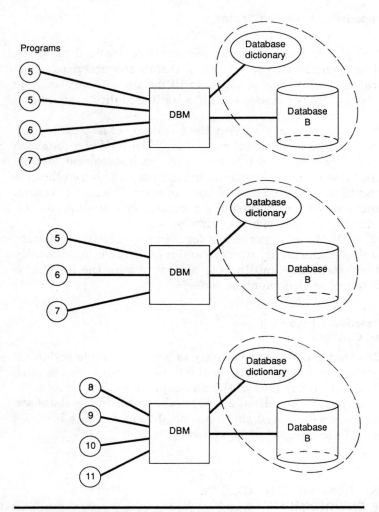

Figure 6.4   Example of lack of shared resources.

can be made from the intruders' knowledge of the existing administrative controls. For example, if the intruders know that there is a requirement for the user's name and terminal log-on times to be recorded, then they will very likely not use the terminal.

The probability of accidental threats succeeding decreases with an increase in the user's knowledge of the operating environment and requirements. Clear and precise administrative procedures and assertions help to increase that knowledge and, in turn, decrease the probability of successful accidental threats.

Administrative controls, and security features in particular, should be developed parallel to the actual development of the systems and programs. A group consisting of internal auditors, development team, and users should be assigned to develop these controls and standards.

Administrative controls can be defined in the following areas:

- *Top-level management decisions:* Decisions pertaining to the selection and evaluation of safeguards.

- *Security risk assessment studies:* Identify and rank the events that would compromise the security of the database and the information stored in it.

- *Personnel management:* Decisions pertaining to employee hiring and firing procedures, employee rules of conduct, and enforcement.

- *Data-handling techniques:* A well-defined set of rules describing the precautions to be used and the obligations of personnel during the handling of all data.

- *Data-processing practices:* The methods to control accountability for data, verification of the accuracy of data, and inventories of storage media.

- *Programming practices:* The discipline employed in the specification, design, implementation, program coding, and debugging of the system.

- *Assignment of responsibilities:* Assign individuals a specific set of responsibilities toward carrying out certain security functions for which each is held responsible.

- *Procedure auditing:* An independent examination of established security procedures to determine their ongoing effectiveness.

6.6 AUDITING AND MONITORING THE DATABASE

Auditing and monitoring are integral features of database management and control. Should a violation be attempted, the system must be able to detect it and react to it effectively. Detection then implies that the system has a threat-monitoring capability. Threat monitoring requires the following actions:

- Monitoring the events of the systems as related to security
- Recognizing a potential compromise to the security system
- Diagnosing the nature of the threat

- Performing compensatory actions
- Reporting and recording the event

While threat monitoring is an active form of surveillance, an equally important, but more passive form, is auditability of the database. A security audit should be able to cover the past events of the system and, in particular, cover all security-related transactions.

Audit trails that can lead to the identity of users, terminals, and authorizing bodies should be a feature of all applications. The monitoring process within an organization should include the ability to determine whether:

- The controls over the database administration function are effective
- The process by which sensitive data is determined is adequate
- The procedure by which security violations are detected is in place and effective
- The extent to which data access is restricted to only authorized individuals is workable
- The ability to restrict access by a program to the database, other programs, and catalogs exists
- Terminal security features, such as log-on, log-off, and restart, are adequate and effective
- The procedures to follow during processing interruptions are effective

The importance of keeping records and logs of events affecting the database and its environment cannot be overemphasized. The events recorded should include performance data, all error or abnormal events, all transactions related to sensitive information, and all overrides of established system control.

Several DBMSs provide logging capabilities as part of their package. These logs should be investigated for their adequacy and ability to meet the auditing requirements of the environment. Organizations should not be hesitant about designing and implementing their own in-house logging facilities if the vendor's facilities prove inadequate.

Any security effort in an organization should eventually involve internal auditors. This involvement becomes mandatory because of the changing requirements for evaluating and verifying controls in a secure database environment. Personnel responsible for security can offer considerable assistance to the auditors in determining the accuracy, integrity, and completeness of systems.

Researchers are now suggesting that internal auditors become involved in the development phases of system design, not only in the post-implementation evaluation. The auditor's experience should provide the development teams with an insight into the various methods they can use to approach their responsibilities in controlling and auditing the total information processing systems.

Because of the rapidly changing database technology, internal auditors need to consistently upgrade their skills. System development teams with current knowledge should assist the auditors in filling in the gaps in their knowledge of techniques and concepts of integrated database systems design. The development teams should strive to increase management's awareness of changes in the database environment as they affect internal audit and the controls governing data processing.

Finally, the following list of management activities should enhance the internal auditing capabilities within an organization and, especially, how they affect the database environment:

- Ensure that all staff realize the importance of internal auditing in the database environment

- Ensure that there is a clearly defined internal audit mandate that specifies the responsibility of internal audit as it relates to all phases of the security of the database environment

- Clearly define the working relationship among users, internal auditors, and development teams responsible for database management and control

- Encourage the development of new techniques and internal audit approaches to ensure the security, privacy, and integrity of the database

- Require the development of security control guidelines

- Ensure that internal auditors participate in the security effort

6.7 PROTECTION MECHANISMS IN THE DATABASE ENVIRONMENT

Protection mechanisms can be defined as the techniques and methods used to ensure security, integrity, and privacy in the database environment. There are two types of protection mechanisms, those built into the computer operating system, also known as internal mechanisms, and those not linked to the operating system, or external mechanisms. This section discusses two protection mechanisms.

6.7.1 Resource Access Control Facility (RACF)

RACF is a program product of IBM that is designed to identify system users and control their access to protected resources. Its authorization structure can be contrasted with a dataset password mechanism. With typical password protection, a password is assigned to a specific dataset. The system ensures that the dataset can be accessed only when that password is supplied.

Protected datasets can be accessed by anyone who knows the password. Obviously, there are control problems associated with restricting knowledge of the passwords. There are also problems in withdrawing access to datasets. If three people know the password for a particular dataset and an administrator wants to take away one person's access rights, the password must be changed and the new password communicated to the users.

The RACF authorization structure is based on other principles than password protection. RACF eliminates the need for dataset passwords. With RACF, an administrator can tell which users are authorized to access which datasets. A user's right to access datasets can be withdrawn by changing the profile.

RACF authorization structure contains three kinds of elements: (1) users, (2) groups of users, and (3) protected resources. It stores descriptions of users, group, and resources in profiles contained in a special dataset called the RACF dataset.

RACF interfaces with the operating system in the following three main areas:

- Identification and verification of users
- Authorization checking for access to protect resources
- Monitoring to provide both immediate notification of security problems and a log for post de facto analysis

6.7.2   The Access Matrix, or Authorization Table

The access matrix, or authorization table, is an internal mechanism built into the operating system. It is essentially a set of tables that indicate who has access to what data. The access matrix consists of the following components:

- Objects that are to be protected
- Subjects seeking access to these objects
- Different protection levels for each object
- Rules that determine how the subjects access each object
- A monitor that mediates all access of a subject to an object
- Directories containing information about the objects and subjects

The interaction between objects and subjects can be represented by an access matrix (see Fig. 6.5). The objects that are protected are the new components of the matrix. The subjects seeking access to the objects are the column components of the matrix. Each entry in the access matrix determines the access rights of the subject to the object and is defined as the access attribute in the model. The access matrix is dynamic enough to include any class of objects or subjects within the database environment. It can provide a high level of protection for any object irrespective of whatever application the organization's personnel develops and runs against the integrated database.

Each object is placed in a class that is determined by the level of protection for that object. For example, an object may be placed in a read-only protection class. Each subject will be a member of a hierarchy. The hierarchical classifying of the subjects will allow subjects to create object subjects while ensuring that the created subject will not have more privileges than the creator.

In Fig. 6.5, each entry in the access matrix represents the access rights of the subject to the objects. For example, the 01 in the first col-

Employee name	Employee address	Employee phone number	Employee SIN	Employee education	Employee salary	Employee medical	Employee pension	Employee history	
11	11	11	11	11	11	11	11	11	Personnel
01	01	01	01	00	00	00	01	01	Accounting
00	00	00	00	00	00	00	00	00	Marketing
00	00	00	00	00	00	00	00	00	Purchasing
10	00	10	10	10	10	10	10	10	DBA
10	10	10	10	10	10	00	00	00	Maintenance
01	01	01	00	00	00	00	00	00	

Legend

01 — Read
11 — Read and write
00 — No access
10 — Write only

Figure 6.5 Example of access matrix.

umn and the second row indicates that the accounting department can READ the employee name; the 11 in the first column and row indicates that the personnel department can both READ and WRITE to the employee name on the employee database; the 00 in the fifth column and second row indicates that the accounting department can neither READ nor WRITE to the employee education information; and the 10 in the first column and sixth row indicates that the maintenance department can only WRITE to the employee name on the employee database.

The matrix can accommodate several other access attributes such as EXECUTE, DELETE, UPDATE, APPEND, SORT, and CREATE.

Infrastructure Support for the Database Environment

7.1 INTRODUCTION

The introduction of a database management system (DBMS) into an enterprise has an enormous effect on the environment and the way things are traditionally done. Many organizations fail in their efforts to introduce database technology not because of the failure of the software but because of the failure of personnel to offer the infrastructure support necessary to the success of the database environment.

In order for database technology to succeed in an organization, there must be management support for the environment as well as the MIS infrastructure support.

The infrastructure support consists of all efforts by management information system (MIS) personnel to ensure a database operation that runs smoothly and efficiently. It ensures that there is adequately trained personnel not only to operate the environment but to respond to and solve problems as they occur.

The infrastructure support comes from the following areas:

- Data administration (DA)
- Database administration (DBA)
- Technical support
- Physical database designers
- Logical database designers
- Application programmers
- Computer operations

- Input-output data control
- System analysts and designers

7.2 DATA ADMINISTRATION SUPPORT

The infrastructure support for the database environment, which is given by the DA function, consists of, but is not limited to, offering assistance to all functional MIS groups and users in a variety of areas, which include:

- Database design methodologies
- Database security and integrity
- Database access
- Data dictionary support
- Logical database design
- Database audit
- Database performance and maintenance
- Database standards
- Database education and training

7.2.1 Database Design Methodologies

DA provides assistance in the selection of a structured design methodology for the environment. Present design methodologies fall into two main categories:

- Data driven
- Process driven

The primary deliverable from a data-driven design effort is a data model. There are several approaches to producing data models. The one most often used is the entity-relationship approach.

The primary deliverable from a process-driven design effort is a process model or a set of processes which are decomposed into programming specifications. Data-flow diagrams are very often classified as deliverable from a process-driven design effort. In several instances data-driven and process-driven design are done in parallel during the development life cycle. In some instances either one or the other is done.

7.2.2 Database Security and Integrity

The issue of database security and integrity becomes more relevant and important in a database environment. There, the primary objective is to expose the data to the widest audience of users (data sharing) while maintaining the integrity of the data and avoiding abuse of the database (data security).

DA assists in conducting threat analyses and risk assessments to determine the level of protection that will be needed and assists in the evaluation and selection of any required protection mechanisms. DA also establishes data security standards for password protection, database accessing, and program interfacing with the database.

7.2.3 Database Access

DA assists in determining who will access the database, what functions can be performed by authorized users of the database, what terminals can update the database, and whether dedicated terminals should be used in the database environment.

7.2.4 Data Dictionary Support

In a database environment, the data dictionary is a very important tool for systems design, documentation, data management, and data security. It can be used as a repository to collect the user requirements which are used as the primary input to the logical design phase of database development.

Characteristics of the data model can also be stored in the data dictionary as can the input to the physical design phase. And the dictionary can be used to carry out maintenance on the various databases once they are installed.

In the database environment, the data dictionary, as it is currently constituted, cannot support the data-driven design environment outlined above. However, applications that access the database are adequately supported.

7.2.5 Logical Database Design

DA assists system developers in the logical database design phase of database development. During this phase, the system developers produce a data model from the user requirements.

DA also assists in synthesizing the data model to ensure that it meets the needs of the users and assists in the documenting of the entities, attributes, and relationships; the normalization of the entities and tables (in a relational environment); and population of the entities and data dictionary.

7.2.6 Database Audit

DA assists internal auditors, external auditors, and application programmers in developing and maintaining audit trails, audit software, and audit standards. It also provides education and training to auditors and users in database technology and the needs for auditing the database.

7.2.7 Database Performance and Maintenance

Database monitoring and tuning is a very important activity in the database environment. It involves the periodic appraisal of the performance of the database management software. Database tuning involves the adjusting and reorganizing of the database and access methods parameters.

DA does not have the primary responsibility for database monitoring and tuning but generally assists the DBAs, technical support staff, and physical designers in providing guidelines for performing these tasks.

7.2.8 Database Standards

DA assists in the development of standards for accessing the database, naming of tables and table columns, selection of primary and foreign keys, and use of utilities in the database environment, especially in the area of backup and recovery.

7.2.9 Database Education and Training

DA provides input about the education and training needs of the various functional units in the database environment. The immediate needs for the MIS department are in the following areas:

- Data analysis techniques
- Data modeling
- Introduction to SQL
- SQL/DS and DB2 internals
- QMF and other reporting packages
- Introduction to VM/CMS
- Introduction to MVS
- MVS internals
- MVS operating and console messages
- Performance monitoring and database tuning

7.3 DATABASE ADMINISTRATION SUPPORT

The infrastructure support given to the database environment by DBA consists of offering assistance to system designers in a variety of areas, which include, but are not limited to:

- Loading the database
- Reorganizing the database
- Maintenance of the database
- Data storage calculations
- Selection of access paths
- Performance monitoring
- Normalization

The support that DA offers should not be confused with that offered by DBA. DA offers overall data management support to the database environment whereas DBA offers technical support as dictated by the DBMS. That is, the support offered by DA is the same irrespective of the DBMS. The same is not true for DBA. In the database environment DBA support may be offered by the current technical support staff.

7.3.1   Loading the Database

DBA loads both test and production versions of the database. There are several utilities available in both the SQL/DS and DB2 environments for loading the database. The DBA must certainly become familiar with the operation and operational requirements of these utilities.

7.3.2   Reorganizing the Database

It may become necessary because of the database performance or changes in systems design to reorganize the database (i.e., alter the physical storage of data within the database). DBA will accept requests for database reorganization from systems development teams, analyze those requests, and reorganize the database, if necessary.

7.3.3   Maintenance of the Database

DBA has the primary responsibility for maintaining all application and corporate databases where applicable. The database maintenance includes, but is not limited to:

- Restoration or modification of access paths
- Modification of primary and foreign keys
- Reorganizing the database
- Modification of tables and table contents

7.3.4 Data Storage Calculations

DBA is responsible for advising all relevant personnel about space and storage requirements for all databases. That function does the calculations related to space and storage estimates. It also advises about the best access methods to select for each application database.

7.3.5 Selection of Access Paths

DBA assists the systems development teams in determining, on an application by application basis, which columns of a particular row will be used to access the database. The function also assists in determining how frequently these columns will be accessed. DBA also determines what columns are used in joining tables, ORDER by clauses, and WHERE predicates.

7.3.6 Performance Monitoring

DBA is responsible for monitoring the performance of application and corporate databases. The function will establish measures to calculate database performance. One such measure is the response time for online access of the database.

7.3.7 Normalization

DBA assists systems developers in ensuring that the relationships between entities, association of attributes within entities, and the data model itself is optimized. The function also assists with the normalization process which is conducted to reduce data redundancy and problems with inserting, updating, and deleting data from the database.

7.4 TECHNICAL SUPPORT

The infrastructure support for the database environment, which is given by technical support, consists of, but is not limited to, offering assistance in the following areas:

- Software installation, including DB gens
- Application of PTFs
- Software maintenance
- Performance tuning
- Backup and recovery
- Utilities maintenance

7.4.1 Software Installation

The technical support staff is primarily responsible for installing all of the DBMS and relevant software. The installation includes database, gens, utilities, operating system interfaces, communication handlers, and editors.

7.4.2 Application of PTFs

The DBMS vendor will, from time to time, send PTFs to the database that should be applied to the various software programs. It is the sole responsibility of technical support to apply these fixes as they come in.

7.4.3 Software Maintenance

Technical support is responsible for ongoing maintenance of database software. The maintenance requirements, to a large extent, may be confined to software upgrades, changes in versions or levels, installation of new releases, and addition of utilities.

7.4.4 Performance Tuning

DA, DBA, and technical support share responsibility for monitoring the performance of the database and taking steps to tune it wherever necessary. Performance tuning in the database environment must begin during the design process. It will be reflected in the way queries are structured and will be taken into consideration during application and utility processing.

Some performance tuning considerations that must be taken into account are:

- Applications using DDL commands for table spaces, tables, and indexes should have their own databases.

- Unless very small tables are being developed, have only one table per table space.

- Attempt to keep all of the data in a table space within its primary location.

- Keep the table row length less than 4 kbytes of storage.

- Minimize the use of variable-length columns, unless you are saving an average of 20 bytes per row.

- Do not select columns you do not need.

- Avoid using subroutines for I/O, if possible.

7.4.5   Backup and Recovery

The vendor provides several utilities that can be used to backup and recover the database; they are:

- LOAD. Loads data into tables from datasets
- COPY. Creates copies of tables for recovery purposes
- MERGE COPY. Combines partial and full image copies
- MODIFY. Removes recovery information from CATALOG
- RECOVER. Recovers a table or index
- REORG. Resequences rows of tables
- REPAIR. Fixes bad data or pointers
- RUNSTATS. Records information about data in tables and indexes in CATALOG
- STOSPACE. Records space information in the CATALOG

Technical support must become familiar with the use of these utilities, the JCL required to run each of them, and the occasions when they will be used. They must also become involved in the management and judicious use by others of these utilities.

7.4.6   Utilities Maintenance

The management and maintenance of utilities in a database environment are very critical issues. Technical support is responsible for making changes to the utilities and the JCL required to run the utilities and for maintaining correct and up-to-date versions of each utility.

The management of database utilities requires that only authorized users have access to them. Technical support must ensure that there is no illegal use of these utilities.

7.5   PHYSICAL DATABASE DESIGNERS

In a database environment, physical database designers may often perform the duties of application DAs or may even be called application DBAs.

In the database environment, the role of the physical database designers may be more appropriately given to the senior systems analyst who demonstrates a fondness for the technical aspects of database design.

The duties of the physical database designer include several of the tasks outlined for the DBA in addition to the following:

- Development of storage formats
- Normalization
- Table creation
- Key selection
- Input to programming specifications
- Data integrity considerations
- Data security considerations
- Useful physical design knowledge

7.5.1 Development of Storage Formats

The physical database designer is responsible for determining how the database will be physically stored and how many tables will occupy a table space, building storage groups, and determining whether indexes should be built. The physical designer also determines what data will be stored in the primary area of the direct access storage device (DASD) and what data will be stored in the overflow area and must be or become familiar with the fundamentals of disk structures and the storage requirements of the database.

Disk space calculations are very often carried out by the DBA; however, there may be times when the physical designer may be called on to do space calculations.

7.5.2 Normalization

Normalization is an activity that is generally done during the logical data design phase of systems development. However, because of performance considerations and storage requirements, the physical designer may be asked to contribute to normalizing and synthesizing of databases and also denormalizing of normalized data.

7.5.3 Table Creation

Physical database designers are responsible for all table and index creation in the environment. This activity is carried out on an application by application basis. During table creation, the physical designer takes several performance considerations into account, including:

- Whenever it is practical, create one table per table space.
- Limit the table to less than 300 columns.
- Unique indexes should be created based on columns that are not updated frequently.

- Table names may be up to 18 characters in length.
- Unique indexes should not be created from columns whose data type is specified as VARCHAR since the software will reserve spaces for the longest occurrence of the data irrespective of the actual length.
- Create composite indexes for columns which are frequently used together in a WHERE clause.

7.5.4   Key Selection

The physical database designer along with the logical database designer selects the primary and foreign keys for the databases. The key selection should not only be based on performance and integrity considerations but also on the business function usage and requirements of the access methods.

7.5.5   Input to Programming Specifications

The primary input to programming specifications comes from the systems designers who consist of project leaders, systems analysts, and programmer analysts. However, the physical designers still have some input to the specifications. This includes recommendations to:

- Store keys and attributes in related tables
- Store derived data
- Use partitioned table spaces for very large tables
- Minimize the number of tables with rows whose defined length is greater than 4056 bytes
- Only use VARCHAR when the field is at least 18 bytes in length and there is a 30 percent savings per row length
- Use numeric data types if a column's data is restricted to numeric data
- Eliminate duplicate key rows before creating a unique index on an existing table
- Avoid indexes on VARCHAR columns

As shown above, the input to programming specifications from physical designers mainly concerns performance issues.

7.5.6   Data Integrity Considerations

Data integrity issues for physical designers is limited to ensuring that whenever a query is made to the database, the results obtained from the database are always the same as long as there were no modifications made to the database. The physical designers ensure data integrity through the judicious selection of unique indexes and access paths.

7.5.7 Data Security Considerations

Physical designers advise the users of the database about the various protection mechanisms available in relational databases to ensure that threats against the data will not succeed. They advise the users about the various locking mechanisms and view creations that are available to protect the data from illegal use.

7.5.8 Useful Physical Design Knowledge

The physical designers must be willing to educate users on various topics pertinent to the effective operations of the database including:

- Referential integrity
- Fundamentals of disk structures
- Primary and secondary access methods
- Indexing for performance and integrity
- Indexing, B-trees, and hashing
- Data clustering
- Locking mechanisms

7.6 LOGICAL DATABASE DESIGNERS

The logical database design phase of database development includes all activities which produce a data model from the user requirements.

In the database environment, the role of the logical database designers may be more appropriately given to the senior systems analyst who demonstrates a fondness for understanding and interpreting the business functions of the organization.

The duties of the logical database designer include several of the tasks outlined for the DA in addition to the following:

- Analysis of formulated user requirements
- Development of a data model
- Mapping the data model to a relational model
- Normalization of the relational model

7.6.1 Analysis of Formulated User Requirements

The logical database designers analyze the user requirements collected by the systems development team for relevant entities and relationships. The known entities and relationships are represented in the form of a data model (E-R diagram).

7.6.2 Development of the Data Model

The data model that results from the analysis of the user requirements is revised several times until it adequately represents the users' needs. The logical database designers assist in the selection of unique identifiers for the entities and establishing definitions for the attributes, entities, and relationships.

7.6.3 Mapping the Data Model to a Relational Model

The logical database designers convert the entities of the data model into tables. They analyze the table columns for uniqueness and establish which columns will be used for primary keys and which will be used as foreign keys. The logical database designers also assist the systems developers in selecting column names that can be referenced in queries by all users.

7.6.4 Normalization of the Relational Model

The logical database designers assist systems developers in the three major steps involved in the normalization process: First Normal Form, Second Normal Form, and Third Normal Form.

7.7 APPLICATION PROGRAMMERS

Application programmers are responsible for developing the programs that access the database. They work from specifications developed by systems designers to produce reports requested by various users.

Application programmers support the database environment by:

- Prototyping for specification debugging
- Testing the interfaces to the database
- Assisting in the development of programming standards and naming conventions

- Testing the application software
- Educating the environment about specific application requirements

7.7.1 Prototyping for Specification Debugging

Application programmers support the environment through prototyping applications at an early stage of systems development to ensure correctness and adequacy of the systems design.

7.7.2 Testing the Interfaces to the Database

Application programmers support the environment by testing applications that access the database. The test includes CALLS to the database from COBOL, queries to the database through QMF, and access through utilities.

7.8 OPERATIONS SUPPORT

Operations support is very critical to the success of the database environment. The support includes but is not limited to:

- Generation of activity logs
- Generation of operating procedures and manuals
- Administration of the operating environment and software
- Maintenance of hardware manuals
- Creation of operating and override logs (e.g., SYSLOG, SMF, and JOB scheduling)
- Running of utilities to monitor integrity (e.g., LOAD, REORG, REPAIR, and CHECK)

The database environment has little impact on the way operations is run in a traditional data processing environment. The additional requirements and activities of the database environment are usually transparent to the operations staff. Therefore, with this proviso, the author will not discuss these activities at any length.

7.9 INPUT-OUTPUT DATA CONTROL SUPPORT

As with operations, the activities and requirements of data control in a database environment do not differ to any significant degree from those in a traditional data processing environment. It is, therefore, not my intention to discuss these activities any further.

7.10 SYSTEM DESIGNER'S SUPPORT

In a database environment, the system designer's role parallels that of the systems analyst in the traditional data processing environment. However, the designer's role may be divided into logical design and physical design in larger organizations. With this in mind, the author would like to refer the readers to the sections on logical and physical database designers earlier in this chapter for coverage of system designers' activities in a database environment.

Relational Database Issues

2

Relational Database Issues

8

Administration of the Database Environment

An earlier text, *Data Administration*, established the premise that data is a resource in much the same way as employees, products, natural resources, finances, and other material products are resources. The same text defined information resource management (IRM) as a discipline that deals with planning for, allocating, maintaining and conserving, prudently exploiting, effectively employing, and integrating the data resource. Data resource management (DRM) is another name for IRM.

This chapter deals with three aspects of IRM. It deals with the effective management of the data resource, emphasizes the fact that in order to effectively manage data, it is necessary to obtain as much data about the data resource as is possible, and deals with planning for the data resource, with emphasis on the strategic, tactical, and operational aspects of IRM planning. In the area of control of the data resource, the chapter deals with establishing lines of authority and responsibility for the data and emphasizes the importance of having common procedures for collecting, updating, and maintaining the data. Finally, it establishes that in order to control the data resource, the organization must evaluate, mediate, and reconcile the conflicting needs and prerogatives of its functional departments.

8.1 MANAGEMENT OF THE DATA RESOURCE

To repeat, in order to manage data effectively as a resource, it is necessary to obtain as much data about the data resource as possible. There must be stringent procedures for collecting, maintaining, and using the resource. The next several sections of this chapter will discuss various tools that can be used in the effective management of the data resource.

8.1.1 The Data Dictionary

The data dictionary may be defined as an organized reference to the data content of an organization's programs, systems, databases, collections of all files, or manual records. It may be maintained manually or by a computer. Sometimes, the term *data dictionary* may refer to a software product that is used to maintain a dictionary database. The data dictionary contains names, descriptions, and definitions of the organization's data resource.

8.1.2 The Data Dictionary as a Management Tool

The data dictionary is perhaps the most important tool that information resource managers have at their disposal. The data dictionary allows management to document and support application development and assist in designing and controlling the database environment. It allows managers to set standards and monitor adherence to those standards.

In the database environment, the data dictionary can be used to document the single-user view of the organization's data or several integrated views. It can document the related data models of those views, the logical databases that result from those views, and the physical representation of those logical models.

The organization can store complete representations of its data architecture in the data dictionary. This data architecture can be used to indicate how adequately the data resource supports the business functions of the organization and to also show what data the company will need to support its long-range plans for expansion.

The dictionary allows information managers to respond quickly to upper-level management's needs for data in a decision support environment. It supports the organization's need for consistent data definitions and usage.

The data dictionary can be used to indicate management's desire to control access to the organization's data resource. Managers can now state who can access the data and the level of access assigned to the individual. They can use the data dictionary, in consort with the operating system, to deny access to unauthorized individuals.

The data dictionary can provide managers and other users with concise definitions of entities and data items that are important to the organization. It can indicate where data is used, what uses it, how it is used, and what else is dependent on that data.

Management can indicate, via the dictionary, who is responsible for changing the characteristics of the data resource and the procedures for effecting the change. On the other hand, managers can use the dictionary to control changes to the data resource and readily assess the effect on systems, programs, and user operations when such changes are made.

8.1.3 The Database as a Management Tool

Today's highly competitive business climate, characterized by more educated consumers and shorter product cycles, forces companies to be information-driven. Corporate decision-makers derive information by analyzing raw data, gathered internally or externally, in a particular business context. Therefore, to be successful, a company must ensure that this raw data is captured and readily available for analysis in various forms. If such data is easily accessible, various levels of support must be built before meaningful information can be obtained.

Various tools have evolved over the past two decades to facilitate data resource management. When first introduced, database management systems (DBMSs) were thought to offer a panacea to the growing lack of control over the company data resources.

The database can be defined as a collection of interrelated data items that can be processed by one or more application systems. The database permits common data to be integrated and shared between corporate functional units and provides flexibility of data organization. It facilitates the addition of data to an existing database without modification of existing application programs. This data independence is achieved by removing the direct association between the application program and physical storage of data.

The advantages of the database are:

- Consistency through use of the same data by all corporate parts
- Application program independence from data sequence and structure
- Reduction and control of redundant data
- Reduction in application development, storage, and processing costs

Database technology has permitted information resource managers to organize data around subjects that interest the company. It has allowed for data sharing among divergent parts of the organization and has introduced new methods of managing data and new, sophisticated logical and physical design methodologies. By having a central pool of data, the organization can now secure the resource more efficiently and in more cost-effective ways. Access to the data can be more readily controlled while making it available to a wider audience of diverse users.

The technology has allowed management, through decision support systems (DSS), to more readily adjust to the changing environment of their respective businesses and reduce the impact of these changes on the organization's economy.

8.1.4   Managing the Corporate Database

Effective management of the corporate database requires that the following activities be addressed consistently and logically:

- *Planning:* The corporate database must be planned according to the specific needs of the company.

- *Organization:*   A data-driven company requires new organizational entities.

- *Acquisition:* Once the corporate database has been planned, the needed data must be acquired.

- *Maintenance and control:*   The data in the corporate database must be securely, accurately, and completely maintained. In addition, proper control must be exercised over access to the database. Data ownership, use, and custodianship issues must also be addressed.

- *Usage:* The corporate database must be available to all authorized users in the company.

Planning.   Planning entails the preparation of all corporate data models. This is best achieved through interviews with the department heads of each functional area in the company. These managers should be asked to determine what data influences their functional areas and what information is required to successfully operate and manage their departments. After all the interviews are completed, the collection of data items must be analyzed and distilled into a model that can be understood, presented, and accepted by corporate management. This analysis should include a determination of the source of the data as well as its characteristics and interrelationships with other data items. This corporate data model must then be compared with currently held and maintained data. The difference between what is currently available and what is ultimately required determines what data must be collected.

Organization. There are two distinct aspects of organizing the corporate database. The first is the business aspect, identifying which data is relevant to the company, its source and method of capture, and the interrelationships among the data items. The second is the technical aspect, storing data on computer-readable media in a form readily accessible by the corporate decision-makers. The business tasks of organizing the corporate database required the creation of the relatively new position, chief information officer (CIO), and the more traditional data administration function.

The CIO is the executive in charge of the information systems department and is responsible for formulating an information strategy that includes all systems development, computer operations, and communications planning and operation.

The data administration function links computer systems and the business functions they are designed to serve. The group responsible for data administration builds and maintains the corporate data model. A properly constructed data model places the system to be developed into a proper business perspective. This model is instrumental in the preparation of the information systems department's strategic plan.

Acquisition. In a data-driven organization, information strategy is derived from the corporate data model. Systems planned for development should provide information or a level of service that was previously unavailable. In a typical systems development project, a major part of the effort is spent acquiring and storing the data that is used to produce the required information.

Although data analysis and design is defined as a separate activity in the definition of information resource management, application programs to collect and validate data items and add them to the appropriate database must still be written. The interactions among systems development, data administration, and database administration must be in place to ensure that the corporate database effectively acquires data.

Maintenance and control. Maintenance tasks include making changes to the corporate data model, reflecting these changes in the data dictionary, and properly communicating changes to all users who must know the model's current status. Given the degree of data independence that can be achieved in today's DBMSs, changes to the database should not necessitate changes to application programs. However, the addition of new data items and changes or deletions to existing data items must be controlled as vigorously as are changes to application systems. That is, the change control principles applied to application programs must be applied to changes in data definitions used by these programs.

Data security issues are critical in data-driven organizations. The data is used and relied on by all corporate users, including high-level decision-makers. Procedures must be established that define what level of access an individual should be granted. Unauthorized access must be detected and reported. The cause of the infraction also must be determined, and action taken to prevent its recurrence.

The distinction must be made between data owners—those with update authority—and data users—those with read-only access or limited update authority.

The computer operations group is the custodian of all data. This group must ensure that proper monitoring is performed and that backup and recovery procedures are in place and functioning. The data administrator should also have sufficient authority to arbitrate any ownership disputes between rival users.

Maintenance and control activities should also monitor systems performance and the time required to access needed data items. The database administration group should monitor system performance and take whatever corrective action is needed to provide an adequate level of response to users or systems requiring access to particular data items.

Usage.   Procedures that clearly define how to use the database must be established. First, potential users must know what data exists. Then, tools must be provided to enable users to easily access selected data items. For example, query languages that provide flexible database access and allow what-if questions to be presented and answered are implemented in many companies. Another area of great potential is the ability to interface selected data items with business software tools. These interfaces provide users with more meaningful presentations of the extracted information.

The delivery vehicle used to bring the data to the users must also be considered. Many companies have established information centers to provide a user-friendly environment for data access. This access may be provided through interactive query languages that enable users to view results online or through batch report generators that enable users to obtain preformatted printed reports.

Downloading segments of the database to a microcomputer is another method of information delivery that is becoming more common. The microcomputer environment typically provides the user with interactive access to the data as well as easy-to-use and powerful software. With the continuing emergence of local area networks (LANS), more and more data will be downloaded to microcomputers for use by the end-user community.

8.1.5 The Data Model as a Management Tool

A data model is defined as a logical representation of a collection of data elements and the associations among those data elements. A data model can be used to represent data usage throughout an organization or can represent a single database structure. A data model is to data what a logical data flow diagram is to a process.

The data model can be used by management to:

- Develop new systems
- Maintain existing systems
- Develop data structures for the entire organization
- Set priorities for the data needs of the organization
- Assist in planning for expansion into new markets or business areas
- Delegate authority for data usage
- Classify data by data areas or business functions
- Determine security needs of the data and implement protection mechanisms

Develop new systems. Data models are fast becoming a very important tool in the development of new systems in an organization. The advent of new structured design methodologies, especially data-driven methodologies, saw the birth of data models as tools for systems development. The traditional approach to developing computer systems focuses on the processes to be performed, particularly with operational-type systems. However, process-oriented system designs generally do not fulfill subsequent tactical or strategic information needs. In many cases, information requests go unanswered because either the source data does not exist or building custom software that supports ad hoc inquiries is too costly and time-consuming. This is a major disadvantage of many conventional systems.

The data resource management approach overcomes this limitation by focusing on data and information requirements during systems planning and building. The data model now becomes the vehicle by which application systems are built and it addresses the above limitations.

Maintain existing systems. It is now determined that 80 percent of an organization's programming resources is expended during maintenance of existing systems. This expenditure is consumed by programmers trying to determine where changes should be made to existing systems and what data is best suited to test the modified programs. The expenditure may even occur before the changes are made. Programmers may spend (it varies depending upon their experience) a considerable amount of time determining how the application meets the requirements of the business function. This expenditure in time and financial resources can be minimized if there are data models of all existing systems in place.

The programmers can determine from the data models of the section or the user view what must be modified. Then, with the data model section or user view as a guide, the parts of the application programs that must be changed will be more readily identified and programming maintenance expenditure will be less costly.

Develop data structures for the organization. The organization, by undertaking a business system plan (BSP), can identify business processes and data classes required to design databases for its informational needs. Various charts showing the relationship between business processes and classes of data can be prepared. This relationship is the backbone of the data architecture for the organization. The data architecture, in turn, is obtained through a single data model or set of data models.

Set priorities for the data needs of the organization. It is impossible in most organizations to implement systems to satisfy their data needs all at once. Priorities must be set and phased implementation of these systems undertaken. The data model can show what data is available, where it is available, and where it is needed. Data managers can use this information to determine the cost and complexity of implementation of systems and hence set priorities for the implementation of these systems.

Assist in planning for expansion of business. Whenever an organization expands its business into new markets or business areas, data is needed to aid or even implement the expansion. Data models are very useful tools that management can use to determine what data is needed and where it can be obtained for the expansion program.

Delegate authority for data usage. Data models can indicate to an organization what business function uses what data. They can also be used to indicate the common uses and functions of corporate data. Corporate management can use this information to delegate authority for data usage throughout the organization. Managers can also use this information to control access, on a need to know basis, to the corporate data.

Classify data by data areas.   Data is very often classified by the business function it serves. For example, data that serves an accounting function is very often classified as accounting data. Data models, by showing the relationship between business functions and business entities (data), can assist in the proper classification of corporate data.

Determine the security needs of data.   Data models allow an organization to determine what data is available, who uses it, and where it is being used. They allow the organization to determine the common usage of data and the parameters that are needed to allow data usage across organizational boundaries. Armed with this knowledge, an organization can now plan for its data security needs. It can determine what protection mechanisms are needed to control access to the data and the level of authorization to be given to users of corporate data.

8.1.6   Data Flow Diagrams as a Management Tool

Data flow diagrams help the systems analysts determine where data is being held from one transaction to the next or is stored permanently because the diagrams describe some aspect of the world outside the system. They indicate how the data flows from process to process. They assist the analysts in determining what immediate accesses to each data store will be needed by the user.

Data flow diagrams are powerful tools that can be used by organizations to develop process-flow architectures for their environment. Management can use this tool to determine where data is created, where it is being used, and who uses it.

Management can use the data flow diagrams to build complete databases to store the required data for users' needs and to transform flows of data. The processes can be decomposed into functions and activities from which programs can be coded to manipulate the data stores.

Data flow diagrams are currently being used on a worldwide basis as the major deliverable from process-driven structured systems analysis and development. Several organizations are using data flow diagrams as a deliverable of a basic BSP. Data flow diagrams are also being used by several organizations to demonstrate and illustrate their corporate data needs.

Management can use the ability to break down processes into several levels to determine the operational processing requirements of each data store in the process architecture. For example, one organization is currently using data flow diagrams to determine whether operational processing, such as sorting, dumping to other storage media, deleting files, and creating backup files, is consuming too much of the corporation's operational budgets and time. This same organization is using data flow diagrams to illustrate where various reports are distributed to other users, whether current users should have access to the reports, and where reports are produced but never distributed.

Management can use existing data flow diagrams to audit the corporate data dictionary for completeness and currency. For example, a complete data dictionary should have data about all the processes and data stores that exist in the organization. By checking the data dictionary content against existing data flow diagrams, the completeness of the data dictionary can be determined. The assumption here is that the data flow diagrams are in themselves complete and represent the entire information and process architecture of the corporation.

Data flow diagrams can be used to create functional specifications for systems development. The data flow diagram shows the sources and distinctions of data and hence indicate the boundaries of the system. It identifies and names the logical functions, the data elements that connect the function to another, and the data stores which each function accesses. Each data flow is analyzed and its structures and the definitions of its component data elements are stored in the data dictionary. Each logical function may be broken down into a more detailed data flow diagram. The contents of each data store is analyzed and stored in the data dictionary.

These documents make up a comprehensive account of a system that can be used by management to build systems or set priorities for the building of systems. The documents and the data flow diagrams may also prove very useful in the maintenance of existing systems.

Finally, data flow diagrams can be used by systems designers to prepare functional specifications that are:

- Well understood and fully agreed to by users
- Used to set out the logical requirements of the system without dictating a physical implementation
- Useful in expressing preferences and trade-offs

Several organizations are attesting to the fact that data flow diagrams can prevent very costly errors in systems development. Figure 8.1 is an example of a data flow diagram.

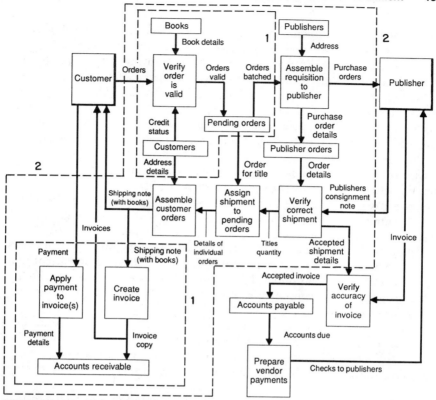

Figure 8.1   A data flow diagram.

8.1.7   Managing Information through CASE Tools

More and more organizations are looking to computer-aided software engineering (CASE) tools to improve the effectiveness of analysts and designers, increase the role of end users in systems design, reduce programming and maintenance time, and manage data more effectively.

CASE is the automation of software development and a combination of software tools and systems development methodologies. CASE is different from earlier software technologies because it focuses on the entire software productivity problem, not just on implementation solutions. CASE attacks software productivity problems at both ends of the life cycle by automating many analysis and design tasks, as well as program implementation and maintenance tasks.

CASE offers full support for the systems development life cycle. At the analysis phase, CASE allows the designer to collect user requirements either through conventional interview methods or by the use of Structure English. The collected user requirements are entered into a CASE repository or data dictionary and become the input to the design phase. The deliverables from the design phase can be data models, such as entity-relationship (E-R) or data flow diagrams. The tools have the ability to explode the data flow diagrams down to several levels and balance the data stores at each level. The deliverables are checked against the data dictionary entries for accuracy, consistency, and completeness.

Most of the CASE tools have a prototyping capability and can create screens of the user requirements and models of the systems so that users can review the design at a very early stage of systems development. During prototyping simulated reports can be produced that reflect the actual reports required by the users.

CASE tools use the entries in the data dictionary and the processes from the design phase not only to develop programming specifications for application programmers, but some tools can even generate the actual program code compatible with standards for several programming languages.

At the moment, the major weakness of CASE tools is their inability to maintain program code in and changes to existing systems over the life of the system. Several manufacturers of CASE tools are now developing solutions to this problem and the answers may not be too far off.

CASE tools have become very important tools for managers to use in their efforts to manage data more effectively and prudently exploit the data resource. They now represent the most rapidly growing sector of the software industry.

8.1.8 Managing Information through Reverse Engineering

Reverse engineering is defined as the act of taking unstructured programs or systems not designed using one of the current structured design methodologies and either structuring the programs or producing deliverables more appropriate to the structured systems development life cycle (SDLC).

Reverse engineering accomplishes the following:

- Produces programs that are structured and less costly, both in time and money, to maintain

- Enhances the quality of programs, program documentation, and informational content

- Increases the useful life of program code and identifies sections of programs that can be reused as subroutines

- Removes or identifies unreachable or unexecutable codes in programs

- Indicates problem areas in unstructured programs which could be responsible for seemingly inexplicable processing behavior

Although most of the effort of reverse engineering is now centered on producing structured program code from unstructured code, a considerable amount of effort is being expended on producing more appropriate deliverables with a structured SDLC. For example, there are efforts being undertaken to produce E-R diagrams from the data division of COBOL programs. These E-R diagrams are then used along with the major processes defined by the COBOL programs to populate data dictionaries, produce logical and physical design schemas, provide better documentation for programming specifications and maintenance, and build relevant databases. Managers can now use the data dictionary content, the documentation, and the databases to more effectively manage the data resource.

8.1.9 Project Management Tools and Management of Data

There are now several automated project management tools on the market that seek to aid in the development of systems and indirectly in the management of data. Project management tools are used in the following areas:

- Project planning
- Project duration
- Costing
- Personnel scheduling
- Personnel allocation
- Project reporting

8.2 PLANNING FOR THE DATA RESOURCE

Planning for the data resource is done at three levels: strategic, tactical, and operational.

- *Strategic planning:* Defines the data environment's mission and objective in achieving the goals of the organization. The strategic plan is driven by the current and future information needs of the business. Strategic planning helps businesses share the data resource.

The strategic data plan defines the organization's data requirements and states the benefits of data resource management and how it differs from database technology management. The strategic plan serves as the baseline for data resource management and directs all subsequent data-related activities. It also defines the target toward which all subsequent data-related activity is directed.

- *Tactical planning:* Identifies a resource and directs the way in which it will be managed to achieve goals set forth in the strategic plan. Because each resource is to be managed in its own life cycle, each should ideally be governed by its own plan. The tactical planning window is 12 to 18 months, with a review cycle of 9 to 12 months.

- *Operational planning:* Describes the details of the tactical plan and identifies the tasks to be carried out in a scheduled time frame, the expected deliverables, and the assigned responsibilities. The operational planning window is 3 to 9 months, depending on the size of the project.

8.2.1 Contents of the Strategic Plan

The strategic plan should address the broadest context under which data sharing will exist and should contain the sections outlined below:

- *Mission statement:* Statements of an overall direction for data resource management from a single, high-level perspective. It defines the scope of the data environment. For example, a mission statement may read as follows: To provide data about shared corporate entities to all regional offices in a timely and controlled manner.

- *Goals:* The expected results to be gained in that domain. For example, a goal of data resource management may be to build a strategic data architecture that will ensure the integrity of data as it is integrated across application systems.

- *Strategies:* General statements of direction for achieving data resource management goals. Strategies are generally applied across goals to identify how the goals will be achieved. For example, a strategy for data resource management may be to train systems staff and end users in data-oriented systems design and database development or to provide effective data security with minimal interruption to end-user service.

- *Critical success factors:* Broad statements of achievements in data resource management. For example, a critical success factor may be the management of data through a data dictionary. Success is achieved with the implementation and effective use of the data dictionary.

- *Constraints:* Data resource management may be constrained by the evolution of the business, the state of the technology in the environment, and the availability of staff. Current business operations and the role of information in the organization's planning may force constraints on the scope of data resource management.

Planning for the data resource must include acquisition of data through application systems, employment and exploitation of data through end-user reports, maintenance of data through the technology tools, and disposition of the data depending on the life cycle of the business subject matter. The deletion of the data element is determined by its relationship to other elements.

Planning for the data resource must identify the tools to manage the data resource including database management systems, data dictionaries, data modeling tools, CASE tools, and database auditing, journaling, and recovery tools.

8.3 CONTROLLING THE DATA RESOURCE

The third component of IRM is the control of the data resource. Although the other two components, management and planning, were discussed first, this is no indication of their relative importance in the triumvirate. Management control of the data resource includes the following:

- Common procedures for access control to the data
- Establishing lines of authority and responsibility for the data
- Common procedures for collecting, updating, and maintaining the data
- Common formats and procedures for data definition
- Identifying entities that are important to the enterprise
- Evaluating, mediating, and reconciling the conflicting needs and prerogatives of functional departments
- Ensuring that the data and all transactions against the data can be audited
- Control the data in order to measure and evaluate the corporation and predict its reaction to change in its environment and in its own internal organization

The above list, although quite extensive, is by no means all inclusive. Readers can expand on this list and also to research the various activities that must be performed for each item in the list.

Coexistence of Relational and Nonrelational Databases

Because of the financial investment that an organization may have in an older database management system (DBMS), it may be necessary for that organization to have dual DBMSs, one of which is the relational DBMS. Furthermore, an application that is running well, is already paid for, and has little or no need to exchange information with a relational database may never be rewritten to a relational database structure. Again, here is a necessity for dual DBMSs.

This chapter discusses the coexistence of relational and non-relational databases and the issues involved in operating and maintaining these two environments.

9.1 THE DUAL DBMS

The application of dual databases to DBMS software centers on performance, usually online. Can a single piece of DBMS software satisfy the need for high-performance online processing as well as the need for flexibility and rapid development all within the structure of a single DBMS technology? Aside from the specifics of teleprocessing monitors and database management software, much controversy exists regarding whether or not high-performance and high-flexibility capabilities can coinhabit the same DBMS technology.

Undoubtedly, a single DBMS is desirable for both performance and flexibility. Every new technology, DBMS or otherwise, requires its own support training period and costs. Having multiple technologies in one environment is a manager's nightmare. For many reasons, the fewer technologies a company has, the stabler and more streamlined the organization. DBMS technology is no exception to this rule. A single DBMS technology that serves both performance and flexibility objectives is much more desirable than a separate set of DBMS technologies.

9.1.1 The Dual Database

For a dual database, the first issue is whether any DBMS technology will suffice to secure both performance and flexibility. Even if a DBMS technology exists that can serve both needs, the next issue is whether it can be done simultaneously for the same data on the same processor. A DBMS technology may well be able to be used for both performance and flexibility needs but not for the same data at the same time. For example, one group of end users may well be using the technology for decision support system (DSS) processing and another group may be using it for performance systems, but they cannot do this on the same processor on the same data at the same time. This issue differs from the larger, more fundamental issue.

In using a single DBMS to handle both performance and flexibility needs, it is necessary to separate data—to have one collection of data to serve the need for flexibility and another to serve the need for performance.

The primary division of data in the dual database environment is along the lines of online, operational database systems and flexible, easy-to-build DSSs. This split of data appears to be a result of the performance conflict between the operational and DSS environment.

It is unreasonable to expect that the same data can or should be so widely accessed in many different ways at the same time. Even if the same DBMS technology could be used, or even if the nature of the basic input-output operation—the main impediment to performance—was fundamentally changed to be able to accommodate some degree of performance for simultaneous set-at-a-time and record-at-a-time data use, the differences in data use are so diverse and so severe that there must be a separation of data under even a limited amount of processing.

In light of these very fundamental differences in data use and processing, it is not surprising that the world is evolving to the dual database approach. Given the nature of I/O operation as it is currently known, the performance needs for access and control over any given data element is such that no processor can keep up with the totality of demand. However, the performance differences are only the forerunner of many deeper differences in the use of data.

9.1.2 The Historical Orientation of DBMS Software

Ideally, a single DBMS technology would be malleable enough to provide adequate facilities for both operational and DSS processing; however, software has traditionally been designed to service one function or the other. Considering the fundamental differences in operational and DSS environments and the limitations of traditional software, the direction for traditional software is duplicate databases—one serving the operational needs of a company and one serving the DSS needs.

With dual databases the issue of data redundancy must be addressed. The redundancy that exists in the dual database environment is across the operational and DSS environments. The summarized, historical nature of DSS processing does not mandate the use of up-to-the-second data. Indeed, most forms of DSS processing (e.g., trend analysis, projections, and demographic analysis) require that detailed data be frozen as of some time. The implication is that redundancy across the DSS and operational environments is not only acceptable but desirable, and for some types of DSS processing it is absolutely mandatory.

Redundancy within the DSS environment is a different matter. On the one hand, redundancy within the DSS environment is necessary if the end user is to have the flexibility of processing that is inherent to the end-user computing environment. On the other hand, uncontrolled redundancy in the DSS end-user computing environment leads to inconsistent results, which potentially undermine its original purpose.

Despite the deep differences between operational and DSS data, there is always a temptation to assume that a more effective use of technology can bridge the gap.

9.1.3 System Performance and the Dual Database

The primary performance issue of the dual database centers on data use. In particular, end-user computing access and use of data usually operate on indeterminate or large amounts of data in an unstructured fashion. Operational processing typically accesses limited, determinate amounts of data, and data use is generally structured. This difference in use is perhaps the main performance difference between the online operational and DSS end-user computing systems using conventional I/O operations.

DSS systems typically access data a set at a time, which results in the consumption of an indeterminate amount of resources. Accessing a small database would consume few resources; however, for large databases, set-at-a-time processing can consume a huge amount of resources using conventional inboard I/O operations.

Unlike DSS processing, rapid online processing usually accesses data a record at a time. Unquestionably, record-at-a-time processing is more difficult and time consuming to encode and develop. Resource consumption can be contained, however, when records are processed under the current standard operation of I/O. In addition, when resource consumption can be measured and contained, effective online performance is the result.

For optional performance, longer running processes (i.e., set-at-a-time processes) are not mixed with short running processes (i.e., record-at-a-time). In this case, performance can be consistently maintained at a high level. However, managers are still in conflict with software developers who seek to mix long- and short-running processes in the same jobstream, when there is a fair load on the processor on which conventional I/O is being run and efficient performance is still the objective.

9.2 COMPARISON OF RELATIONAL AND NONRELATIONAL MODELS

In comparing relational and nonrelational databases, we must differentiate between two types of database languages: high-level languages that operate on sets of records and low-level languages that operate on a single record at a time.

Most high-level database languages are associated with the relational model, whereas the network and hierarchical models are associated with record-at-a-time low-level languages. Several high-level query languages have recently been proposed for the entity-relationship (E-R) model, and an E-R algebra has been specified, but we will not discuss these languages because they are not available commercially and are not well established yet.

The relational model has several high-level languages. The formal operations of the relational algebra apply to sets of tuples, so they are high-level operations. A query is specified by a sequence of relational algebra operations on relations. In relational calculus, a single expression—rather than a sequence of operations—specifies a query. We specify what we want to retrieve but not how to retrieve it. The relational calculus is considered to be at an even higher level than the relational algebra because in the latter we specify a certain order among the high-level operations. This order specifies how the system should retrieve the desired information. The formal basis of the relational calculus is provided by a branch of mathematical logic called predicate calculus. The basic set of relational algebra operations has been shown to have expressive power equivalent to that of the relational calculus.

Commercial languages for the relational model—such as SQL, QUEL, and QBE—are based primarily on relational calculus. QUEL is based on tuple relational calculus, as, to a lesser degree, is SQL.

Both languages resemble some aspects of relational algebra. They also incorporate facilities for aggregate functions, grouping, sorting, keeping duplicate tuples, and arithmetic, which are outside the realm of basic, relational algebra of calculus. QBE is based on domain relational calculus. These are high-level languages that retrieve a set of tuples by a single query.

The network and hierarchical DML (data language management) commands are low-level because they search for and retrieve single records. We must use a general-purpose programming language and embed the database commands in the program. In both these languages, the concept of current record is crucial in the interpretation of the meaning of DML commands because the effect of a command depends on the current record.

The network model DML uses additional currency indicators such as currency of set types and currency of record types, which also affect the outcome of DML commands. Although these currency concepts facilitate record-at-a-time access, the programmer must be thoroughly familiar with how the different commands have their origin in traditional file processing commands.

For the network model, the user must understand the effect of the various variations of the FIND command for record and set access. The effect of the FIND command depends on the current values of the various currency indicators and will also change the values of any affected currency indicators.

For the hierarchical model, the programmer must understand the concept of hierarchical sequence of records. Records are generally accessed in that sequence forward from the current record. Records of different types in the hierarchy must, therefore, be processed along hierarchical paths from left to right within the tree. Again, exceptions do occur. For example, IMS allows stepping back within one hierarchical occurrence tree and then proceeding forward again within the tree.

From the above discussion, it is clear that the relational model has a distinct advantage as far as languages are concerned. Both the formal and commercial languages associated with the relational model are quite powerful and are high level. In fact, several network and hierarchical DBMSs, such as IDMS/R and IMS, have implemented high-level query languages that are similar to the relational languages for use with their systems along with the traditional DML commands. Both high-level query language interfaces and traditional embedded DML commands are available in the systems.

Table 9.1 contains a comparison of the terminology used by each of the data models. Table 9.2 contains a summary of the modeling power of the various data models.

TABLE 9.1   **Comparison of Terminology**

E-R model	Relational	Network	Hierarchical
E-R schema	Table	Record type	Record type
Entity type	Table	Record type	Record type
Entity instance	Row	Record occurrence	Record occurrence
1:N relationship		Set type	Parent-child relationship
Attribute	Column	Field	Data item
Value set	Data type	Data type	Data type
Key	Candidate key		
	Primary key	Key	Sequence key
Multivalued Attribute		Repeating group	

TABLE 9.2   **Summary of Modeling Power**

E-R model	Relational	Network	Hierarchical
Weak entity type	As a relation, but include the primary key of the identifying relation	As a record type that is a member in a set with record type as owner	As a record that is a child of the record type
1:N relationship type	Include the primary key of the "1-side" relation as foreign key in the "N-side" relation	Use a set type	Use a parent-child relationship
M:N relationship type	Set up a new relation that includes as foreign keys the primary keys of the participating relations	Set up a linking record type and make it a member in set types owned by the record types	Use a single hierarchy and duplicate records

9.3   COMPARISON OF STORAGE STRUCTURES

For the relational model, the general technique is to implement each base relation as a separate file. If the user does not specify any storage structure, most relational DBMSs will store the tuples as unordered records in a file. Many relational DMBSs will allow the user to specify dynamically on each file a single primary or clustering index and any number of secondary indexes.

The network model is usually implemented by using pointers and ring files. This file structure is suitable for implementing sets. Most network DBMSs will also present the option of implementing some sets by clustering; that is, the owner record is followed by the member records in physical contiguity for each set instance.

The hierarchical model is usually implemented using hierarchical files, which preserve the hierarchical sequence of the database. In addition, a variety of options including hashing, indexing, and pointers are available, so we can have efficient access to individual records and to related records.

9.4 COMPARISON OF INTEGRITY CONSTRAINTS

The relational model is generally considered weak on integrity constraints. Two standard constraints are now considered to be part of the model—entity integrity and referential integrity. Commercial DBMSs implement entity integrity via the key constraint by disallowing null values on a key attribute. Unfortunately, many relational DBMSs combine the specification of a key with that of a physical index. Referential integrity has not been generally available in relational DBMSs. However, some of the newer DBMSs, like DB2, are allowing the specification of this integrity.

The hierarchical model has the built-in hierarchical constraints that a record type can have at most one real parent in a hierarchy. Other constraints exist in each individual DBMSs; for example, IMS allows only one virtual parent for a record type. There is no provision for enforcing consistency among duplicate records; this must be enforced by the application programs that update the database. The implicit constraint that a child record must be related to a parent record is enforced; also, child records are automatically deleted when their parent or ancestor is deleted.

The network model is the richest among the three implementation models in the types of constraints it specifies and enforces. The set retention option specifies constraints on the behavior of member records in a set with respect to the owner record, such as whether every record must have an owner or not. Automatic set types with SET SELECTION BY STRUCTURAL match the key field of an owner with a field in the member record. The CHECK option can be used to specify a similar constraint for MANUAL nonautomatic set types. Key constraints are specified by a DUPLICATES NOT ALLOWED clause. Hence, many structural constraints on relationship types can be specified to a network DBMS.

9.5 ADVANTAGES AND DISADVANTAGES OF THE MODELS

From the above discussions, it is clear that the relational model has a more formal mathematical foundation than the other two—both in the description of its structures and in the languages specified for it. The network and hierarchical models were developed originally as representations of specific commercial systems. Hence, it is understandable that their record-at-a-time languages are close to traditional file system commands.

The relational DBMSs generally provide more flexibility. Most relational DBMSs make it easy to expand a schema by adding new relations or by adding new attributes to a relation. In addition, it is usually quite easy to add or drop indexes dynamically as needed. Another advantage of relational DBMSs is that most provide high-level query language interfaces as well as a programming interface. For these reasons, a relational DBMS is more suitable for many small and medium-sized database applications where flexibility and quick system development are important.

However, for large databases that have well-defined applications, relational DBMSs sometimes do not provide the high performance that may be required. This is because the access to the database is always through the query language and DBMS system optimizer. Hence, programmers often do not have the capability to access the data in the method they know is most efficient.

Network and hierarchical systems are good for designing and implementing large databases with well-defined queries, transactions, and applications. The database designers and users can spend enough time during system implementation to choose appropriate storage structures and ensure that their applications are programmed in the most efficient way. However, unforeseen future applications may cause very expensive system reorganization.

10

Distributed Relational Database Management System

Since the early 1980s, centralizing an organization's data in a large and expensive computer has been the single approach to data processing. Recent developments in these areas of database technology, computer networks, mini-, and microcomputers have made the distributed database approach a practical alternative. A distributed database in a collection of logically related data distributed across several machines interconnected by a computer network. An application program operating on a distributed database may access data stored at more than one machine.

A distributed database has four main advantages. First, each group having a computer has direct control over its local data, resulting in increased data integrity and more efficient data processing. Second, compared to the centralized approach in which the data must be transferred from each group to the central computer, the communication overhead is reduced. Third, the distributed approach is the natural solution to data processing in a geographically dispersed organization. Fourth, performance and reliability may be increased by exploiting the parallel processing and redundancy capabilities of multiple machines.

The need to integrate and share the data located and managed on different computers is the basis for a distributed database. Such data sharing requires the interconnections of the various computers through a local or general network and specific software support to manage and process distributed data. Such software must provide high independence from the distributed environment. Relational database technology has been successful at providing data independence, making transparent to the application programs any change in the physical or logical data structure. Therefore, it has been the natural support to distributed data sharing. As a result, most relational database systems today offer the option of sharing distributed data.

10.1 DISTRIBUTED DATABASE CAPABILITIES

The distributed database capabilities offered by current database systems range from a remote database access to a heterogeneous distributed database. A more recent use of the distributed database approach is to distribute the data across the modes of a multiprocessor computer so that performance and reliability are increased.

A remote database is a database located on a computer other than where the user is executing. In general, the user is aware of the remote database location, which must be specified to access the data. A data communication component is necessary for accessing the remote database.

A local database may also reside on the computer which the user is running. The user can then download remote database data to the local database. Recent developments in microcomputer technology have favored the workstation and server organization, in which the remote database is managed on a mainframe server by a DBMS and private databases are managed on workstations by a micro-version of the same DBMS. The interconnection between server and workstation is typically handled by a local network. The remote database approach provided little functionality and does not address the problems of distributed databases.

A distributed database is a set of cooperating databases residing on different machines, called sites, interconnected by a computer network. A user at any site can access the data at any other site.

The main difference from the remote database is that the user is not aware of data distribution and perceives the distributed database as a nondistributed database. The management of a distributed database requires the following system components at each site: a data communication component, a local DBMS, and a distributed DBMS. The main functions of the distributed DBMS are:

- Management of a global data dictionary to store information about distributed data

- Distributed data definition

- Distributed semantic data control

- Distributed query processing, including distributed query optimization and remote database access

- Distributed transaction management including distributed concurrency control, recovery, and commit protocol

A distinguishing property of a distributed database is that it can be homogeneous or heterogeneous. A homogeneous distributed database is one in which all local databases are managed by the same DBMS. This approach is the simplest one and provides incremental growth, making the addition of a new site in the network easy, and it increases performance by exploiting the parallel processing capability of multiple sites. A good example of homogeneous distributed databases is illustrated by the R* system.

A heterogeneous distributed database is one in which the local databases need not be managed by the same DBMS. For example, one DBMS can be a relational system while another can be a hierarchical system. This approach is by far more complex than the homogeneous one but enables the integration of existing independent databases without requiring the creation of a completely new distributed database. In addition to the main functions, the distributed DBMS must provide interfaces between the different DBMSs. An example of heterogeneous distributed database is illustrated by the INGRES/STAR system.

10.2   OBJECTIVES OF DISTRIBUTED SYSTEMS

A distributed database may provide various levels of transparency; however, each level of transparency has the same goal: making the use of the distributed database equivalent to that of a centralized database. All of the following objectives are rarely met by a single system. Rather, depending on the targeted applications, a distributed DBMS will meet only a subset of these objectives. For example, a homogeneous distributed DBMS will provide DBMS transparency.

10.2.1   Site Autonomy

Site autonomy is an important objective that enables any operational site to control and process its local data independently from any other site. Therefore each site must store all data dictionary information necessary to be autonomous, without relying on a centralized global data dictionary and a global database administrator. The immediate advantage of site autonomy is that the administration of the distributed database need not be centralized. Each local database may be independently controlled by a local database administrator. Intersite cooperation requires coordination among the local database administrators using specific capabilities of the distributed DBMS. The support of site autonomy can range from no autonomy to full site autonomy (decentralized control).

10.2.2   Location Transparency

Location transparency is the primary objective of a distributed database. It hides the fact that the data may not be stored at the user site. The database user does not need to know the location. Therefore queries involving relations stored at different sites need not specify the relation locations. Location transparency provides physical independence from the distributed environment. The data location information is maintained in the data dictionary and is used by the distributed DBMS to find the data. The main advantage is that the database may be physically reorganized by moving relations to different sites without having any impact on the application programs that access them.

10.2.3   Fragmentation Transparency

The simplest way to store a conceptual object (relation) in a distributed database is at a single site. However, for performance reasons, it is often desirable to divide a relation into smaller fragments, each stored at a different site. A fragment is generally defined by restriction and/or projection and is therefore another relation. Thus, fragmentation is particularly simple in the context of the relational model. Fragmentation enhances the performance of database queries by increasing the locality of reference. For example, consider an EMPLOYEE relation in a database distributed between New York and Paris. The optional fragmentation is probably to store the American employee tuples in New York and the European employee tuples in Paris. The fragmentation definition is application dependent.

Fragmentation transparency makes fragmentation transparent to the user, who sees only nonfragmented relations. Fragmentation information is stored in the data dictionary and used by the distributed DBMS (DDBMS) to automatically map queries on conceptual relations, called global queries, into queries on fragments, called fragment queries.

10.2.4   Replication Transparency

Data replication in the same form is the single solution to reliability. In a distributed database, data replication can be used for reliability, availability, and performance. In general, the unit of fragmentation is the fragment or the relation if fragmentation is not supported. A fragment is replicated when it is stored as two or more copies, each at a different site. The immediate advantage of replication is high availability. If a site fails, the fragment copy is still available at another site. Furthermore replication may enhance performance by increasing locality of reference. The main problem of replication is the complexity and overhead required to keep the copies identical. The update to one copy must be propagated to all its copies. Furthermore when a site recovers from a failure, all its replicated fragments must reach the same state as the other copies that might have been updated while the site was down. The trade-offs between retrieval and update performance make replication definition a difficult problem, which is highly application dependent.

Replication transparency makes such replication invisible to the user, who sees only nonreplicated relations. Replication information, stored in the data dictionary, is used by the DDBMS for mapping global queries into fragments and to manage copy consistency for update queries and recovery after failure.

10.3 DISTRIBUTED DATABASE ISSUES

The database system issues became much more complex in a distributed environment because of specific aspects of distributed databases.

First, relations of the same database may reside at more than one site. In addition, a conceptual object can be fragmented and/or replicated. Fragmentation and replication are necessary for performance and availability reasons. They have a strong impact on data dictionary management, data definition, semantic data control, and query processing.

Second, a user transaction that involves data resident at several sites can be executed as several subtransactions, each at a different site. Therefore each site has only partial information to decide whether to commit the subtransaction's updates. Transaction management and, in particular, concurrency control and commit processing are a must to ensure synchronization among all participating sites.

Third, since data copies may continue to be updated at various sites while one site is down, the recovery of a failed site requires the cooperation of other sites in order to keep replicated copies identical.

Finally, the support of DBMS transparency adds another translation mechanism between the different models and languages. This translation mechanism must be combined with several other functions, such as data dictionary, data definition and control, and query processing.

10.3.1   Data Dictionary

The data dictionary includes information regarding data descriptions, data placement, and semantic data control. It can itself be managed as a distributed database. The data dictionary can be centralized in one site, fully replicated at each site, or fragmented. Its content can be stored differently according to kind of information; some information might be fully replicated while the rest might be distributed. For example, information that is most useful at query compile time, like security control information, could be duplicated at each site. The implementation of the data dictionary depends on the degree of site autonomy that must be supported. For example, full site autonomy is incompatible with a centralized data dictionary.

10.3.2   Data Definition

Data definition in a distributed database is much more difficult than in a centralized database. Data definition includes the introduction of new database objects and their placement in the network. The way a new object is created depends on the degree of site autonomy and management of the data dictionary. With a centralized data dictionary, the data definition command involves only one site, the one that stores the data dictionary. With a fully replicated data dictionary, all sites of the network must be synchronized to perform the data definition operation. If the data dictionary is fragmented, data definition must be done on a site pair basis whereby two sites, the site at which the object is created and another site, cooperate to exchange data definition information. In this case, only the sites that are aware of the new object definition will be able to access it.

10.3.3   Data Control

Semantic data control typically includes view management, security control, and semantic integrity control. The complexity added by the distributed environment concerns the control definition and enforcement. The problem of managing semantic data control rules is similar to the data definition problem.

In a distributed database, a view can be derived from fragmented relations stored at different sites. The mapping of a query expressed on views into a query expressed on conceptual relations can be done as in centralized systems by query modification. With this technique, the qualification defining the view is found in the data dictionary and merged with the query to provide a query on conceptual relations.

The additional problems of authorization control in a distributed environment stem from the fact that objects and subjects are distributed.

These problems are remote user authentication, management of distributed authorization rules, and handling of user groups.

The main problem of semantic integrity control in a distributed environment is that the cost incurred in communication and local processing for enforcing distributed assertions can be prohibitive.

10.4 ARCHITECTURES OF DISTRIBUTED DBMSs

Similar to centralized databases, distributed databases may be implemented in many different ways depending on their objective and design choices. However, for our purposes, it is useful to consider a reference architecture and a functional architecture for distributed databases. These architectures are illustrated in Figs. 10.1 and 10.2.

The reference architecture provides an ideal organization of a distributed database that implements all possible levels of transparency. This architecture is given in terms of schema levels and mapping.

The typical functional architecture is grouped into two different components: the user component that handles interaction with the users and the data component that manages the data. A single-user query involves the user component at the user site and the data component at one or more sites. The user component consists of four modules while the data component consists of three.

The user interface analyzes user queries and returns the result. Semantic data control performs view, authorization, and semantic integrity controls. Global query processing maps a query enriched with semantic data controls into a set of local queries, each for a different site. Transaction management coordinates the distributed execution of the query.

In the data component, local query processing performs decomposition and optimization of a local query. Subtransaction management cooperates with the user components and other data components to synchronize the execution of the subtransaction of the same transaction. Local data access includes the remaining functions for database management.

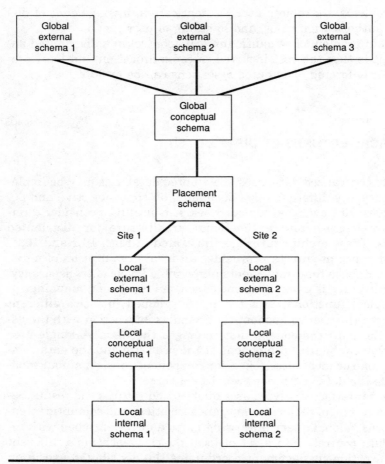

Figure 10.1   Reference architecture for distributed databases.

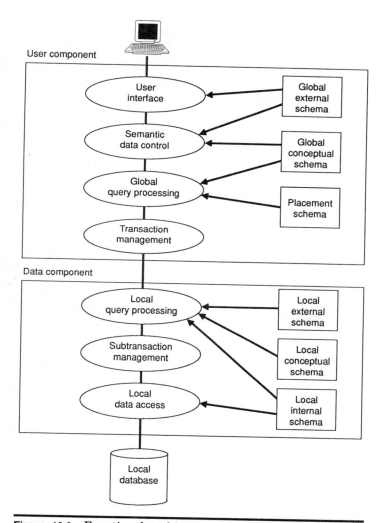

Figure 10.2   Functional architecture for distributed databases.

Introduction to DB2 and SQL/DS

DB2 and SQL/DS have become the flagships of relational database management systems (DBMSs). The universal acceptance of these two products coupled with the strong support of IBM has made them the DBMSs of the future.

The vendor, IBM, has indicated that these two DBMSs are compatible database engines and differ in only the operating system that supports them. DB2 is supported by MVS, whereas SQL/DS is supported by DOS/VSE and VM/CMS. With this in mind, this chapter will treat them as one and will only differentiate between them when the differences are significant enough to merit highlighting them.

11.1 BACKGROUND OF DB2

In June 1983, DB2 was announced. Delivery was said to be 15 months away, so IBM was executing its normal gambit to discourage customers from defecting to third parties or to give sites the opportunity to plan ahead, depending on one's viewpoint. The new product was intended to run under MVS/370 and MVS/XA, although it was clearly intended to cooperate with the latter and could be seen as another incentive to opt for this operating environment. DOS/VSE users already had their own relational DBMS, SQL/DS, and the new product was very similar to it. The main differences were that DB2 supported much larger databases, had the IMS interface, and, of course, was tightly coupled with MVS/XA.

Two packages were also announced to provide support for DB2 in the MVS environment. Query Management Facility (QMF) uses Structured Query Language (SQL) and QB2 to provide interactive extraction, manipulation, and generation.

Data Extract (DXT) uses ISPF menu-driven panels to enable data to be extracted from IMS/VS and DL/1 databases and from VSAM and SAM datasets in readiness for loading into DB2.

The intriguing thing about DXT, apart from the fact that it was scheduled to be available 3 months before DB2, was the implication that MVS users were expected to run both IMS and DB2. This makes business sense from IBM's point of view. However, IMS was supposed to be the corporate DBMS, and one of the primary reasons for implementing a DBMS, particularly a corporate one, is to reduce data redundancy. Issues such as data integrity, support, security, DASD requirements, and programmer productivity also arise.

In April 1985, IBM announced that DB2 was generally available and at the same time extended its data dictionary to give support to DB2. The main objective of the data dictionary was to improve system and application programmer productivity. Interestingly, IBM was already beginning to suggest that DB2 was not entirely unsuitable for production applications. IBM also started to produce throughput figures for DB2, which suggested that it might be suitable as a general-purpose DBMS, and to push IMS into a more specialized high-throughput role.

In February 1986, Release 2 of DB2 was announced, with the stated intention of giving the product a large-scale production role, as well as an information center one. This message was reinforced by the introduction of the DB2 Performance Monitor (DB2PM) and a more flexible version of DXT.

11.2 A DB2 PERSPECTIVE

Before discussing techniques for development under DB2, it is useful to step back for a perspective on what makes up a DB2 development environment. This section discusses the various components of IBM's environment for DB2 development and the relative strengths and weaknesses of that environment. This will lay the basis for later discussion of the techniques needed to supplement that environment.

A useful parodying for the evaluation of DB2 is called a Comprehensive Information Management System (CIMS). Such a system provides a fully integrated environment revolving around a repository. Closely tied to the repository are a distributed DBMS, a systems designer system, a systems implementor system, and interactive end-user access.

A CIMS environment enhances and simultaneously constrains the development of systems. It constrains development because it provides the structures and architectures that are vital to a highly productive environment. At the same time, it enhances development by allowing

designers and implementors to concentrate their efforts on creative
and responsive solutions to business problems rather than reinventing
interfaces to the technical environment.

True integration in a CIMS environment means that systems will
be built in new and more rigorous ways.

The CIMS components are shown in Fig. 11.1. The integration between them will be developed later. This section will simply summa-
rize the features of each component, as a basis for describing the DB2
environment.

11.2.1 Repository

The repository is the heart of the CIMS environment. The dictionary
provides the descriptions of the processing that is required and the
data that is required for the processing. It provides common definitions for all users of the same data item, whether it is a screen, report,
database, or other file type or program processing.

The repository allows the DBMS to do more than just identify its
objects. It contains information about all the data that is of interest to
the enterprise. Therefore, it includes database elements, screens, reports, programs, and systems. In order to provide the level of functionality required, a repository must provide both a standard set of entities, which are useful in most environments, and an extensibility
feature that allows individual enterprises to include entities of unique
interest to that organization.

11.2.2 Distributed DBMS

The CIMS environment provides a powerful DBMS, which services
data in a fashion analogous to that provided by the repository for
metadata. All master information of interest to the organization resides under the control of the DBMS. It ensures integrity and security
of the data while providing access to authorized users. In today's world
of far-flung enterprises, the DBMS must be distributed if it is to

END-USER SYSTEM	MAINFRAME	DISTRIBUTED DBMS	SYSTEM DESIGNER SYSTEM
	MICRO	DATA DICTIONARY (repository)	
		SYSTEM IMPLEMENTOR SYSTEM	

Figure 11.1 CIMS components.

achieve its objective. The definition of distributed DBMS is now evolving. However, it is clear that a distributed DBMS must provide location transparency, partitioning, and replication around the network with full integrity and location independence.

11.2.3 System Designer Systems

System designer systems are commonly called CASE tools. Such tools provide facilities to improve designer productivity by automating designer tasks. These include word processing integrated with graphics, functional prototyping, data modeling, database design, and performance prototyping. A critical aspect of CASE tools is that they must provide multiuser access to a central design dictionary to provide vital cross-team communication.

11.2.4 System Implementor Systems

System implementor systems are increasingly being labeled CASE tools. More recognizable labels include 4GLs and workbenches. Facilities of a truly complete system implementor would include:

- A standardized architecture for online and batch processes, incorporating standard interfaces to the technical environment
- Code generation
- Screen and report generation
- Database generation
- Test data generation
- Test data and testing management
- Configuration management for systems moving through unit testing, system testing, and production

11.2.5 End-User Systems

End-user systems require a wide variety of options. For high-volume systems, such as order processing or reservations, a high-performance TP monitor such as CICS or IMS/DC is needed. For simple ad hoc requirements, a query tool that has a short learning curve for nondedicated users is necessary. For complex ad hoc requirements, a powerful decision support product is required. In today's world of microcomputers, interface software to download and/or upload between microcomputer and mainframe is increasingly necessary.

11.3 DB2 AS A DATABASE MANAGEMENT SYSTEM

As described earlier, DB2 is a powerful DBMS. Its primary weakness under the CIMS model is its lack of distributed capabilities. In this section, we discuss DB2's capabilities in more detail.

Today, we expect a DBMS to be relational and to provide all the advantages promised by relational theory. First and foremost, the advantage expected from relational theory is that of programmer productivity. The characteristics of a fully relational system may be summarized as follows:

- Data is always presented to users as tables consisting of rows and columns.

- The DBMS provides the functions of the relational algebra, especially SELECT, PROJECT, and JOIN.

- The DBMS enforces the integrity of primary and foreign keys.

- The databases are managed strictly through relational capabilities of the DBMS.

DB2 maintains data integrity during multiple user accesses; it provides security against unauthorized access from programs or end users; it provides roll-back in the event of program or system failure and roll-forward in the event of medium failure. And DB2 provides that functionality at a speed suitable for most online transaction processing systems.

DB2 has two weaknesses when viewed from a traditional perspective. For batch processing, DB2 seems to ignore the typical situation of batch posting to master files while creating audit trail records for a batch report. The DB2 integrity features do not encompass sequential files of the type typically used for report records. Therefore, there is an integrity exposure if a batch program fails and is subsequently restarted. The state of the sequential file may not match the state of the master files. Techniques for overcoming this weakness tend to require one of the following:

- Use of Assembler programming, which is increasingly unacceptable to today's data processing management

- Use of DB2 for report records, which leads to significant performance degradation when the volume of report records is large

The second weakness in DB2 is the structure of the security system. The system is inherently hierarchical, assuming that the system administrator should have full authority to manipulate all DB2 objects. In fact, security has been implemented for many decades under the principle of separation of duties, so that no one individual has full access to sensitive assets. Within data processing, someone in operations typically needs enough authority to fix problem programs in the middle of the night and put them back into production. Ensuring that this same individual does not also have the authority to dynamically change sensitive production data can be problematic under DB2. The difficulty is heightened by the fact that DB2 does not provide any audit trails of interactive changes.

11.4 APPLICATION DEVELOPMENT USING DB2

The major advantage of a relational DBMS is application programmer productivity gains, which have been reported as 2 to 4 times better than with a traditional DBMS. My own experience with relational databases supports these claims. Not only are these gains found when writing new applications, but they are even greater when modifying existing relational DBMS applications.

There is absolutely no question that the application programmer productivity gains of a relational DBMS are significant; they are possible because of two fundamental differences between a relational DBMS and a traditional DBMS.

The first difference is that a relational DBMS uses the values in the data fields themselves to relate data items rather than using physical pointers or indexes to connect data items. In fact, a relationship can be made dynamically between two data items. When you ask for data, you don't have to know whether or not there are predefined access paths. This truly separates the application program from having to know about the physical structure of the data, unlike a traditional DBMS. Thus, the application programmer can focus on building applications and does not have to waste time working out how to navigate through the database. Usually, changes to data structures and changes to applications are independent of each other; this rarely happens in a traditional DBMS. Although using the values in the data fields to connect the data items together does introduce more data redundancy than a traditional database, it can be dealt with by the application.

The second difference is that, unlike a traditional DBMS, which deals with data one record at a time, a relational database is set, or multirecord, oriented. When you ask for data from a relational DBMS, you don't have to know how many records, if any, satisfy the criteria. With one single statement, you get all the data to satisfy your request. You do not have to write application program statements to determine if and when you have all the data. When you ask for data from a traditional DBMS, you get only one record at a time.

This is why a relational database, like DB2, is ideal for ad hoc query and report writing applications, which are sometimes called information center or decision support applications. Ad hoc query and report applications typically have the following attributes:

- Cannot be preplanned
- Create data relationships dynamically
- Require rapid turnaround
- Tend to be run infrequently

Since a relationship between two data items can be made dynamically, and predefined access paths are not required, ad hoc query and report applications are ideal for implementation under DB2.

Conversely, with a traditional DBMS, data can only be retrieved using predefined access paths. You might not even be able to write a particular query or report application until the database administrator builds the particular predefined access path required by that application. This can take days or even weeks to accomplish.

11.4.1 CICS-DB2 Transaction Processing

Implementing a new CICS transaction processing application for DB2 is easier than doing the same for a traditional DBMS. To obtain good performance in a relational DBMS, it is mandatory that the application deal with sets of records at a time, not single records. This section describes some of the problems that can occur when implementing CICS transactions that use DB2.

In order to process a CICS transaction under DB2, you issue SQ1 "select" statements in your application program and pass control to DB2. DB2 then involves the optimizer to determine how the request will be handled.

Having a predefined index available does not necessarily mean that DB2 will use it. DB2 searches for the records that meet the selecting criteria and puts the records in DB2's virtual memory and transfers control back to the application program. If the data must be reordered, the answer set must be sorted before control is returned to the user. This can take a long time.

The application program will issue "fetches" for as many records as it can deal with; typically a screenful. After it gets them, it writes to the screen. Writing to the screen is the end of the transaction, which means CICS will release all those records you just found. Your selection criteria should be very specific so that all the selected records can fit on one screen.

But what if one screen could only hold 20 records and the selection criteria found 100 records? The application program has to remember the key of the last record found and save that key in the transaction work area. Then you must reissue the "select" statement with a "where" clause asking for records with a higher key value. This is passed to DB2. It does the entire search over again and stores the records in virtual memory—not all of the records, just 21 to 100. Your application then must process 20 more records and you have to repeat the entire process again for records 41 to 60. This continues until you process the hundredth record. Note that you have read records 81 to 100 five times and only displayed them once.

11.5   LOGICAL DATABASE DESIGN FOR DB2

There are three parts to database design under DB2:

- Data normalization
- Logical database design
- Physical database design

11.5.1   Data Normalization

Over the last decade, data normalization techniques have demonstrated their value. Normalized data structures survive corporate growth and reorganization. This stability in data structure brings commensurate stability to the applications that use the data while allowing development of new applications using the old data.

There are many texts on data normalization, so we will not attempt to define techniques for normalization here. Suffice it to say that a rigorous approach to data normalization is strongly encouraged. Researchers need not be in third normal form; first normal form is all that is required.

However, there is no substitute for rigorous data analysis for understanding the business relationships of data elements. Therefore, we recommend that the first stage of database design should take the data to third normal form, at a minimum. Fourth or fifth normal form may be preferable where data relationships are complex.

11.5.2 Logical Database Design

Logical database design has four steps:

- Define tables
- Define referential integrity requirements
- Denormalize the table designs
- Define views

Table definition begins by assuming that each normalized entity from the data analysis will become a DB2 table. The first step is to define all the columns that will be contained in the table, recognizing that additional columns will typically be identified during programming.

DB2 column names may contain 18 characters, including the 26 letters of the alphabet, the 10 digits, the special COBOL characters, and the underscore (__). It is helpful to use COBOL data names for the column names.

The data characteristics of each column must be identified at this stage. This includes defining alphabetic versus numeric format as well as the use of nulls or variable-length fields. When there are frequent opportunities to conserve at least 20 bytes by making the field length variable, and the field will not increase in size during the life of any specific row occurrence, VARCHAR is appropriate. For example, when four address lines are allowed, but normally only two are used, it is appropriate to use VARCHAR for lines 3 and 4. However, if a long text field is normally omitted at the time of entry, but keyed into the system at some subsequent time, it is not appropriate to use VARCHAR. There are four types of fields available for defining numeric fields in DB2:

- Integer (halfword or fullword)
- Decimal (packed decimal)
- Float (fullword or doubleword)
- Calendar (date, time, or timestamp)

Nulls are occasionally used for numeric data. They are appropriate when functions need to know a minimum, nonempty value, but empty values are permissible. For example, it may be necessary to know the smallest salary, excluding unknown salaries. Nulls are also appropriate when the function must compute an average by excluding empty values. Once you have defined the data types of all columns, the next step is to define the primary keys of all DB2 tables. Generally, these will be the primary keys defined during data analysis. Primary keys should guarantee uniqueness of each row of the table. They should also be acceptable as the primary means for accessing the data. DB2 can always retrieve data, regardless of what criteria are defined. As a practical matter, though, only one access path will give better performance than any other, and transaction processing systems should maximize use of that path. All columns included in primary keys should be defined as NOT NULL. Default values should never be acceptable.

Once the initial table designs are complete, it is necessary to identify the relationships between tables that must be maintained by the applications. For example, in a receivable system, it will be important to ensure that customer numbers are always valid and that no customers are deleted from the customer file while they still have outstanding receivables in the receivable file. This is called "referential integrity."

Referential integrity is enforced by identifying columns that contain data that serves as a primary key to another table. For example, the receivables table will contain the customer number, which is the primary key to the customer table. Therefore, customer number is called a foreign key in the receivables table. Referential integrity says that all foreign keys must be valid.

Rows may not be inserted to the secondary table if the related row does not exist in the primary table. If a key is updated on the primary table, all occurrences of that value in secondary tables are updated as well. A value cannot be changed in a primary table if there are any occurrences of that value in secondary tables. The matching values in the secondary tables are set to null and the primary is then updated. A foreign key cannot be changed to a value that does not exist on the primary tables. If a primary key is deleted in the primary table, all occurrences of that value in secondary tables are deleted as well.

The third step of logical database design is to denormalize the data. During this phase of denormalization, look for opportunities to minimize the number of tables that must be accessed to complete a single application. Typically, this will be made possible by creating redundant data in certain tables in order to avoid accessing other tables for those columns. The reduction in accesses for the application must be balanced with the cost of maintaining redundant data. Therefore, it is desirable to replicate only stable data that will not require maintenance.

Another common technique for reducing the number of tables accessed is the compaction of two or more tables into a single table. This is particularly useful when tables have a one-to-one relationship. It is also useful when only a small amount of data must be replicated if tables are combined. For example, if data analysis defines a very narrow order header table and a wide (many columns) order line table, the two tables can be combined at relatively little cost. Typically, the order header data would appear on every associated table, and the order header table would disappear.

Data analysis, when completed to third normal form, can produce too many tables to be supported effectively. Comparison of third normal form data structures to first normal form structures may suggest additional denormalization that will improve performance.

11.5.3 Physical Database Design

During the physical database design task, there are seven steps for DB2:

- Group tables into databases
- Group tables into table spaces
- Analyze requirements for partitioning large table spaces
- Define unique indexes
- Create a project storage group
- Create databases, table spaces, tables, and primary indexes
- Identify additional indexes

Begin with the data model of the logical database that was developed during the logical database design. Each such grouping of tables defines a database. Typically, databases hold 6 to 10 tables. These databases are typically defined along traditional database lines (i.e., customer, product, order, and inventory).

You may expect a one-to-one correlation between table spaces and tables. The only exception are small tables that can more easily be grouped together and managed as a single unit. It is possible to load several related tables into a single table space so as to force the clustering of related rows from different tables into common data pages.

Large table spaces are typically partitioned by key range. Partitioning allows faster backup, reorganization, and recovery of large table spaces. It also allows key ranges that are accessed frequently to be placed on faster devices. I/O bottlenecks may be reduced by placing partitions of frequently accessed tables on different devices and/or different controllers.

However, partitioning has its disadvantages. It prevents programmers from updating the columns that are used as the basis of partitioning. For example, if a table is partitioned by region ID, region ID cannot be updated. The row must be deleted and inserted with the new ID.

The final step in physical database design is to define unique indexes. Usually, the primary keys defined during normalization will be the unique indexes. It is very important for each table to have a unique key. Because of the set processing nature of DB2, it is impossible to delete a single erroneous row of a table unless uniqueness of the key can be assured.

Indexes should be smaller than 40 bytes; 8 to 12 bytes is the preferred range of index sizes. In addition to the unique indexes, it is necessary to define the partitioning index at this time. This is the index that DB2 will use to create the table space partitions.

The partitioning indexes have two special features:

- They define the physical sequence of the data in the table.
- The data columns used for partitioning indexes cannot be updated.

There are several parameters that should be specified when defining table spaces. These include:

- Database that holds the table space
- Partitioning
- CLOSE—whether the table space should be closed when the program using it terminates
- PRIQTY—primary space allocation in kbytes
- SECQTY—secondary space allocation in kbytes
- ERASE—whether to rewrite DASD space with binary zeros whenever the table space is dropped
- Locking level
- Buffer pools
- Password

11.6 THE DB2 CATALOG

DB2 as a database manager is required to manage data that is defined to it. DB2 uses tables to manage the data that it keeps. In addition to keeping track of every object defined in the relational system, information is recorded that pertains to who can create new objects or access the existing ones. All of these tables are grouped into what is known as the DB2 Catalog or the DB2 System Catalog. The DB2 Catalog contains approximately 30 tables.

Let's identify what some of these objects are that have to be managed by the DBMS. These objects include buffer pools, storage groups, databases, table spaces, tables, indexes, views, synonyms, and plans. DB2 keeps track of not only the just mentioned objects in the Catalog but also who has access and control over these objects.

Execution of various DB2 utilities, such as COPY, RECOVERY, REORGANIZATION, LOAD, RUNSTATS, and STOSPACE, will either retrieve or update information contained in columns in one or more of the DB2 Catalog tables. This information is valuable to DB2 when determining data access strategies and recovering tables. The DB2 Catalog tables are unlike normal tables, in that SQL operations to perform inserts, updates, or deletes are not allowed. Instead, the DB2 Catalog is updated indirectly through special SQL data definition statements, such as create, alter, and drop.

DB2 uses buffer pools when building temporary tables to store data resulting from sorts and joins. There are only four buffer pools available. They are PF0, BP1, BP2, and BP32K. DB2 uses DP0 to store its data pages. Performance-critical applications can process in their own buffer pools such as BP1 and BP2.

DB2 Performance Implications

When an organization considers making a strategic decision to use IBM's DB2 database management system (DBMS), one of the many factors to appreciate is the potential performance implication of using DB2 compared with the benefits to be gained through ease of data access and the high degree of data transparency. For organizations who are introducing DB2 for decision support systems (DSS), the fact that end users are able to get to a variety of business data in an unplanned fashion (through dynamic SQL) often outweighs the significant performance overhead that may be incurred. For production online transaction processing systems (OLTPs), however, the need to understand how DB2 behaves and to plan for the best performance cannot be overstated. This chapter reviews DB2 with regard to performance optimization and makes a comparison of the controls one has with DB2 with those available for other DBMSs.

12.1 WHAT INFLUENCES DB2 PERFORMANCE?

The performance of a DB2 application depends on many factors. Like most database systems, poor database and application design will usually lead to poor performance. The common factor in most cases is the inability of the database and I/O subsystems to respond to the demand of the application to access and manipulate data. Unlike record-level processing DBMSs (DL/I, IDMS), DB2 retrieves data at the set level. In essence, this means that a single database call made by a program could retrieve or update every row within a DB2 table. One has to appreciate the power of such a call against the cost and impact of its execution. The management of the power and performance of DB2 can be considerably influenced by factors under direct user control.

12.2   PHYSICAL DATABASE DESIGN

DB2 holds data in simple table structures (rows and columns). Indexes may be defined on columns in a table to improve data access, and tables may be grouped together in a table space (segmented or partitioned) for efficient storage management. With the implementation of referential integrity in DB2 Version 2.1, table columns may have data integrity relationships with one another. This simplified view of how DB2 stores data conceals the following facts:

- The order of rows in a table has no logical significance.
- There are no user-defined pointers to improve the linkage to related data.
- The use of indexes is transparent to the application.
- The access path to the data is selected by DB2 (the Optimizer) and not the application (or database administrator).

For these reasons, careful attention must be given to table design, degree of data normalization, and data process requirements in order to ensure database design efficiency.

12.3   INDEXES

The use of indexes remains the most common performance option. Indexes can be created dynamically or during table load and may be built from a combination of up to 16 columns (ascending or descending). A DB2 table may have any number of indexes that can be used to enforce uniqueness. Indexes may also be used to partition large tables.

12.4   TABLE DESIGN

Some of the subtleties around DB2 table design are worth mentioning, in particular, when to use variable columns and the positioning of fixed and variable columns within a row. The impact of implementing referential integrity is discussed below. The use of VARCHAR is recommended only when the average space saving for a column is greater than 20 bytes. For retrieval performance, fixed-length columns should be at the beginning of a row. To reduce data logging when fixed-length columns are updated, variable-length columns should be at the beginning of a row.

12.5   STATIC VERSUS DYNAMIC SQL

DB2 provides a Structured Query Language (SQL) to define, manipulate, and control the objects, data, and access within the DB2 environment. The SQL within an application can be either static or dynamic. Static SQL (complied) offers better performance than dynamic SQL because it uses a prebuild PLAN (containing the data navigation path) for execution. With dynamic SQL, there is significant overhead in catalog contention, view decomposition, and authorization. Generally, static SQL is used for OLTP and dynamic SQL is used for decision support.

12.6 SQL EFFICIENCY

Through SQL, applications may retrieve and update vast amounts of data in relatively few database calls. DB2 and SQL together provide an assortment of options and techniques which may be used singly or may be combined to manipulate the data. These options and techniques include:

- Table JOINs and UNIONs (application, or DB2, invoked)
- Queries and subqueries
- Correlated and noncorrelated queries
- Cursor and noncursor operations
- Predicate sequencing
- Cursor stability (CS) and repeatable read (RR)

Misunderstanding, misuse, or abuse of these options and techniques may achieve the correct application result at the expense of performance. Frequent use of the DB2 EXPLAIN statement (which reports on DB2's chosen navigational path, discussed below) together with quality assurance procedures on SQL code (whether generated by hand or through CASE methods) will lead to SQL efficiency. The key points to remember when developing SQL code are that only required columns must be selected and that the minimum number of rows are processed.

12.7 DATABASE VOLUMETRICS

The set-processing mechanisms within DB2 can begin to affect performance as the size of production DB2 tables increases. To alleviate performance constraints, tables may be physically spread (partitioned) over different direct-access storage device (DASD) volumes (and device types) by a range of values for a single or column combination of columns. Logically, DB2 considers the multivolumed table as a single table, allowing most volatile or frequently accessed data to be held on the fastest devices. As an alternative approach to limiting table size, a database archiving strategy may be adopted which removes historical data (which may be infrequently or no longer accessed) from primary production tables in order to reduce the length of table and index scans. DB2 supports table sizes of up to 64 Gbytes.

12.8 LOCKING STRATEGIES

A DB2 subsystem may be accessed from many different environments (TSO, CICS, IMS) concurrently. In order to allow sharing of the same collection of data and maintain update integrity, DB2 adopts a concurrency control mechanism locking technique under the same guidelines as for other DBMSs:

- Modified data must be committed (or rolled back).
- Data that has been updated by one application cannot be accessed by another application until it is committed (or rolled back). The type, level, access mode, and duration of locking necessary to maintain data integrity will obviously influence system performance.

The four lock attributes within DB2 are:

1. *Object:*   Type of resource (table, page, table space, index space).
2. *Granularity:*   The level at which the resource is locked (page instead of a table space). The smaller the lock, the more granular the lock is said to be. DB2 can modify a lock during execution (lock escalation).
3. *Mode:*   The type of access permitted to concurrent users of the locked object. S locks (shared) allow other applications to access the resource in read-only mode. Applications with update intent are locked out. X locks (eXclusively) prevent any application from accessing the locked object. During execution, a lock can be promoted from S to X (lock promotion).
4. *Duration:*   Depends on when the lock is required and released. The activation of a resource lock requires storage and processing time. Smaller locks (at the page level) offer maximum concurrency whereas larger locks (at the table space level) offer maximum performance. DB2 locks are released when a transaction reaches a synchronization point.

12.9 BUFFER USAGE

Most database systems with high transaction volumes are primarily constrained by the level of physical I/O. To reduce physical I/O, database systems rely on the use of buffers to hold frequently used data.

DB2 is no exception and its buffer pool acts as an "intelligent cache," giving preference to randomly retrieved data over sequentially prefetched data, and is managed on a least recently used (LRU) basis. The current practical maximum buffer size is 2 Gbytes, although there is a theoretical maximum of 8 Tbytes. Large buffer pools are effectively managed through hashed access mechanisms, small synonym chains, and sophisticated LRU processing, which contribute to a low pool management cost. The benefits of large buffer pools are:

1. *Fewer physical I/Os:* Gives faster application response with reduced DASD contention.

2. *Sequential prefetch:* Asynchronous reading of up to 64 chained pages (10 times more than sequential read I/O).

3. *Asynchronous write:* Write I/O does not contribute to transaction performance and allows multiple updates in the buffet before a physical write (see physical I/O).

4. *Chained write:* Gives fewer DASD contention issues and more effective use of 3380K devices.

12.10 THREAD UTILIZATION

A subsystem or batch address space must establish connection with DB2 before it can access any of its resources. The connection establishes the communication path and within the connection a thread establishes the bidirectional path when the application in the subsystem makes its first SQL call. DB2 sets up control blocks and allocates resources to the thread. It tracks the execution of the thread through its system interactions until the thread ends when connection is made (see Fig. 12.1):

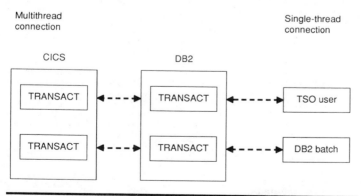

Figure 12.1 Single-thread and multithread connection.

- *Single-thread:* Only one thread is allowed per connection (TSO or batch).

- *Multithread:* Multiple threads are possible between the subsystem and DB2. Each thread services the calls of one transaction. Threads may be defined as protected or unprotected. Protected threads are not terminated when not in use, thereby avoiding the overhead of thread creation and termination for each transaction. Note that any thread will be terminated if it remains unused for any two consecutive 30-second periods.

12.11 REFERENTIAL INTEGRITY

DB2 Version 2.1 introduced the implementation of referential integrity (RI). The RI rules state what should happen when an SQL update request (INSERT, UPDATE, or DELETE) that affects columns involved in an RI relationship is processed. The definition of RI rules is through the DDL for primary keys and foreign keys. Support for system-enforced RI (via the DB2 Data Manager) removes the responsibility of enforcing referential constraints from the application developer (via SQL). There are, however, performance and application consideration to be examined before using DB2 to enforce RI. Enforced RI offers:

- Application development productivity, no need for additional programs.

- Greater integrity and consistency of data; RI enforced for all environments.

- DB2 RI is likely to be equal to or better than user-enforced RI: fewer SQL calls are needed in the application program. In some situations where the user has informed knowledge of the application and data, user-enforced RI has an associated performance cost (see Fig. 12.2).

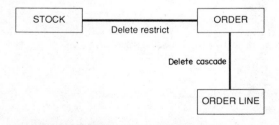

Figure 12.2 RI as an associated cost.

12.12   PERFORMANCE CONSIDERATIONS
OF REFERENTIAL INTEGRITY

The existence of a primary key is checked by a lookup of the primary index. The checking of a foreign key is done by an index (if it exists, or if the foreign key is the first part of an index). If no index exists, a table space scan with sequential prefetch is carried out. Implementing RI may increase page reference and path lengths and therefore affect performance; additional locking and checking must be done by DB2, and there will be an additional cost in taking and releasing locks and checking for dependent and parent rows to enforce RI.

Our recommendations for better performance and throughput when referential integrity is in use are:

1. Create an index of foreign keys.

2. Minimize the lock size and duration.

3. Consider LOCK TABLE for batch processing.

4. Consider user-enforced RI where applicable.

12.13   COMPARISON OF DB2
PERFORMANCE INDICATORS

Having considered some of the factors which influence DB2 performance, it is now worth taking some comparisons of database structures of other DBMSs and looking at how their performance indicators (design, I/O efficiency, etc.) compare with those of DB2. Table 12.1 shows the equivalences among these four systems.

12.14   IMS VERSUS DB2

The IMS database system manages its database as a collection of records, where each record can contain a hierarchy of segments (see Fig. 12.3). The physical design of the IMS database is usually more complex than that for DB2 in that it can be represented in all manner of structures (up to 16 levels deep), including logical relationship and secondary indexing. On top of this, the choice of physical design criteria is plentiful, ranging from the selection of which physical database access method to use (HDAM, HIDAM, HISAM, etc.) and the system access method (VSAM, OSAM) through to the specification of segment pointers (parent pointers, twin pointers, etc.). Unlike DB2, IMS database designers are provided with many more options and thus require more understanding of the application requirements and typical call activity in order to judge the best performance options. Performance of

TABLE 12.1 **Equivalents between Database Systems**

DB2	IMS	IDMS	ADABAS
Database		Database	Database
Table space		Area	
Table	Database	Set	File
Row	Record	Record	Record
Column	Field	Field	Field
Set process	Record process	Record process	Record process
Indexes	Indexes		Descriptor ISN
	Pointers	Pointers	
	Ordering	Ordering	
RI system/user	System/User	User	Data compression/ User
Integrated DD			

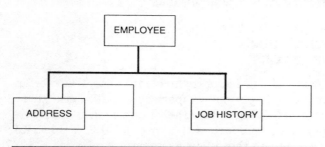

Figure 12.3 Hierarchy of segments.

the application is under tighter control too, in that the data access requirements for high-volume transactions are closely linked to the databased design. This is because access profiles are predefined and can be accommodated in database design. Navigation of the database is usually via a root segment (EMPLOY), which can be found quickly through an index (or hashing algorithms). Thereafter, scanning related dependent segments is efficient because of either locality of reference (HISAM) or internal pointers (HDAM). As with DB2, the specification of large buffer pools assists in reducing the physical I/O.

12.15 IDMS VERSUS DB2

The IDMS database system manages its database as a collection of records in a network architecture. The physical design of the database

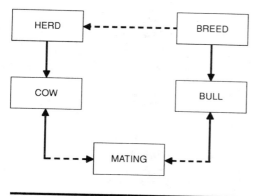

Figure 12.4 Logical data model.

can closely resemble the logical data model with little compromise for data denormalization (see Fig. 12.4). Unlike DB2, the choice of physical design criteria is plentiful, ranging from the selection of location modes (CALC, VIA DIRECT) to specification of record pointers (owner, first and last, etc.). IDMS database designers are provided with more options for improving performance than they would be with DB2. Examples are the selection of page sizes for areas (to suit the location modes) and the ability to use VIA for optimum clustering of related member records to a particular owner occurrence. As with IMS, databases can be designed to meet transaction performance needs. The programming database method is record oriented, usually with initial entry to the database by the CALC key followed by sequential navigation through a series of record pointers. As with DB2, the specification of large buffer pools for the most heavily accessed areas (by page size) assists in reducing the physical I/O.

12.16   ADABAS VERSUS DB2

The ADABAS database system manages its database as a collection of records indexed through inverted lists (see Fig. 12.5). The Association contains direct pointers (ISNs) to the records within the data area. Indexes can be defined on the data (descriptors, superdescriptors, hyperdescriptors) to improve access efficiency. ADABAS provides data compression facilities which reduce I/O volumes at the expense of CPU to decompress the record. ADABAS is designed for high buffer efficiency and allows the user to set the criteria for buffer flushes (forced physical writes). The use of NATURAL (from TSO or CICS) also plays a part in performance efficiency, providing a range of database access statements which allow direct record and set processing to be combined. Like DB2, NATURAL uses threads to establish a con-

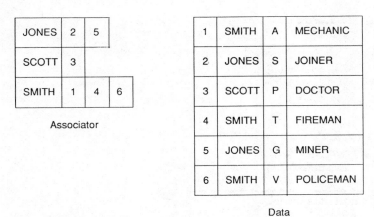

Figure 12.5   Records indexed through inverted lines.

nection with ADABASE and thread utilization requires monitoring and control. With ADABAS Version 4 only one thread is available for update transactions, which can limit throughput. With ADABAS Version 5, however, this restriction has been removed.

12.17 DB2 PERFORMANCE MANAGEMENT

DB2 comes with a number of rules, formulas, and policing methods for managing the performance of DB2 application.

12.18 THE GOVERNOR

For dynamic SQL only, the Governor (Resource Limit Facility) provides policing control on excessive resource usage. The controls, held within DB2 tables, specify time constraints for user-program combinations. Applications that exceed the time constraints are terminated by the Governor. The Governor can, in addition, prevent execution of certain QMF commands, limit time of day when commands may be executed, limit the length and activity of QMF sessions (by CPU time, number of rows), and keep track of a user's usage (elapsed/CPU time, DB activity, etc.).

12.19 USE OF THE EXPLAIN STATEMENT

The EXPLAIN statement provides details of the access path that the DB2 Optimizer will select in order to process an SQL request. The use of the EXPLAIN statement is a common tuning tool for database administrators (DBAs) in that they can decide, for example, that an SQL request requiring a table scan can be avoided by introducing a new index. The information provided from the EXPLAIN statement gives details about access type, indexes that are used, order of table access, order of table join, the join method (nested loop or merge scan), sort information, and the locking strategy. The explain information is provided by using the EXPLAIN statement interactively, as follows:

```
EXPLAIN PLAN
        SET QUERYNO = 1
     FOR
           SELECT  PROD_NO. ORDER_NO. ORDER_SALESPERSON
              FROM PRODTAB. ORDERTAB
           WHERE PROD_NO = ORDER_PROD_NO.
           AND ORDER_SALESPERSON = 'SMITH'
```

or by specifying the EXPLAIN option on BIND or REBIND. The information is stored in a PLAN_TABLE for use as and when required.

12.20 TRACING FACILITIES

DB2 provides a sophisticated trace facility that can show which resources are being used and how. A trace may be activated at startup time or explicitly from a trace command. Up to 32 traces may be activated at any one time. There are six different types of trace:

1. Statistics (STAT)
    a. Systemwide DB2 execution measurement
    b. Minimal overhead
    c. CPU times represent activity in DB2 address space
2. Accounting (ACCTG)
    a. Measurement of individual DB2 users (threads)
    b. Used for application and system tuning
    c. CPU represents user TCB or SRB
    d. Three classes: total application time, in DB2 time, I/O and lock/latch suspension time
3. Performance (PERFM)
    a. Measurement of specific BD2 events (e.g., start I/O)
    b. For detailed investigation, causes large amounts of output
4. Monitor (MON)
    a. Buffered trace output so that it can be used by the Instrumentation Facility Interface (IFI)
    b. Used for online monitoring
5. Audit (AUDIT)
    a. DB2 audit and security trace
6. Global (GLOBAL)
    a. Serviceability trace (IBM use)

DB2 can write its trace output to different destinations (GTF, SMF, etc.). The use of any tracing facility causes a performance overhead, so its use should be limited.

12.21   THE ROLE OF THE DB2 CATALOG

The DB2 Catalog is a system database (DSNDBO6) that contains information about various objects (table spaces, tables, columns, views, indexes, privileges, plans, etc.) that are defined, used, and manipulated by DB2. The Catalog tables are accessed and updated by DB2 during normal operations, in response to SQL data definition (DDL), data control (DCL), data manipulation (DML), and utilities. The Catalog assists in managing the DB2 environment, optimizing of navigation paths, recovery, and security. Statistics in the Catalog can be used for tuning purposes and should be updated on a regular basis. To update these statistics, it is necessary to execute the utilities RUNSTATS and STOSPACE, which will do table and index space scans and enquire on datasets and VSAM catalogs:

- RUNSTATS—gives information about space utilization and row clustering so that DB2 has current information for access path determination

- STOSPACE—gives information about space allocated by storage groups and related table spaces and indexes

12.22   THE DB2 OPTIMIZER

The DB2 Optimizer contains the navigation logic to determine the optimum access path to satisfy an SQL request. The access path optimization techniques are based on the System R prototype and make full use of rules, cost algorithms, and Catalog statistics to produce an efficient access path strategy. It is essential that the DB2 Catalog is frequently updated to reflect any changes in table sizes (by use of RUNSTATS utility) in order to maximize the effectiveness of the Optimizer. The access path selection is based on:

- Cost model (CPU, I/O, data manager calls, Relational Data System, or RDS, calls, predicates, etc.)
- Available access paths (table space scans, index and data, index only, multiindex access, sequential and list prefetch)
- Statistics about the data stored in the Catalog

- Assumptions made (CPU and I/O weighting factors, DASD types, uniform distribution of values)

12.23 DB2 EXPLOITATION OF HARDWARE AND SOFTWARE ARCHITECTURE

The development of DB2 continues to take advantage of the latest hardware and software features announced by IBM. This "tight fit" approach to the development of DB2 and its integration operating environment will ensure that any shortcomings that may exist now with DB2 are likely to be overcome in the future. Specific areas in which DB2 takes advantage of this operating environment are discussed below.

12.24 DB2 AS AN MVS TASK

DB2 under Version 2.1 runs under three address spaces:

1. *SSAS:* System Services Address Space for system-oriented services (connections, logging, etc.).
2. *DBAS:* Database Services Address Space for all database services.
3. *IRLM:* IMS/VS Resource Lock Manager for all locking services. DB2 is an authorized subsystem of MVS/XA and ESA and uses MVS subtasking facilities.

12.25 MVS/ESA FEATURES

The use of expanded storage offers a significant reduction in transaction response times by limiting the physical I/O activity for database access, page and swap processing, and system I/O. The specification of large database buffer pools (up to 100 Mbytes) backed by processor storage has a significant impact on reducing database I/O. The high degree of residence on frequently referenced index and data pages (e.g., DB2 Catalog and QMF datasets) assists in increasing the transaction throughput capability. Furthermore, sorts from certain SQL functions (ORDER BY and GROUP BY) will require less disk I/O. The reduction in page and swap I/O is less significant, affecting the calling task only while DB2 remains available to concurrent users, enabling priority of preplanned transaction throughput capability. Furthermore, sorts from certain SQL functions (ORDER BY and GROUP BY) will require less disk I/O. The reduction in page and swap I/O is less significant, affecting the calling task only while DB2 remains available to concurrent users, enabling priority of preplanned transactions to be guaranteed. System I/O can be reduced by increasing the Environmental Description Manager (EDM) pool to a reasonable size. When a DB2 transaction executes the SQL statements, the "sections" of the plan are transferred from the DB pool to the EDM pool. Section loading can take up to 30 ms and an average plan may have at least 10 sections. Since the EDM pool is managed on an LRU basis, it should be set large enough to hold the most popular plans. Typically, 100 plans require an EDM pool of 5 to 10 Mb in order to minimize plan dataset I/O. DB2 exploits Advanced Address Space Facility (AASF) for further improvements in performance.

12.26   VIRTUAL STORAGE UTILIZATION

In an MVS/370 environment, virtual storage can be a major problem especially if there are many concurrent users and transactions requiring services of the database services ordering space (DBAS). For MVS/XA environments, most of DB2 is above the 16-Mb line, thus reducing virtual storage constraint problems (see Table 12.2).

12.27   CROSS MEMORY SERVICES

DB2 makes full use of Cross Memory Services (CMS) to provide efficient communication between address spaces and once again takes advantage of ESA performance enhancements. CMS allows SQL code to be executed under the TCB of the user's address space.

12.28   VSAM USAGE

Physical data access within DB2 is based on a special VSAM format, Linear Data Sets (LDS), which provides a privileged fast path for ex-

TABLE 12.2   Virtual Storage Utilization

		MVS/XA (below 16 Mb)	MVS/XA (above 16 Mb)
	MVS/370		
SSAS	AMS 0.5M DB2 code 1.0M	AMS 0.5M	DB2 code 1.0M
IRLM	Code Locks	Code	Locks
DBAS	DB2 code 3 VSAM CBs Working storage Buffer pool EDM pool	DB2 code 0.5M VSAM CBs Working storage	DB2 code 2.5M Working storage Buffer pool EDM pool

ecution and allows DB2 to manage its own buffer pools. LDSs are used for user databases, the DB2 Catalog, and the DB2 Directory; ESDs are used for DB2 active logs; and KSDSs are used for the bootstrap dataset (BSDS). DB2 takes one CI (4K) as the physical record size. An LDS does not contain VSAM Control Internal Definition Field (CIDF) or a Record Definition Field (RDF), enabling all space to be used for data. In order to keep control over its physical data structure, the DB2 Data Manager holds the relationship between internal and external objects in the DB2 directory.

12.29 OTHER SUBSYSTEM COMPONENTS

DB2 is integrated with the various components of System Managed Storage (SMS). DFMS storage groups can be used for DB2 STOGROUPS enabling automatic use of MIGRATE and RECALL functions for archived logs and image copies of DB2 table spaces. DB2 optimizes the use of cache by dynamically changing the operating mode of the cache (sequential or random) to suit the actual pattern of usage.

12.30 PERFORMANCE IMPROVEMENTS IN DB2 VERSION 2.2

DB2 Version 2.2 became available in October 1989. The main areas of enhancement were in system performance and in the initial implementation of distributed database.

12.30.1 Multiple Indexing

Prior to Version 2.2 the DB2 Optimizer would only use one index on a table to process a single SQL query. With Version 2.2, multiple indexes on a table are now used, for example:

```
PRODTABLE (PROD_NO. PROD_DESC. PROD_TYPE. PROD_MAT.
                                               PROD_PRC)
PRODX1 INDEX ON PRODTABLE (PROD_NO)
PRODX2 INDEX ON PRODTABLE (PROD_TYPE)
PRODX3 INDEX ON PRODTABLE (PROD_MAT)
SELECT *
    FROM PRODTABLE
    WHERE PROD_TYPE = 'BOLTS'
    AND PROD_MAT = 'STEEL'
```

Under Version 2.1 both PRODX2 and PRODX3 provide good access paths, but only one is chosen by the Optimizer. With Version 2.2, however, improved access path selection is made (see Fig. 12.6).

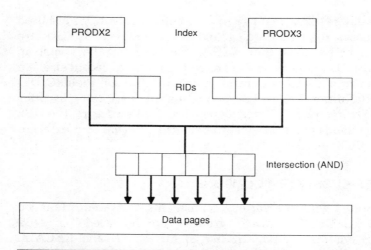

Figure 12.6 Benefits for queries using multiple indexes and nonclustered indexes.

12.30.2 Optimizing the DB2 Optimizer

Several steps have been taken to introduce programming efficiency within the DB2 Optimizer; they are:

- Column function evaluation (AVE, MIN, MAX, SUM, etc.).
- Correlated subquery processing by using results from a previous subquery.
- Query optimization for frequently occurring data values. The Optimizer now uses statistics on data value distribution to determine the optimal join sequences, index usage, and path selection. DB2 chooses one index over another based on the statistics generated and maintained by the RUNSTATS utility.

Prior to Version 2.2 data was assumed to be uniform across a table. With Version 2.2, statistics can now be generated for the 10 most frequent values in the first key column of nonunique indexes and multicolumn unique indexes. These statistics hold the occurrence percentage of the frequent values. The Optimizer looks at these statistics to improve the access path selection, giving benefits to queries for columns compared to constant, simple predicates (=. between, – . > . < . <), data skewed to a few values.

12.30.3 Unclustered Indexes

A clustered index has the physical order of records near the order of the index. A nonclustered index can have a physical order of records different from that of the index. Version 2.2 has improved support for access via unclustered indexes that enables data to be retrieved in physical record ID sequence (rather than in random sequence), which leads to fewer data pages read and more efficient access.

12.30.4 Programming Enhancements

DB2 Version 2.2 offers improved performance in the following areas:

- Noncorrelated subqueries used in a quantified predicate involving either Any or All in a range.
- Comparison against certain subqueries is arguable.
- Correlated subqueries.

12.30.5 Transaction Management

DB2 offers improvements by reduction of the initialization and termination process of each transaction, including faster plan authorization checking and improved commit processing for read-only transactions.

12.30.6 Authorization Caching

Prior to Version 2.2, plan authorization required Catalog access every time (except if the plan is too PUBLIC for Version 2.1). With Version 2.2, on the first execution of the plan, the Catalog is checked and an authorization cache block is created. More users are added to the cache upon their initial execution of the plan. Subsequent execution by a user first checks cache for authorization. The cache will utilize as much as a 1K block of EDMPOOL per plan.

12.30.7 Read-Only Commit

Prior to Version 2.2 the full two-phase commit was always used. In Version 2.2 one-phase commit is used for read-only transactions, enabling significant reduction of path lengths for a major part of commit processing and for CICS transactions and the bypassing of some of the CICS logging.

12.30.8 Index Field Retrieval

Index-only access is more efficient when querying a table when:

- All fields to be retrieved are in the index
- All fields to be retrieved are of fixed length
- An index scan is used

12.31 CONCLUSIONS

Database systems such as IMS, IDMS, and ADABAS have evolved from traditional data processing requirements which have predefined access patterns based on perceived user requirements. The database suppliers have, where possible, given the database designers, database administrators, and application developers a wide range of options to design and program for performance efficiency. With DB2, however, the need for flexibility in the way users can access data has simplified data structures (by using tables) and provided a reduced set of options for the database designer to design for performance. In addition, the database navigation path is no longer selected by the DBA (or programmer) but by the DB2 Optimizer, which takes into account the database statistics to determine, dynamically, access path selection. To compensate for this reduction in performance control, DB2 is being continually enhanced to take full advantage of state-of-the-art technology and has become the de facto DBMS for the implementation of relational database technology. Only the DB2 user community will be able to judge whether, for its specific application requirements, DB2 is able to meet the performance expectations.

Introduction to SQL

The standard language for handling data stored in relational databases is called Structured Query Language (SQL). SQL commands can be entered directly from display terminals, used as database system (DBS) utility program input or embedded in application programs written in COBOL, PL/1, FORTRAN, C, or Assembler language. Any operation that can be done with SQL commands from a terminal can be done with SQL commands embedded in an application program. Some SQL commands can be used only in application programs.

Relational databases present all data as tables in a simple row and column format, as illustrated in Fig. 13.1. This table has three rows and four columns. The data value in row 1 and column 2 is 06/06/1988.

SQL commands can do many common data processing tasks, such as:

- Selecting and updating some items
- Sorting data
- Calculating values using stored data
- Copying data from one table into another
- Combining tables based on values in the tables themselves

CHECK	DATE	RECIPIENT	AMOUNT
101	06/06/1988	C. Clark	262.00
102	06/07/1989	M. Bass	40.50
103	06/08/1990	M. Cook	478.35

Figure 13.1 SQL table.

13.1   SQL DATA TYPES

SQL supports 12 types of data as listed in Fig. 13.2. All the field values of a column must be exactly the same.

Name	Description	Range
SMALLINT	Binary integer of 16 bits	−32768 to +32767
INTEGER	Binary integer of 32 bits	−2147483648 to +2147483647
FLOAT(n) OR REAL	Single precision floating-point number. n is in the range of 1 to 21.	5.4E − 79 to 7.2E + 75
FLOAT(n) DOUBLE PRECISION	Double precision floating-point number. n is in the range of 22 to 53.	5.4E − 79 to 7.2E + 75
DECIMAL(p,s)	Decimal number with precision p and scale s.	−999999999999999 to +999999999999999
DATE	Values consist of three parts for year, month, and day.	0001-01-01 to 9999-12-31
TIME	Values represent a time of day in hours, minutes, and seconds.	00.00.00 to 24.00.00
CHARACTER(n)	Fixed-length character strings represented using EBCDIC 1 n 254	
VARCHAR(n)	Variable-length character strings represented using EBCDIC.	
LONG VARCHAR	Variable-length character strings represented using EBCDIC.	
GRAPHIC(n)	Fixed-length graphic strings containing DBCS data. n is in the range of 1 to 127.	
VARGRAPHIC(n)	Variable-length graphic strings containing DBCS data.	
LONG VARGRAPHIC	Variable-length strings containing DBCS data.	

Figure 13.2   SQL data types.

13.1.1 Date and Time Data Type Formats

The following table describes the available date and time data type formats.

Data type	Description	Format
DATE	ISO	yyyy-mm-dd
	JIS	yyyy-mm-dd
	EUR	dd.mm.yyyy
	USA	mm/dd/yyyy
	LOCAL	user defined
TIME	ISO	hh.mm.ss
	JIS	hh:mm.ss
	EUR	hh.mm.ss
	USA	hh:mmxm
	LOCAL	user defined
TIMESTAMP		yy-mm-dd
		hh.mm.ss (nnnnn)

where ISO = International Standards Organization.
  JIS = Japanese Industrial Standard.
  EUR = European IBM Standard.
  USA = U.S. IBM Standard.
  yyy is the year.
  mm is the month.
  dd is the day.
  hh is the hour.
  mm is the minute.
  ss is the second.
  nnnnn is the microsecond.
  XM is a.m. or p.m.

13.2 CLASSIFICATION OF SQL COMMANDS

SQL commands consist of command verbs, one or more optional clauses, language keywords, and parameter operands. The structured use of verbs and keywords in SQL syntax permits exact specification of data requests in a readable fashion. The language allows single and double-byte characters to be used in identifiers and character string constants and variables.

SQL commands have many types. Some are for handling the data itself. Others are for controlling administrative matters, such as who can access what data. The most commonly used commands are shown in Fig. 13.3.

DATA MANIPULATION COMMANDS	
SELECT	Retrieves data from one or more tables.
INSERT	Places one or more rows into a table.
UPDATE	Changes field level data in one or more rows of a table.
DELETE	Removes one or more rows from a table.
DATA DEFINITION COMMANDS	
CREATE TABLE	Defines a new table and its columns and optionally specifies a primary key and referential constraints
DROP TABLE	Drops or deletes a table.
ALTER TABLE	Adds a new column to a table. It may also add or drop a primary key and add, drop, deactivate or activate referential constraints.
DROP INDEX	Drops or deletes an index.
CREATE INDEX	Defines an index that enables accessing the rows of a table in specific sequence. A table can have many indexes.
CREATE VIEW	Defines a logical table from one or more tables or views in terms of a SELECT command.
DROP VIEW	Drops or deletes a view definition.

Figure 13.3   Classification of SQL commands.

13.3 STRUCTURE OF THE SELECT COMMAND

The SELECT command is used to retrieve data from a table. The basic form of the SELECT command is:

SELECT some data
FROM some table
WHERE specific conditions are met.

13.3.1 Examples of the SELECT Command

If we consider the data in Fig. 13.4 from which to SELECT data, we can illustrate the following examples of that statement.

Example 1

SELECT * FROM SCHEDULE1

In this example, all the data shown in Fig. 13.3 will be selected and returned.

SCHEDULE1

CO	FLT	Origin	Dest	Depart	Arrive	Stops
A	100	New York	LA	12.30.00	16.40.00	0
A	101	New York	LA	09.00.00	16.00.00	2
B	978	New York	LA	18.30.00	22.30.00	1
C	50B	New York	LA	08.00.00	12.00.00	0

Figure 13.4   Table of flight and destination.

Example 2

```
SELECT * FROM SCHEDULE1
WHERE ORIGIN = 'NEW YORK' AND
DEST = 'L.A.'
```

In this example, the following data will be returned:

```
A    100    New York    LA    12.30.00    16.40.00    0
A    101    New York    LA    09.00.00    16.00.00    2
```

Example 3

```
SELECT CO, FLT, DEPART, ARRIVE
FROM SCHEDULE1
WHERE ORIGIN = 'NEW YORK'
AND DEST = 'SF'
AND DEPART BETWEEN '08.00.00' AND '10.00.00'
AND STOP = 0
```

In this example, the following data will be returned:

```
C    50B    08.00.00    12.00.00
```

The BETWEEN key word in this example is one key word used in SQL to denote a special type of qualifying phrase. Some other key words are IN, LIKE, IS NULL, and EXISTS. IN tests for values from a user-specified list of values. LIKE searches for character string data that fully or partially matches a user-specified character string. IS NULL looks for null values. EXISTS tests for the existence of a row.

Example 4

```
SELECT COUNT(*)
FROM SCHEDULE1
WHERE ORIGIN = 'NEW YORK'
AND DEST = 'LA'
```

In this example, 2 will be returned. The expression COUNT(*) means count all the rows that satisfy the selection rules given in the WHERE clauses of the SELECT command. COUNT is one of the SQL's column functions. Others are MAX, MIN, AVG, and SUM.

Example 5

```
SELECT ORIGIN, COUNT(*)
FROM SCHEDULE1
WHERE DEST = 'LA'
GROUP BY ORIGIN
ORDER BY ORIGIN
```

In this example, the following data will be returned:

ORIGIN	COUNT
New York	2

The WHERE clause determines the rows of the table that are to be counted. The GROUP BY clause causes the counting to be done for each group of rows that has a common ORIGIN value. The ORDER BY clause presents the results in alphabetic order by ORIGIN. The data for ORDER BY is either in ascending or descending order. Ascending order is the default. The key word DESC can be appended to one or more of the columns referred to in the ORDER BY clause.

13.4   STRUCTURE OF INSERT COMMAND

The SQL INSERT command lets the user put a row of values into a table.

13.4.1   Examples of INSERT Command

Example 1
```
INSERT INTO SCHEDULE1
VALUES ('A', '100', 'New York', 'Chicago',
        '12.30.00', '16.00.00', 0)
```

The above INSERT command would enter values into the table of Fig. 13.4 in the order in which they appear in the command. Values that go into columns that hold character, graphic, date, or time data are enclosed in single quote marks.

Example 2

```
INSERT INTO SCHEDULE1
SELECT * FROM SCHEDULE2
```

The above example will copy all the rows from SCHEDULE2 and add them to SCHEDULE1.

13.5 STRUCTURE OF THE UPDATE COMMAND

The SQL UPDATE command lets you specify the columns to be updated and the rows on which the updating should be done.

13.5.1 Examples of the UPDATE Command

Example 1

```
UPDATE SCHEDULE1 SET FLT = '602'
WHERE CO = 'A'
AND FLT = '101'
```

The above UPDATE command would cause the second row of Fig. 13.3 to be changed as follows:

CO	FLT	Origin	Dest	Depart	Arrive	Stops
A	602	New York	LA	12.30.00	16.40.00	0

Example 2

```
UPDATE SCHEDULE1 SET DEPART = '09.15.00'
WHERE CO = 'A'
AND FLT = '101'
AND ORIGIN = 'NEW YORK'
```

The above UPDATE command will affect more than one row in Fig. 13.4. The updating affects the table in such a way as to change it as follows:

CO	FLT	Origin	Dest	Depart	Arrive	Stops
A	101	New York	LA	09.15.00	16.00.00	2

13.6 STRUCTURE OF DELETE COMMAND

The SQL DELETE command lets the user drop a row of values from a table. The following is an example of the command:

```
DELETE FROM SCHEDULE1
WHERE FLT = '50B'
AND CO = 'B'
```

In this example, all rows of Fig. 13.4 that satisfy the WHERE clause criteria will be deleted.

13.7   STRUCTURE OF CREATE COMMAND

The CREATE command defines the format of a table, but it does not put any data into the table.

13.7.1   Examples of CREATE Command

Example 1

```
CREATE TABLE SCHEDULE1
        (CO CHAR(1) NOT NULL,
        FLT CHAR(3) NOT NULL,
        ORIGIN     VARCHAR(11),
        DEST       VARCHAR(11),
        DEPART TIME,
        ARRIVE TIME,
        STOPS SMALLINT)
```

The above example will create a table in the format shown in Fig. 13.4. However, no data will exist in the table. In order to put data into the table, one must use the INSERT command.

Example 2

```
CREATE INDEX SICOFLT
ON SCHEDULE1
(CO, FLT)
```

The above example will create an index SICOFLT and specify the columns to be used for the data access path.

13.8   STRUCTURE OF THE ALTER COMMAND

The ALTER command allows the users to add columns to a table. The following is an example of the command:

```
ALTER TABLE SCHEDULE1
ADD FOOD CHAR(1)
```

This example will add a new column to the table in Fig. 13.4. The new table looks as follows:

CO	FLT	ORIGIN	DEST	DEPART	ARRIVE	STOPS	FOOD
A	100	New York	LA	12.30.00	16.40.00	0	

It should be noted that there is no data entered into the FOOD column. One would use the UPDATE command to add data to the FOOD column.

13.9   REFERENTIAL INTEGRITY

Two tables are joined or related through columns which have equal values in the columns of both tables. That is, every value of one column in one table must be the same as the value in the other table. To ensure referential integrity, one follows the rules below:

- Do not add a row to one table unless one column in it matches one of the columns in the other table.
- If a row is deleted from one table, set the dependent rows in the other table to null values.
- If a value is changed in one row of one table, no row in the next table can contain the old value of the other table.

13.10   INTERACTIVE SQL FACILITY (ISQL)

User of SQL/DS can access and manipulate data directly from display terminals. This capability is provided through the Interactive SQL (ISQL) facility of SQL/DS.

ISQL runs as a CMS application in multiple-user mode. The ISQL facility is controlled by CMS in the VM system. ISQL works with a variety of display terminals, including the larger screen sizes offered by some models of IBM 3270 and 3279 devices. ISQL enables the users to:

- Enter SQL commands and observe the results on the display screen
- Obtain an estimate of the processing resources needed to run a query
- Control for display screen
- Write data from query results
- Enter data into tables in bulk
- Display online reference information (HELP)
- Create and run stored SQL commands
- Create and run stored routines
- Control logical units of work
- Cancel commands in progress
- Use the SHOW and COUNTER operator commands

13.11 EMBEDDED SQL COMMANDS

Languages such as COBOL, PL/1, FORTRAN, C, or Assembler allow SQL statements to be embedded in their languages. These embedded statements are executed as part of the language and produce the same results as stand-alone SQL.

The reader should refer to the numerous books on the subject to see how the host language is altered to accommodate the SQL statements.

14

Introduction to QMF

The Query Management Facility (QMF) is a licensed interactive product offered by IBM to supplement DB2 in the TSO environment. QMF is a must because it allows each user to manage SQL statements. To many users, QMF is inseparable from DB2. QMF provides the user-friendly interface to DB2 necessary to make DB2 usable by nonprofessionals and professionals alike.

The user can develop, test, and store SQL queries for future use. QMF displays the rows retrieved in reports and charts. The user can then modify the report to suit his or her own needs. Not only will QMF allow users to execute stored queries, it allows users to share queries with others.

Queries can be developed to serve multiple functions by allowing the development of SQL statements in such a manner that the user is prompted for variables to complete the query. One query could serve the needs of many users, thus reducing redundant development. Through QMF variables, different tables can be accessed by the same stored query. QMF allows a person to select a subset of rows from a large table, save the selected rows in a new table, and proceed to analyze the new table. QMF is also suitable for ad hoc user requests.

14.1 QMF SYSTEM TABLES

QMF contains several system tables. Availability of the system tables will vary according to the controls placed by the installation. The content and use of these tables are outlined below:

- *Q.COMMAND_SYNONYMS:* Allows the installation to make additional commands available to users. Commands such as SAVE and ERASE allow users to save and remove their stored queries.

- *Q.ERROR_LOG:* Used automatically by QMF to record information when a user encounters resource, system, or QMF program errors.
- *Q.OBJECT_DATA:* Contains information describing the item stored. A stored item could be a procedure, form, or query.
- *Q.OBJECT_DIRECTORY:* Describes what kind of object is being stored and whether others are allowed to access the stored object.
- *Q.OBJECT_REMARKS:* Gives the individual saving the query the ability to record comments about the stored object.
- *Q.PROFILES:* Contains information about how an individual's QMF session is structured.
- *Q.RESOURCE_TABLE:* Gives individuals responsible for QMF administration a method of treating QMF users differently.

14.2 ISSUING QMF COMMANDS

There are four ways to issue QMF commands:

- On the COMMAND line
- On a PROMPT panel
- By pressing a PF key
- From a Procedure

14.3 THE PROGRAM FUNCTION (PF) KEYS

The following PF keys are used in QMF processing:

PF1	HELP
PF2	RUN
PF3	END
PF4	
PF5	
PF6	QUERY
PF7	
PF8	
PF9	FORM
PF10	PROC
PF11	PROFILE
PF12	REPORT

```
FORM.COLUMNS         ENTMS099.QMF084_0

                                  REPORT WIDTH IS NOW: 69
  NUM   COLUMN HEADING                        USAGE    INDENT   WIDTH   EDIT
  ---   -----------------------------------   -------  ------   -----   -----
   1    DEPT._NUMBER                                      2        6      L
   2    JOB                                               4        5      C
   3    EMPLOYEE_NAME                                     4        9      C
   4    SALARY                                            2       10      L2
   5    COMMISSIONS                                       2       11      L2
   6    TOTAL_EARNINGS                                    2       12      L2
        *** END ***
 1=HELP      2=CHECK     3=END       4=FORM.MAIN    5=FORM.OPTIONS  6=QUERY
 7=BACKWARD 8=FORWARD 9=FORM.PAGE  10=FORM.FINAL  11=FORM.BREAK1 12=REPORT
 OK, FORM.COLUMNS IS DISPLAYED.
 COMMAND ===>
                                                    SCROLL ===> PAGE
```

Figure 14.7

complish this in Figures 14.5 and 14.6 by changing the 2 to 4. The results are shown in Figs. 14.7 and 14.8.

14.5.4   Editing the Column Headings

We can edit the column headings by using the following codes to change the EDIT column on the FORM panel:

```
REPORT
   DEPT.                                    LINE 1      POS 1     79
   NUMBER    JOB       EMPLOYEE                         TOTAL
                        NAME      SALARY  COMMISSIONS  EARNINGS
 ++------+++-----+++----------++----------++----------++----------++++++++

   DEPT.               EMPLOYEE
   NUMBER    JOB        NAME      SALARY  COMMISSIONS  TOTAL
                                                      EARNINGS
   ------   -----   ----------  ---------- ----------- -----------
      15    SALES   ROTHMAN      16502.83    1152.00    17654.83
      15    CLERK   KERMISCH     12258.50     110.10    12368.60
      15    CLERK   NGAN         12508.20     206.60    12714.80
      20    SALES   PERNAL       18171.25     612.45    18783.70
      20    CLERK   JAMES        13504.60     128.20    13632.80
      20    CLERK   SNEIDER      14252.75     126.50    14379.25
      38    SALES   O'BRIEN      18006.00     846.55    18852.55
      38    SALES   QUIGLEY      16808.30     650.25    17458.55
      38    CLERK   ABRAHAMS     12009.75     236.50    12246.25
      38    CLERK   NAUGHTON     12954.75     180.00    13134.75
 1=HELP       2=          3=END       4=PRINT    5=           6=QUERY
 7=BACKWARD   8=FORWARD   9=FORM     10=LEFT    11=RIGHT     12=
 OK, REPORT IS DISPLAYED.
 COMMAND ===>
                                                    SCROLL ===> PAGE
```

Figure 14.8

Code	Definition
C	Character
L	Numeric, no decimal
L1	Numeric, one decimal
D	Dollar amount, no cents
D2	Dollar amount, with cents
P	Percent, no decimal
P1	Percent, one decimal

Figures 14.9 and 14.10 illustrate the editing of columns.

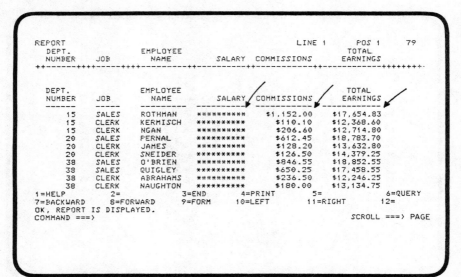

```
FORM.COLUMNS          ENTMS099.QMF085_0

                            REPORT WIDTH IS NOW: 69
 NUM  COLUMN HEADING                                USAGE    INDENT   WIDTH   EDIT
 ---  ------------------------------------------    -------  ------   -----   -----
   1  DEPT._NUMBER                                               2       6       L
   2  JOB                                             4         5       C
   3  EMPLOYEE_NAME                                   4         9       C
   4  SALARY                                                     2      10       D2
   5  COMMISSIONS                                                2      11       D2
   6  TOTAL_EARNINGS                                             2      12       D2
      *** END ***
1=HELP      2=CHECK      3=END          4=FORM.MAIN    5=FORM.OPTIONS  6=QUERY
7=BACKWARD 8=FORWARD  9=FORM.PAGE   10=FORM.FINAL   11=FORM.BREAK1  12=REPORT
OK, FORM.COLUMNS IS DISPLAYED.
COMMAND ===>                                            SCROLL ===> PAGE
```

Figure 14.9

```
 REPORT                                     LINE 1      POS 1     79
 DEPT.                     EMPLOYEE                      TOTAL
 NUMBER     JOB              NAME      SALARY  COMMISSIONS  EARNINGS
+-+------+++-----+++----------++----------+--------------+-----------+++++++-

 DEPT.                     EMPLOYEE                      TOTAL
 NUMBER     JOB              NAME      SALARY  COMMISSIONS  EARNINGS
 ------     ----          --------     ------  -----------  --------
     15     SALES         ROTHMAN      **********  $1,152.00   $17,654.83
     15     CLERK         KERMISCH     **********    $110.10   $12,368.60
     15     CLERK         NGAN         **********    $206.60   $12,714.80
     20     SALES         PERNAL       **********    $612.45   $18,783.70
     20     CLERK         JAMES        **********    $128.20   $13,632.80
     20     CLERK         SNEIDER      **********    $126.50   $14,379.25
     38     SALES         O'BRIEN      **********    $846.55   $18,852.55
     38     SALES         QUIGLEY      **********    $650.25   $17,458.55
     38     CLERK         ABRAHAMS     **********    $236.50   $12,246.25
     38     CLERK         NAUGHTON     **********    $180.00   $13,134.75
1=HELP        2=            3=END      4=PRINT      5=              6=QUERY
7=BACKWARD    8=FORWARD    9=FORM    10=LEFT      11=RIGHT       12=
OK, REPORT IS DISPLAYED.
COMMAND ===>                                          SCROLL ===> PAGE
```

Figure 14.10

14.5.5   The USAGE Code

The USAGE code shows how a column is used. The following table shows the codes and their meanings.

Usage Code	Meaning
BLANK	Display or print the column
OMIT	Do not display the column
SUM	Display the column and add it to the total at the bottom of the column
CSUM	Show the cumulative total for each line of the report
AVERAGE	Average the values in a column
MAXIMUM	Choose the maximum value in a column
MINIMUM	Choose the minimum value in a column
COUNT	Count the nonnull values in a column
PCT	Show the percentage that each line represents of the total for the column in the report

The results of the USAGE code in a column are shown in Figs. 14.11 and 14.12.

14.5.6   Formatting with the USAGE Code

The USAGE code determines where subtotals are taken in the report. In this instance, the control column is used to control the display of results from another column. Control columns which are used as breaks must appear in the ORDER BY clause in the sequence in which the breaks are taken. The sequence of the breaks are:

```
FORM.COLUMNS        ENTMS099.QMF086_0

                                  REPORT WIDTH IS NOW: 70
  NUM  COLUMN HEADING                              USAGE   INDENT  WIDTH  EDIT
  ---  ------------------------------------------  ------- ------  -----  -----
   1   DEPT._NUMBER
   2   JOB                                                   2       6      L
   3   EMPLOYEE_NAME                                         4       5      C
   4   SALARY                                                4       9      C
   5   COMMISSIONS                             SUM           2      11      D2
   6   TOTAL_EARNINGS                          SUM           2      11      D2
       *** END ***                             SUM           2      12      D2
  1=HELP       2=CHECK      3=END          4=FORM.MAIN     5=FORM.OPTIONS  6=QUERY
  7=BACKWARD 8=FORWARD   9=FORM.PAGE    10=FORM.FINAL   11=FORM.BREAK1  12=REPORT
  OK, FORM.COLUMNS IS DISPLAYED.
  COMMAND ===>
                                                 SCROLL ===> PAGE
```

Figure 14.11

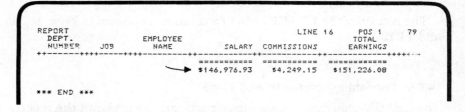

```
REPORT                                        LINE 1      POS 1    79
    DEPT.                                                 TOTAL
    NUMBER     JOB        EMPLOYEE                         EARNINGS
                          NAME         SALARY  COMMISSIONS
+-------+++-----+++-----++----------++-----------++-----------++---------------+++++++-

    DEPT.                 EMPLOYEE                         TOTAL
    NUMBER     JOB        NAME         SALARY  COMMISSIONS EARNINGS
    ------     -----      ----------   -----------  -----------   -------------
        15     SALES      ROTHMAN      $16.502.83   $1,152.00    $17,654.83
        15     CLERK      KERMISCH     $12,258.50   $110.10      $12,368.60
        15     CLERK      NGAN         $12,508.20   $206.60      $12,714.80
        20     SALES      FERNAL       $18,171.25   $612.45      $18,783.70
        20     CLERK      JAMES        $13,504.60   $128.20      $13,632.80
        20     CLERK      SNEIDER      $14,252.75   $126.50      $14,379.25
        38     SALES      O'BRIEN      $18,006.00   $846.55      $18,852.55
        38     SALES      QUIGLEY      $16,808.30   $650.25      $17,458.55
        38     CLERK      ABRAHAMS     $12,009.75   $236.50      $12,246.25
        38     CLERK      NAUGHTON     $12,954.75   $180.00      $13,134.75
1=HELP         2=            3=END        4=PRINT       5=          6=QUERY
7=BACKWARD     8=FORWARD     9=FORM      10=LEFT      11=RIGHT     12=
OK, REPORT IS DISPLAYED.
COMMAND ===>                                          SCROLL ===> PAGE
```

```
REPORT                                        LINE 16     POS 1    79
    DEPT.                 EMPLOYEE                         TOTAL
    NUMBER     JOB        NAME         SALARY  COMMISSIONS EARNINGS
++------+++-----+++-----++----------++-----------++-----------++--------------++++--
                                      ===========  ===========  =============
                                      $146,976.93  $4,249.15    $151,226.08

*** END ***
```

Figure 14.12

- BREAK1 is the major sort key.
- BREAK2 is the minor sort key.
- BREAK6 is the lowest level sort key.

Figures 14.13 and 14.14 illustrate formatting by the USAGE code.

14.5.7 Adding a Subheading to a report

Subheadings are added to a report by using HEADING, FOOTING, and TEXT entries of the FORM.MAIN panel. For example, if we wanted to add (1) Division Earnings Report, (2) Company Confidential, and (3) Totals to the report in Fig. 14.15, we would make the entries to the FORM.MAIN panel as shown in the figure. The results of those entries are shown in Fig. 14.16(a) and (b).

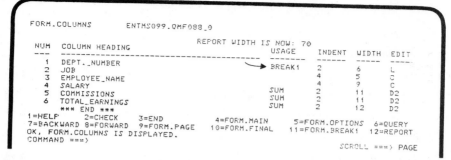

```
FORM.COLUMNS          ENTMS099.QMF088_0

                                     REPORT WIDTH IS NOW: 70
 NUM  COLUMN HEADING                           USAGE    INDENT  WIDTH  EDIT
 ---  -----------------------------------      -------  ------  -----  ----
   1  DEPT._NUMBER              ----------> BREAK1     2       6      L
   2  JOB                                              4       5      C
   3  EMPLOYEE_NAME                                    4       9      C
   4  SALARY                                           2
   5  COMMISSIONS                          SUM         2      11      D2
   6  TOTAL_EARNINGS                       SUM         2      11      D2
      *** END ***                          SUM         2      12      D2
1=HELP      2=CHECK      3=END          4=FORM.MAIN      5=FORM.OPTIONS  6=QUERY
7=BACKWARD 8=FORWARD  9=FORM.PAGE     10=FORM.FINAL    11=FORM.BREAK1  12=REPORT
OK, FORM.COLUMNS IS DISPLAYED.
COMMAND ===>                                                    SCROLL ===> PAGE
```

Figure 14.13

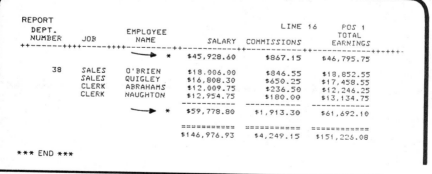

```
REPORT
   DEPT.                               LINE 1      POS 1
   NUMBER    JOB     EMPLOYEE                       TOTAL
                     NAME        SALARY COMMISSIONS  EARNINGS
 ++------+++-----+++---------++------------++-----------++-------------+++++-

   DEPT.
   NUMBER    JOB     EMPLOYEE                       TOTAL
                     NAME        SALARY COMMISSIONS  EARNINGS
   ------   -----   ---------   ----------- -----------  -------------
     15     SALES   ROTHMAN     $16,502.83   $1,152.00    $17,654.83
            CLERK   KERMISCH    $12,258.50     $110.10    $12,368.60
            CLERK   NGAN        $12,508.20     $206.60    $12,714.80
                       ---->  * ----------- -----------  -------------
                               $41,269.53   $1,468.70    $42,738.23

     20     SALES   PERNAL      $18,171.25     $612.45    $18,783.70
            CLERK   JAMES       $13,504.60     $128.20    $13,632.80
            CLERK   SNEIDER     $14,252.75     $126.50    $14,379.25
1=HELP      2=           3=END        4=PRINT       5=         6=QUERY
7=BACKWARD  8=FORWARD    9=FORM      10=LEFT      11=RIGHT     12=
OK, REPORT IS DISPLAYED.
COMMAND ===>                                               SCROLL ===> PAGE
```

```
REPORT
   DEPT.                               LINE 16     POS 1
   NUMBER    JOB     EMPLOYEE                       TOTAL
                     NAME        SALARY COMMISSIONS  EARNINGS
 ++------+++-----+++---------++------------++-----------++-------------+++++-
                       ---->  * $45,928.60     $867.15    $46,795.75

     38     SALES   O'BRIEN     $18,006.00     $846.55    $18,852.55
            SALES   QUIGLEY     $16,808.30     $650.25    $17,458.55
            CLERK   ABRAHAMS    $12,009.75     $236.50    $12,246.25
            CLERK   NAUGHTON    $12,954.75     $180.00    $13,134.75
                       ---->  * ----------- -----------  -------------
                               $59,778.80   $1,913.30    $61,692.10

                               =========== ===========  ============
                               $146,976.93  $4,249.15   $151,226.08

*** END ***
```

Figure 14.14

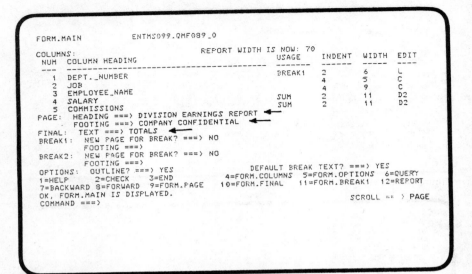

```
FORM.MAIN              ENTMS099.QMF089_0

COLUMNS:                         REPORT WIDTH IS NOW: 70
  NUM  COLUMN HEADING                                  USAGE    INDENT  WIDTH  EDIT
  ---  ----------------------------------------        ------   ------  -----  ----
   1   DEPT._NUMBER                                     BREAK1    2       6      L
   2   JOB                                                        4       5      C
   3   EMPLOYEE_NAME                                              4       9      C
   4   SALARY                                           SUM       2      11      D2
   5   COMMISSIONS                                      SUM       2      11      D2
PAGE:   HEADING ===> DIVISION EARNINGS REPORT
        FOOTING ===> COMPANY CONFIDENTIAL
FINAL:  TEXT ===> TOTALS
BREAK1:  NEW PAGE FOR BREAK? ===> NO
         FOOTING ===>
BREAK2:  NEW PAGE FOR BREAK? ===> NO
         FOOTING ===>
OPTIONS:  OUTLINE? ===> YES                    DEFAULT BREAK TEXT? ===> YES
1=HELP     2=CHECK     3=END        4=FORM.COLUMNS  5=FORM.OPTIONS  6=QUERY
7=BACKWARD 8=FORWARD  9=FORM.PAGE   10=FORM.FINAL   11=FORM.BREAK1  12=REPORT
OK, FORM.MAIN IS DISPLAYED.
COMMAND ===>                                          SCROLL == > PAGE
```

Figure 14.15

```
                                              LINE 1      POS 1     79
REPORT
  DEPT.                   EMPLOYEE                        TOTAL
  NUMBER    JOB           NAME         SALARY  COMMISSIONS  EARNINGS
++------+++-----+++-----------+------------+-----------+------------++++++
                     DIVISION EARNINGS REPORT

             DEPT.                   EMPLOYEE                 TOTAL
             NUMBER    JOB           NAME      SALARY  COMMISSIONS  EARNINGS
             ------    -----         ---------  ------  -----------  --------
               15      SALES         ROTHMAN   $16.502.83   $1,152.00  $17,654.83
                       CLERK         KERMISCH  $12,258.50     $110.10  $12,368.60
                       CLERK         NGAN      $12.508.20     $206.60  $12,714.80
                                               -----------  ---------  ----------
                                          *    $41,269.53   $1,468.70  $42,738.23

               20      SALES         PERNAL    $18,171.25     $612.45  $18,783.70
                       CLERK         JAMES     $13,504.60     $128.20  $13,632.80
                       CLERK         SNEIDER   $14,252.75     $126.50  $14,379.25
1=HELP      2=              3=END      4=PRINT       5=            6=QUERY
7=BACKWARD  8=FORWARD      9=FORM     10=LEFT       11=RIGHT      12=
OK, REPORT IS DISPLAYED.
COMMAND ===>                                        SCROLL ===> PAGE
```

(a)

Figure 14.16a

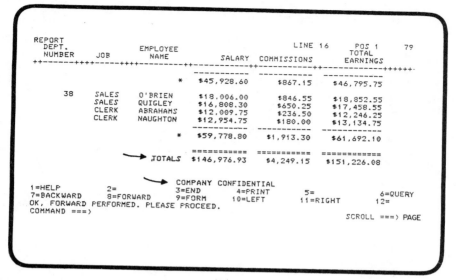

```
REPORT
    DEPT.                EMPLOYEE                        LINE 16      POS 1      79
    NUMBER    JOB          NAME          SALARY  COMMISSIONS       TOTAL
                                                                   EARNINGS
++------+++++------+++----------++------------++------------++------------+++++++-
                                    -----------    -----------    ------------
                             *       $45,928.60        $867.15      $46,795.75

        38    SALES   O'BRIEN        $18,006.00        $846.55      $18,852.55
              SALES   QUIGLEY        $16,808.30        $650.25      $17,458.55
              CLERK   ABRAHAMS       $12,009.75        $236.50      $12,246.25
              CLERK   NAUGHTON       $12,954.75        $180.00      $13,134.75
                                    -----------    -----------    ------------
                             *       $59,778.80      $1,913.30      $61,692.10
                                    ===========    ===========    ============
                    →   TOTALS     $146,976.93      $4,249.15     $151,226.08

                                COMPANY CONFIDENTIAL
1=HELP          2=          →   3=END        4=PRINT      5=              6=QUERY
7=BACKWARD      8=FORWARD       9=FORM      10=LEFT       11=RIGHT        12=
OK, FORWARD PERFORMED. PLEASE PROCEED.
COMMAND ===>                                              SCROLL ===> PAGE
```

(b)

Figure 14.16b

Introduction to ORACLE

At the heart of ORACLE is a set of fourth-generation environment (4GE) tools. These include:

- ORACLE RDBMS
- SQL*PLUS
- SQL*FORMS
- CASE*METHOD
- CASE*DESIGNER
- SQL*MENU
- SQL*REPORT WRITER
- SQL
- PRECOMPILERS

At the heart of ORACLE's 4GE toolset is SQL*FORMS, with the high-level screen painter and forms application generator. Via a menu-driven interface, the designer uses SQL*FORMS to automatically generate the basic functionality, or "primitives," for any application— the end-user interface, appropriate field attributes, validation rules to ensure accurate data entry, cursor navigation to control application flow, and the screen manager to direct the flow of data traffic between the screen and the database.

SQL*FORMS is extensible. For more robust application, the default logic supplied by SQL*FORMS can be augmented. SQL*FORMS lets the designer embed SQL statements at various event points in the application to do unique validation checking, perform complex field computations, or retrieve related information from the database. SQL*FORMS provides a macro language for reprogramming function keys, customizing the keyboard layout, calling other forms, performing if-then-else logic on field variables, and passing variable strings between forms with the application.

The other major 4GE tools are as follows:

- *SQL*Report Writer:* A nonprocedural report written for controlling a range of report output formats.

- *SQL*MENU:* A nonprocedural menuing system with a choice of menu styles for application integration.

- *CASE*Method:* A proven, structured design methodology that provides application designers with practical techniques for analyzing users' requirements and then developing systems that fully satisfy those requirements.

- *CASE*Designer:* A multiuser design dictionary to capture application information for system documentation. Information stored in the dictionary can also be used as source input for automatically generating the table design and the application code.

15.1   QUERYING THE DATABASE

SQL is the main query language used by ORACLE to query the database. SQL processes entire groups or sets of records at a time. It is in contrast to procedural languages which perform repetitive processing on single records.

Although powerful, SQL does not offer as much flexibility or programming control as procedural languages do. SQL is not a full programming language; it is a database access and manipulation language.

15.1.1   The SELECT Command

As in all other relational database management systems, ORACLE supports the high usage of the SELECT command. SQL*PLUS is the 4GE tool used by ORACLE to display the results of a SELECT command.

SQL*PLUS displays column names as defined when the table you want to query is created, and truncates them according to column width. When issuing a query, you can change the name of the column on the fly by adding a new name, often called an alias name, after the column name.

While you can change the name of a column in a query, the new name lives only for the life of the query. An alternative approach is to use the COLUMN format command, a SQL*PLUS command that is far more flexible and enduring. The COLUMN format command lets you alter the format of the column and heading, including the column name, its width, its justification position, and whether to wrap or truncate text. This new format endures for the duration of your SQL*PLUS session. A changed column displays the new format any time the column is referred to by any query until it is redefined or until you exit SQL*PLUS.

The COLUMN format command is issued at the SQL> prompt and would look similar to the following example:

SQL > COLUMN TITLE FORMAT A25 HEADING 'Film Title'

The format parameter controls the column width. Different format models are available for character, number, and data fields. As in the above example, the width of a character field is defined with an A, followed by the new width of the column; the width of a number field is defined by the digit n repeated once for each digit of the new width.

The HEADING parameter controls the displayed column name. If the new heading contains blanks or punctuation, it must be enclosed in single quotes.

You can reset a column to its default format, the format originally defined when the table was created, by using the DEFAULT parameter as follows:

SQL > COLUMN title DEFAULT

To view the column format for a given column, simply enter the COLUMN command followed by the column name as follows:

SQL > COLUMN title

15.1.2   Editing SQL Commands

SQL*PLUS temporarily stores the SQL commands you enter in a buffer. The commands remain in the buffer until you enter a new SQL command or explicitly clear the buffer. With the aid of several SQL edit commands, you can examine, modify, or rerun the current SQL command without reentering it.

The SQL edit commands are line-oriented, allowing you to manipulate—change, append, delete, and add—only a single SQL command line at a time. They are handy when constructing a query that is constantly being modified and reexecuted. However, when working with longer queries or highly formatted reports composed of multiple queries, you must use a text editor. The SQL edit commands are listed in Table 15.1.

TABLE 15.1 SQL Edit Commands

Command	Abbreviation	Purpose
APPEND	A text	Add text at the end of a line
CHANGE	C/old/new	Change old text to new
CHANGE	c/text/	Delete text from a line
CLEAR BUFFER	CL BUFF	Delete everything in a buffer
INPUT	I	Add an indefinite number of lines
INPUT	I text	Add a line of text
LIST	L	List all lines in the SQL buffer
LIST n	Ln	List one line
LIST mn	Lmn	List a range of lines (m to n)
RUN	R	Run the current SQL command

15.1.3 Building an SQL Command File

When working with longer queries or designing highly formatted reports, you may want to work with a text editor and build SQL command files. However, while constructing a query online, you can save it to a text file. You can save the contents of the current SQL buffer to disk with the SAVE command, which can be recalled or run directly from the command file. ORACLE appends the suffix .SQL to the saved file unless you specify a different suffix.

The operative commands for working with script files within SQL*PLUS are shown in Table 15.2.

TABLE 15.2 Command File Commands

Command	Purpose
SAVE File	Saves current SQL buffer to the named file
GET File	Retrieves named file to the current SQL buffer
START File	Retrieves the named file and runs it automatically
HOST dir*.sql	Lists the SQL script files stored in the operating system directory

15.2 ADVANCED SQL CAPABILITIES

Character values, such as products, titles, customers, addresses, and other text, are normally displayed in the same form as they were entered into the database. If you entered a title code in uppercase, for example, it will be displayed in uppercase, unless you use one of the many SQL*PLUS character expressions of functions that can transform the way character values appear when displayed.

SQL*PLUS lets you combine character columns and constraints into character expressions. A character expression can be manipulated and selected as though it were a single column.

15.2.1 Field Concentration

One prevalent use of character expressions is to string two or more columns together and display them as a single column. This is called field concatenation. To concatenate fields, you use the concatenate operator (::) in a query as follows:

```
SELECT category :: description
FROM category
```

This would result in the following:

CATEGORY :: DESCRIPTION

100 ADVENTURE
120 COMEDY
135 CLASSICS
140 MUSICALS
165 HORROR
899 SLASHER

When concatenating fields, SQL*PLUS removes any trailing blanks in the first column you specify. To fix the appearance of the display, you might separate the values with literal blanks enclosed in single quotes and perhaps add an alias as follows:

```
SELECT category :: ' ' description "film category"
FROM category
```

The result will be:

FILM CATEGORY

CATEGORY :: DESCRIPTION

100 ADVENTURE
120 COMEDY
135 CLASSICS
140 MUSICALS
165 HORROR
899 SLASHER

15.2.2 Date Functions

SQL*PLUS offers many functions to empower date arithmetic expressions. You can use numbers to add or subtract calendar days to and from dates. With the ADD_MONTHS function, you can manipulate calendar months in arithmetic expressions as well. For example, you can pinpoint the exact date 6 months from April 1, 1991, by entering:

```
SELECT ADD_MONTH ('01-APR-91', +6)
FROM table
```

This returns:

```
ADD_MONTH
01-OCT-91
```

Instead of using a constant, you can plug in the pseudo-column "sysdate." To find the exact date 15 months from today, if today's date is 15-APR-91, enter:

```
SELECT ADD_MONTHS (sysdate, +15)
FROM table
```

This returns:

```
ADD_MONTH
15-JUL-92
```

15.3   THE SQL*FORMS DESIGN PROGRAM

SQL*FORMS contains two parts—the SQL*FORMS (Design) used to design and create forms and SQL*FORMS (Runform) to execute forms built with the Design program. The ability to run a form from the Design program cuts down debugging time because you do not need to log out of the program to generate and execute the form and then log back when you are finished. SQL*FORMS lets you design a form on the screen and modify it interactively until you are satisfied with it.

There are essentially three levels of form design:

- *Creating the blocks and fields:*   The simplest form is merely a window on the base tables that does not have any special validation or functionality.

- *Defining the blocks and fields:*   Once the form is laid out, you can enhance it by adding validation and functionality.

- *Defining triggers:*   At this advanced level, you take the foundation of the form and mold it into a robust application. You provide complex validation by writing "triggers." These are SQL statements.

15.4   GENERATING REPORTS

SQL*PLUS's reporting extensions let you easily control the output format of ad hoc reports, including header and foot titles, line positioning, page size, and page numbering controls. SQL*PLUS provides much finer control of page formatting, margins, spacing, and column layout of the printed output than is offered by SQL. With SQL*PLUS, you can design complex tabular reports, organizing groups of rows in the report on column, row, page, or report breaks and computing subtotals on any combination of breaks.

15.4.1 Specifying Report Breaks

You can organize rows of a report into groups with the BREAK command, and you can dictate special actions a query should take when the report "breaks" on these rows. For example, you can skip a line when the break occurs, start a new page, or compute subtotals on the rows organized by the break.

SQL*PLUS lets you organize rows at the following BREAK points:

On a single column	BREAK on column
On more than one column	BREAK on column
	ON column
Whenever a row is retrieved	BREAK on Page
At the end of the report	BREAK on Report

15.4.2 SQL*PLUS Reportwriter

SQL*Reportwriter is a comprehensive reporting tool which meets virtually all of your production reporting needs. With SQL*Reportwriter, you can develop a full range of business reports and can create the following:

- Versatile tabular and control break reports

- Multisection reports

- Matrix reports, such as cross-tabs with cross-tabulation of data laid out in a spreadsheet format

- Wide reports with repeated columns, spread reports that are wider than a page onto multiple pages

15.5 SQL*MENU

SQL*MENU is based on SQL*FORMS technology and allows you to build a menu that lets you point to and select the menu choices—using the up or down arrow keys to highlight choices—or simply enter the number of the menu choice. The menuing environment can be customized for different groups of users, and several menu commands and macros are available to control menu navigation. SQL*MENU can be linked with SQL*PLUS and SQL*FORMS tools for fast execution of forms and reports.

15.6   ORACLE-SUPPORTED HARDWARE PLATFORMS

The following is a list of ORACLE-supported hardware platforms:

Company	Operating system
AT&T	Unix System V
Altos	Unix System V
Amdahl	MVS/SP, MVS/XA
Apollo	Aegis-Domain/1X
Comparex	MVS/SP, MVS/XA
Control Data	NOS/VE
Convercent Technologies	CTIX
Dansk Data	Unix System V
DDE	Unix
DEC	VMS, Ultrix
Edge	Unix
Encore	Unix
Gould	Unix
Harris	VOS, Unix System V
Hewlett-Packard	HP-VX
Honeywell-Bull	GCOS, Unix System V
IBM	MVS/SP, MVS/XA, VM/CMS
ICL	Unix System V, VME
Motorola	Unix
NAS	MVS/SP, MVS/XA, VM/CMS
NCR	Unix System V
Nixdorf	OSx
Norsk	Sintran
PCS	Unix System V
Plexus	Unix System V
Prime	Prime, Unix
Pyramid	OSx
Sequent	Dynix
Siemens	BS2000, Sinix
Stratus	VOS
Sun	SunOS 3X
Unisys	Unix System V
Wang	VS

16

Performance Issues and Standards

There are very few subjects in the database environment that are more controversial and more ambiguous than performance and standards. The issue of performance of a particular database management system (DBMS) is so important that failure to address it very often results in the lack of commercial acceptance of that DBMS.

Information technology will succeed as a business endeavor only when that technology is standardized and the tools that drive the technology can be evaluated against a common set of guidelines. This chapter looks at some of the most important issues in database performance and standardization and discusses how these two important aspects can be monitored.

16.1 THE DATABASE MANAGEMENT SYSTEM FUNCTIONS

It is generally accepted that all DBMSs should provide most or all of the nine functions, items, and services listed below:

- Storage, retrieval, and updating of data
- Integrity services to enforce database constraints
- A user-accessible catalog of definitions
- Control of concurrent processing
- Support of logical transactions
- Failure recovery
- Complete security provisions

- An interface to communications control programs
- Utility services

The performance of a DBMS, whether relational or nonrelational, must be measured against these nine items.

16.1.1 Controlling Integrity with a DBMS

Application programs that maintain database contents by adding, deleting, and updating data typically have a very high percentage of their logic devoted to ensuring that these operations are valid and the content of the database is not corrupted. This may include code for validating that:

- Certain associated master data is present in the database before a new detail is added. For example, the program may check to ensure that a valid customer exists in the database before recording an order against that customer.
- An input value is placed in more than one location in the database. For example, the program may check to ensure that when the quantity on hand for a particular item is updated, that update is carried to all redundant occurrences of that value.
- Data is not still referencing or depending on data to be deleted from the database. For example, the program may check to ensure that a customer with outstanding orders is not inadvertently deleted from the database.

These integrity constraints should be controlled by the DBMS, not by the application program.

16.1.2 Relational Data Integrity Rules

The primary key provides guaranteed access to a single, unique tuple within a relation. In fact, if the name of the relation, the value of the primary key, and the name of the attribute are known, every attribute value in a relational database is directly addressable. This helps to identify one of the most important properties in electing a primary key from among several candidate keys: the primary key should be one that will definitely remain unique over time. Its important identification role is supported by the first of two relational data integrity rules: no part of the primary key value may be null.

Associations between tuples that occur in the organization, whose data is being modeled by the database, must also be represented. In the relational data model, these associations are represented by storing the referenced tuple's primary key in the referencing tuple. These foreign occurrences of primary key values are called foreign keys. The referencing role played by the foreign occurrences of primary keys is supported by the second of the two relational data integrity rules: the value of a foreign key must reference a valid existing tuple where that value is the primary key.

Relations in a relational database must be normalized. There are multiple levels of normalization, from first normal form, through second, third, Boyce-Codd, fourth, and fifth normal forms. When to stop in the normalization process is a matter of judgment for the designer, but a relational database must be in at least first normal form.

Domains are also central to the enforcement of the integrity of foreign key values. Regardless of the role name of the foreign key attributes, the foreign key's existence can be identified through the knowledge that the domain is the same as an existing primary key. The knowledge of which domains are represented by the attributes of the primary key makes this possible.

Entity integrity ensures that a value is provided for the attributes whenever a new tuple is added to this relation. Domain definition ensures that that value represents a real product for the organization.

Referential integrity ensures that any value provided for an attribute is not only valid for the domain definition but appears as the primary key value to some tuple in the main relation. The ability to define domains directly and associate every attribute with a domain is a cornerstone component of the relational data model.

16.1.3 Relational DBMS's Performance Issues

A relational database system is termed fully relational if it supports:

- Relational databases including the concepts of domain and key and the two integrity rules

- A language that is at least as powerful as the relational algebra and that would remain so even if all facilities for loops and recursions were to be deleted

The combination of the three concepts of fully relational (i.e., relational structure, manipulation, and integrity), a three-schema architecture, and full DBMS capability results in a basic definition of what a relational DBMS should be: a system that functions as a full capability DBMS, based on a three-schema architecture, and that supports relational databases and a powerful relational language.

Because applications are not tied to any one data structuring technique, an organization can use any number of data structures (e.g., indexing, hashing, chaining, clustering, sequential, flat, or coded). The flexibility to choose the most effective data structuring technique for each application translates into improved performance. However, some relational systems require the use of only one data structuring technique, which can yield ineffective performance.

In the absence of a three-schema relational DBMS, many organizations have had to follow a two-database strategy. To improve performance, a nonrelational DBMS typically controls the production environment, and a relational DBMS supports end-user and information center needs.

Another way to improve performance in any DBMS is to provide tools for reducing the number of I/Os needed to access data. As the database is tuned, I/Os should always be minimized. In the relational system, the key is how well the optimizer translates relational operations on the conceptual schema into efficient physical file access.

Designing and tuning the database in the internal schema without changing the definition of views used by applications increases performance. The three-schema architecture used with relational technology and an efficient optimizer provides the performance required in heavy transaction-oriented data processing environments.

16.2   IMPROVING SQL/DS PERFORMANCE

As with any data access method, the proper tuning of the DBMS is essential for the efficient operation of the system. The place to start tuning SQL/DS is on the system level. First, be sure that the Directory dataset is located on a direct access storage device (DASD) device that contains no other SQL/DS datasets. The Directory is constantly being accessed by SQL/DS, so isolating it will speed access times by decreasing DASD contention. Isolation also helps to protect the Directory from DASD failures.

The next step is to look at your log datasets. As with the Directory, the log dataset should be placed on a DASD device that contains no other SQL/DS datasets. The datasets on the DASD device with the log should also be ones that are not heavily accessed.

If you are using dual logging, you are probably doing twice as much I/O for logging than is needed. If you have isolated your log dataset from the rest of the database, you are fairly safe using a single log dataset. If you lose the data, you have the log to recover from. If you lose the log, you have the data and can initialize a new log dataset in order to restart the system.

If you are using a log archiving (LOG MODE = L), automatic log archives will be initiated when the percentage of log space used equals the value of the initialization parameter ARCHPCT. To keep automatic logs from starting, set ARCHPCT at about 90. Also, be sure to regularly take log archives during a time period when the database is not heavily accessed.

16.2.1 Buffer Pool Tuning

SQL/DS operates with two buffer pools in order to increase I/O efficiency. The buffer pools are the Directory block pool and the data page pool, the number of which are specified at initialization time by the parameters NDIRBUF and NPAGBUF, respectively. The 512-byte Directory block buffers contain the most recently used Directory blocks and the 4096-byte buffers of the data page buffers contain the most recently accessed data pages. The tuning of these pools can be one of the most important performance factors and one of the easiest to change.

To determine how effective these values are at reducing DASD I/O in your current system, use the COUNTER* operator command. Calculate the hit ratio for each pool by dividing LPAGBUF by PAGEREAD and LDIRBUF by DIRREAD. This ratio shows you how often the I/O request was able to be satisfied by data already in the buffers. For example, a page pool ratio of 5 means for every five requests for database page data, only one needed to go to the DASD device for the data.

Deciding how large to make the buffer pools can be difficult and is affected by the amount of virtual and real memory available. The default value for both pools is 14 buffers in each. Since Directory blocks are only an eighth the size of page pools, begin by increasing the Directory block buffers by 2 to 3 times. Repeat the process for page pool and observe the LDIRBUR/DIRREAD ratio. If it has increased, you have improved the Directory block buffer performance.

16.2.2 Concurrent Users Tuning

The number of concurrent users (NCUSERS) the system can handle is another important performance consideration. Each user link requires a minimum of 16K of real storage and a minimum of 54K for each ISQL user. The value of NCUSERS might be high enough to allow for the average number of concurrent online users you will have, plus at least one batch user. To determine if your NCUSERS value is appropriate, use the SHOW ACTIVE operator command. If at peak usage times the number of active users tends to be significantly less than the value of NCUSERS, lower the value of NCUSERS. On the other hand, if the number of users tends to be constantly close to the NCUSERS value, you may need to increase the value of NCUSERS if real storage is available.

Again using the COUNTER* command, look at the checkpoint interval, CHKINTVL. For a system with a small database or a large database that is infrequently modified, CHKINTVL should be between 200 and 300. For a large volatile database, the value should be between 50 and 100. The number represents how many log dataset pages may be filled before a checkpoint is taken.

There are two advantages to increasing the checkpoint interval. First, the overhead involved in the checkpointing process may be considerably reduced. Secondly, the frequency of checkpoint delays is reduced by reducing the number of times checkpoints must be taken.

There are also disadvantages to increasing the checkpoint interval. First, the length of time needed to restart SQL/DS after a system failure will increase. Secondly, although the number of times the checkpoint needs to be taken decreases, the length of time the checkpoint will take to complete will increase.

16.3 DATABASE LEVEL CONSIDERATIONS

Indexing tables, data clustering, placement of tables in DDBSPACES, nonrecoverable storage pools, and maintaining table statistics can be done on the database level to improve performance.

Every table should have at least one index, preferably one that is clustered and reflects the method by which the data will most frequently be accessed. If the table does not have one, do a DBSPACE scan to locate the requested data.

There are several techniques which can be used to increase the efficiency of an index. If possible, make the index unique so that each index entry points to only one data row. Also, the index should be clustered. Clustering is simply loading the data so that rows with similar values are located near each other.

A large table should be placed in its own DBSPACE. This avoids DBSPACE scans from searching data from other tables.

Tables which are read-only or are "work tables" should be placed in nonrecoverable storage pools. This eliminates the overhead of logging and checkpoint processing for these tables.

16.4 PERFORMANCE TUNING FOR APPLICATIONS

If no other users are accessing the table during a program's execution, consider issuing the lock table statement to reduce CPU consumption caused by page locks.

Avoid using subroutines for I/O if possible. It is difficult to construct a query that meets the needs of many applications. As a result, there is a tendency to transfer more data, which also means more cross-memory calls. You may find that changing the SQL statements is more desirable than having application programs contain logic to discard unwanted columns and rows.

The parameters specified during the BIND process can have a major impact on the performance of your application program. VALIDATE at BIND time is preferred over VALIDATE at RUN time. The tables and columns will be checked to see if they exist and the individual binder will be checked to determine if the binder has the authority to execute SQL statements contained in the program being prepared for execution. Validation at RUN time causes the validation process to be delayed until the first time the plan is accessed. The first user will experience delays while the validation process is performed.

Use static SQL over dynamic SQL whenever possible. Dynamic SQL has to go through the same BIND functions associated with static SQL for every execution. Dynamic SQL has to be read, verified, prepared for execution, checked for authorization of binder, and then executed. There is significant cost for the SQL flexibility associated with dynamic SQL. If you have to use dynamic SQL, avoid views if possible because SYSIBM.SYSTABLES and SYSIBM.SYS-COLUMNS are accessed once for the view and again for the base table.

Declaring a SELECT...FOR UPDATE OF avoids potential deadlocks with other applications processing concurrently, which would not be the case if you issued the query independently of the SELECT. When performing multiple row updates and deletes, issuing queries to do set processing is the most efficient. Processing online, using the cursor to indicate what field should be updated, will be the next choice followed by multiple update and delete statements. If the column you are updating is contained in an index, you may want to consider deleting the row and reinserting it. Unless the update can use another index, a scan would be required.

16.5 PERFORMANCE MONITORING

Monitoring the applications running on a DB2 system can require many different tools. The first such tool is the DISPLAY command. The DISPLAY THREAD command may be used to display the status of a thread or connection on DB2. Coupled with the DISPLAY DATABASE command, you can determine what plan a particular user is executing and the kind of locks held on the table space and index space datasets. For monitoring utilities, the DISPLAY UTIL command is very useful in following the progress of a large load or reload. It provides information on which of the several phases are currently being executed. In the UNLOAD and RELOAD phases, the number of rows processed is recorded and made available to the DB2 command processor.

The EXPLAIN statement is an excellent tool to analyze a query prior to execution. It displays the access method to be used, what indexes if any will be used, the order in which tables and composite tables are accessed, the order in which multiple tables will be joined, which of the join methods will be used, whether SORT needs to be invoked, and the type of locks to be issued. All queries that expect index usage should be explained.

16.6 DB2 STANDARDS FOR PERFORMANCE

The database world is still struggling to decide on standards for a data dictionary, measurement of productivity, and even performance. This section is not an attempt to establish any elaborate standards but merely lists, in the following table, a few statements about what should be in place in various areas of DB2 processing:

Areas	Recommendation
Denormalization	Denormalize tables if there is a requirement to update joined tables.
Vertical partitioning	Consider vertical partitioning on tables with a large number of columns.
Prejoin tables	When data items from two or more tables are nearly always accessed together, create a single table rather than multiple separate tables.
Allocation of DASD space	Use 4096-page size for DB2 data sets
Create free space	It is better to increase PCTFREE and leave FREEPAGE at the default of zero.
Locking	If row level locking is desired, consider specifying PCTFREE of 90.
Table spaces	Use partitioned table spaces for very large tables.
Null columns	Specify NOT NULL WITH DEFAULT or NOT NULL when defining columns that have no specific need for nullable columns.
VARCHAR	Only use VARCHAR when the field is at least 32 bytes long and there is a 30 percent savings per row length. The use of variable-length columns should be avoided unless there is a potential savings of at least 20 bytes per column.
Variable-length columns	Place variable-length columns at the end of a row.

17

Auditing the DB2 Environment

The introduction of databases and online systems in many businesses has offered several new opportunities as well as new control issues for internal auditors. Some of those generally agreed upon control issues of databases in general and DB2 in particular that exist are identified in this chapter, as are traditional controls for less complex data processing environments.

17.1 AUDITING THE DATABASE ENVIRONMENT

The internal auditor has to become involved in the following activities of the database environment:

- Planning for the database
- System design consideration
- Administration and coordination of the database effort
- Documentation of the database

Planning is a staff function and ensures that top management is committed and involved in the decision to enter the database era and will provide continued support throughout the life of the database. Planning is also useful to determine the initial cost of going to a database environment and the operating cost thereafter. The internal auditor should be actively involved in this phase of the database design because it allows him or her to monitor the cost performance of the database and the application in relation to the planned cost.

One of the major failures of the database environment is neither the technology nor the supporting software, but the conflict that results from the need to share data in an integrated environment. The cause of these conflicts is very often the lack of planning for data sharing in the new environment. The internal auditors should be involved in the coordination of the data sharing effort.

The internal auditor must now assess the corporation's ability to deal with contingencies and must review the plans for recovery and backup of the database and attest to its adequacy. Now that the organization's whole data resource is concentrated in one collection and is more vulnerable to accidental as well as intentional threats, the need for adequate contingency measures is greater than ever. The internal auditor must be an integral part of the team that plans for these contingencies.

Database technology has affected the role of the internal auditor more so than any other single individual. It has now become extremely difficult to audit "around the computer," so the auditor has to develop even greater breadth of data processing expertise than the increasingly specialized systems professional. The internal auditor must now be in a position to monitor the effective and efficient utilization of the new database technology.

The success of the database environment depends upon the discipline introduced by a formal development life cycle which describes the deliverable for each phase of development, clear and well-understood responsibilities, and the role each individual plays in the organization.

The internal auditor must become increasingly involved in systems development, preferably as part of the development team; must review each phase of the development for proper controls, provision for audit trails, backup and recovery plans, and effective testing; and must participate in developing those aspects of data administration planning that involve control and auditability, particularly the data dictionary plan. Internal auditors should understand that their support is essential and can lead to a more efficient, less complex, better controlled database environment.

The internal auditor must be familiar with the commonly implemented controls which now migrate to the DBMS. Some of these controls include:

- Uniqueness checking
- Structure and semantic integrity
- Concurrency control
- Access control
- Restart and recovery
- Audit trail

Access control should include password, sign-on, and user identification verification and authentication. It should also include automatic lock-out of users after at least three attempts to log on to the system and creation of facilities to log those attempts. In addition, access control should include terminal security, logical terminal name usage, and security terminals listing, auditing, and monitoring security violations.

The auditor in the database environment consults with the user on the requirements for edit and validation rules, partial acceptance or rejection of errors, and responsibility for correctness.

The auditor consults with the database administrator on the implementation plan and ensures the existence of procedures for edit and validation maintenance. The auditor determines if the edit and validation rules are sufficient and examines the procedures for adding new data elements.

The auditor specifies what checking of initial content of the database is carried out and may use statistical methods when appropriate to carry out these checks. The auditor also sets objectives for auditing, assessing the environment, and verifies the existence of controls.

The environment control objectives in the database environment should include:

- Adequate documentation
- Recovery and restart procedures
- Adequate security and accessibility
- Complete, accurate, and authorized data

17.2   AUDITING OF ONLINE SYSTEMS

The control issues which are inherent in online systems are categorized into the following basic types:

- Unauthorized access
- Data file controls
- Transmission line controls
- Audit trail considerations
- Output controls
- Failure and recovery considerations

17.2.1   Unauthorized Access

Prevention of unauthorized access to the various stages of the online system is critical to the overall security and accuracy of operations.

The controls against unauthorized access fall into two categories: physical and logical.

Physical controls are measures taken to prevent entry or access to installations. The standard safeguards needed in most installations are security guards, locks and keys, and personal identification.

Logical controls are measures taken to prevent access to the stored data. These include:

- Passwords

- Verification routines

- Audit or management control log

- Restriction on the level or types of access by users

To ensure that logical controls are effectively utilized, a monitoring or review function should also be in existence. A cyclical review of the proper procedures performed each day is usually sufficient and should include the proper sign-on and sign-off procedures, unsuccessful attempts, and attempts to override or patch controls and programs during operations.

17.2.2 Data File Controls

As the transaction process continues from data entry to transmission, the next area of concern is data file protection and controls. The relationship between transaction and programs is reversed in online applications in that it is the transaction that uses a particular program or programs as opposed to the converse in batch systems.

In addition multiple users may need a particular data file at or near the same time, which could lead to a conflict over priorities or errors due to incomplete or inaccurate updating. A supervisory program is usually employed to prevent application programs from getting to the database. This exclusive control function is responsible for granting permission for such access. While one program is using a file, others are prevented from doing so, or locked out, until control is passed back to the supervisory program. This locking mechanism, present in DB2, eliminates the possibility of two programs becoming deadlocked when each has one file or record or rows and needs a second which the other program has, while it waits for what the first program has.

17.2.3 Evaluation of Controls

In the online environment, a proper evaluation of the controls which should be in place as well as those which are in operation is necessary for any reliance on their use.

Proper documentation is one important element required for auditors to understand how and why the system operates as it does. With the loss of many conventional audit procedures inherent in such advanced systems, an adequate description of the steps and stages of processing and record keeping will be the basis for choosing how the subsequent compliance and substantive testing will be done.

17.3 INHERENT DB2 CONTROL FEATURES AND FUNCTIONS

The internal auditor who must audit the DB2 environment must be familiar with some of the following environment control features:

- Provide effective protection of system resources and data from unauthorized intruders of a distributed database processing network
- Provide protection against unauthorized modifications to programs or system code by those responsible for installing and maintaining the system
- Execution of SQL operations and DB2 utilities or commands requires the executor to hold specific authorities
- Properly capture and report on authorization violations and security breaches
- Allow for the definition and enforcement of primary keys and entity integrity constraints
- Maintain an internal catalog integrity control mechanism that does not allow data structure definitions to be at variance or inconsistent with previously defined data objects
- Provide utilities and service aids to verify DB2 internal data structure integrity
- Provide performance monitoring and turning facilities to ensure continuous, reliable DBMS operation and maintenance of service levels
- Provide data relationships by value instead of by pointer

17.4 AUDITABILITY OF DB2

Auditability may be defined as the measures and provisions taken to facilitate the tracking and recording of significant processing events and system changes so that the controls in place can be effectively reviewed and assessed. DB2 has provision for auditability since it provides several of the features necessary for maintaining data integrity and security.

17.4.1   Evidence of Auditability in DB2

Auditability is established by the existence of and consistent use of audit trails. Auditability in DB2 should be established in the following areas:

- *Transaction:*   Verify the complete, correct, and accurate processing transactions as intended
- *System:*   Record and track DB2 and application processing events, authorization activity, access attempts, and access denials
- *Recovery:*   Record DB2 system events and data changes in the event that a failure occurs and the DB2 system and/or its data needs to be restored
- *Program change:*   Record and track changes to the program or DB2 system code, definitions, and installation parameters

17.4.2   DB2 Audit Objectives

The internal auditor bent on auditing the DB2 environment must establish some audit objectives. The following objectives are suggested:

- To examine the trail of DB2 system activity to alert management of potential or real (1) security penetrations and authorization procedure breaches, (2) data integrity problems, and (3) duty segregation issues
- To assess the control techniques used to be reasonably assured that the database environment is conducive to the reliable, complete, and accurate processing of data used to prepare and report information

17.4.3   DB2 Audit Resources

DB2 provides a host of loops, catalogs, utilities, and reports that assist the internal auditor in conducting an audit of the environment. Some of these are:

- DB2 operating environment profile
- DB2 standards and procedures
- DB2 utilities
- DB2 audit trace facility
- DBMAUI reports
- SQL EXPLAIN output
- DB2 display command output
- DB2PM reports and displays

Comparison of Relational DBMSs

This section covers the basic qualifications a product has to have in order to be considered a relational database management system (RDBMS). It then looks at the more detailed list of facilities to be expected in such a system. Charts that compare RDBMS are included. *Does the product include the following features?*

- Database definition separate from programs
- Multiple views possible against same database
- Facilities for administration of shared data
- Access control facilities (i.e., restriction of rights to see or change particular data to those authorized to do so)
- Concurrency control facilities (i.e., prevention of undesirable results or interaction in cases of simultaneous access to data

Some products may be marketed under the database flag while failing to offer the basic facilities for sharing of data. The concept of a single-user database is really a contradiction in terms. Unless this is what you require, you will probably need some facilities under all the headings above.

```
                        Database definition separate from programs
                        | Multiple views
                        |  | Administration of shared data
                        |  |  | Access control
                        |  |  |  | Concurrency control
                        |  |  |  |  |
ADABAS:                 x  x  x  x  x
BL700:                  x  x  x  x  x
CA-UNIVERSE:            x  x  x  x  x
CRESTA/DB:              x  x  x  x  x
DATACOM/DB:             x  x  x  x  x
DB2:                    x  x  x  x  x
FOCUS:                  x  x  x  x  x
IDMS/R:                 x  x  x  x  x
Model 204:              x  x  x  x  x
ORACLE:                 x  x  x  x  x
SQL/DS:                 x  x  x  x  x
SUPRA:                  x  x  x  x  x
Sybase:                 x  x  x  x  x
```

Does the product include the following features?

- Are all commands independent of the existence of any access path support (e.g., indexes)?
- Is all data viewed in third normal form (TNF) relations?
- Does the command language include functional capabilities equivalent to SELECT, PROJECT, and JOIN of relational algebra?
- Is data resulting from any command on existing relations another relation (i.e., the system is closed)?
- Are restructuring commands (ADD/DROP a table or column) included and are executable interactively?

A product that falls seriously short here should not be considered truly relational. Mitigating circumstances might include the following:

1. A product with which hierarchical or network structures are possible, but where a "relational only" subset can be enforced
2. A product which allows "export" of data to other systems may have facilities to create nonrelational data (an extension of the concept of printing a result relation in some report format)

A product with no JOIN functionality (see later question) should not be considered as a serious RDBMS candidate. In conclusion, one is forced to say that the products in the list fall into two classes:

- Those that are relational in the sense that they can *only* be used in a relational manner

- Those that are relational in the sense that they *can* limit usage to being in a relational manner by not using certain facilities or by masking them out by front ends

If the vendors of products in the second group claim to be flying the relational flag but then offer instructions to user staff that involve use of the product in a nonrelational manner (i.e., other than in the questions above), they are not selling a RDBMS.

Does the product permit the use of predefined access path support at the physical level? If so, which types of support are permitted?

- Primary key index

- Secondary indexes (including bit maps, etc.)

- Pointer arrays (index tables listing addresses or keys of records of type B that are related to each instance of record type A)

- Record chains

As stated above, the existence of a predefined access path support at the physical level does not necessarily disqualify a product from the relational club as long as it is invisible to programs and DBA utilities (except for tuning purposes).

	Primary key index	Secondary indexes	Pointer arrays	Pointer chains	Other
ADABAS:	x	x	-	-	$
BL700:	x	x	-	-	-
CA-UNIVERSE:	x	x	-	-	-
CRESTA/DB:	x	x	x	-	-
DATACOM/DB:	x	x	x	-	-
DB2:	x	x	-	-	-
FOCUS:	x	x	-	x	*
IDMS/R:	x	x	-	x	-
Model 204:	-	x	x	-	-
ORACLE:	x	x	-	-	x!
SQL/DS:	x	x	-	-	-
SUPRA:	x	x	x	-	-
Sybase:	x	x	-	-	@

* Choice of above may be program defined.
! Table clustering.
+ Hash random and clustering.
@ Clustered index.
$ Hash random.

Does the product provide the following relational features?

- Enforcement of referential integrity (i.e., allowing specification of constraints on foreign keys)
- Enforcement of entity integrity (i.e., null values not allowed in primary keys)
- Definition of named VIEWS (i.e., virtual relations desirable by normal commands from stored relations or other VIEWS)
- Outer joins
- Greater-than and less-than joins as well as joins based on equality of corresponding attributes

These features are considered part of the mainstream relational theory but are not always included in RDBMS products.

Referential integrity is important because it expresses the way things work in many practical situations. For example, if one is adding orders to an order relation, one should make sure that the customer number on the order already appears in the customer relation. Likewise, when deleting customers, one should ensure that there are no orders in the order relation with the same customer number as that being deleted. Customer number is a foreign key of the order relation, and the referential integrity constraint needed is that the customer number for any order must exist in the customer relation for some customer. In addition, null (i.e., unknown) foreign key values may or may not be permitted. Some older (i.e., prerelational) products are more flexible here than the orthodox products like SQL, although sometimes integrity is forced on insertion but not on deletion.

Views have many uses including access control and increased data independence. Some products offer a macro facility in the language that defines a view, but this is not to be considered equivalent since there is then no named virtual relation that can be treated as the object of further commands.

Outer joins also express the functionality required for many practical instances. When making a join, one often wishes to keep the information about the rows that do not have any match in the other relation. Instead of dropping this information, an outer join creates a row in the joined relation with null values for the attributes of the other relation.

Some of the positive answers to the first two questions may have been based on specifying the conditions within a command language rather than as a constraint embedded within the data definition. Another possibility is that those DBMSs that allow nonrelational structures may be enforcing referential integrity through their linkage mechanisms (e.g., hierarchies or codasyl sets).

```
              Commands independent of access path support
              | Data viewed in TNF relations
              |  | SELECT, PROJECT, JOIN capabilities
              |  |  | Closed system
              |  |  |  | Restructuring commands
              |  |  |  | |
ADABAS:       x  x  x  -  x
BL700:        x  x* x  x  x
CA-UNIVERSE:  x  x  x  x  x
CRESTA/DB:    x  x  x  -  x
DATACOM/DB:   x  x  x  x  x
DB2:          x  x  x  x  x!
FOCUS:        x  x  x  x+ -
IDMS/R:       x  x  x  x  x
Model 204:    x  -  x  -  x
ORACLE:       x  x  x  x  x
SQL/DS:       x  x@ x  x  x^
SUPRA:        x  x  x  x  x
Sybase:       x  x  x  x  x
```

* This is possible but not required.
! Yes; except 'dropping' a column from an existing table is not possible.
+ Optional under program control.
@ Optional.
^ Cannot drop a column.

```
              Referential integrity
              | Entity integrity
              |  | Definition of named VIEWS
              |  |  | Outer joins
              |  |  |  | Greater-than and less-than joins
              |  |  |  | |
ADABAS:       x  x  x  x  x
BL700:        -  x  x  x  x
CA-UNIVERSE:  x  x  x  x  x
CRESTA/DB:    -* x  -  x  -
DATACOM/DB:   x  x  x  x  x
DB2:          x  x  x  -+ x
FOCUS:        x  x  -  x  -
IDMS/R:       x  x  x  x  x
Model 204:    x  x  x  x  x
ORACLE:       -  x  x  x  x
SQL/DS:       x  x  x  -  x
SUPRA:        x  x  x  x  x
Sybase:       x  x  x  x  x
```

* Partially.
+ Except by program offering DB2 outer join.

Does the product provide a freestanding user language in which the database can be accessed and updated without the use of a normal programming language? If so, does it conform to any of the following prospective or de facto standards?

- SQL (as ANSI X3 H2 draft standard)
- SQL superset
- QUEL (Berkeley-type RDBMS language)
- Vendor's own syntax

Whereas previous DBMSs were very often primarily host-language based, the norm with relational DBMSs is to base most access on a user language—which may or may not be very suitable for naive users. Such a user language would be regarded as a requirement, and use of one of the *de facto* standards (SQL, QUEL) is desirable.

```
            SQL
            |  SQL superset
            |  |  QUEL
            |  |  |  Vendor's own syntax
            |  |  |  |  Other
            |  |  |  |  |
ADABAS:     x  -  -  x  -
BL700:      x  -  x  -  -
CA-UNIVERSE: -  x  x  -  -
CRESTA/DB:   -  -  -  x  -
DATACOM/DB:  x  x  -  x  -
DB2:        x  x  -  -  -
FOCUS:      x  -  -  x  -
IDMS/R:     x* -  -  x  -
Model 204:   -  -  -  x  -
ORACLE:     x  x  -  -  -
SQL/DS:     x  x  -  -  -
SUPRA:      x  x  -  -  -
Sybase:     x! x  -  -  -
```

*SQL is retrieval only in current release.
!Transact SQL.

Does the user language (if provided) include the following commands or their equivalent?

- SELECT (WHERE condition)
- PROJECT (all columns, named columns only, all except named columns)
- JOIN
- DIVIDE (join followed by project of first relation's columns only)
- ORDER (by sort key)

- INSERT (new rows)
- DELETE (on selected rows)
- UPDATE (on selected rows)
- UNION (set operations on compatible tables)
- INTERSECTION (set operations on compatible tables)
- DIFFERENCE (set operations on compatible tables)
- GROUP BY (merge rows with same values of the specified attribute)
- HAVING (condition on aggregate value of an attribute in a relation undergoing GROUP BY)

	SELECT	PROJECT	JOIN	DIVIDE	ORDER	INSERT	DELETE	UPDATE	UNION	INTERSECTION	DIFFERENCE	GROUP BY	HAVING
ADABAS:	x	x	x	x	x	x	x	x	x	x	-	-	-
BL700:	x	x	x	x	x	x	x	x	-	-	-	x	x
CA-UNIVERSE:	x	x	x	x	x	x	x	x	x	x	x	x	x
CRESTA/DB:	x	x	x	x	x	x	x	x	x	x	x	x	x
DATACOM/DB:	x	x	x	x	x	x	x	x	x	-	-	x	x
DB2:	x	x	x	x	x	x	x	x	x	x	-	x	x
FOCUS:	x	x	x	x	x	x	x	x	x	x	x	x	x
IDMS/R:	x	x	x	x	x	x	x	x	x	x	x	x	x
Model 204:	x	x	x	x	x	x	x	x	x	x	x	x	x
ORACLE:	x	x	x	x	x	x	x	x	x	x	x	x	x
SQL/DS:	x	x	x	x	x	x	x	x	x	x	-	x	x
SUPRA:	x	x	x	x	x	x	x	x	x	x	x*	x	x
Sybase:	x	.x	x	x	x	x	x	x	-	-	-	x	x

* Not directly with SQL.

These commands are essentially the full range of an orthodox RDBMS user language with respect to data manipulation. One would expect all systems claiming to be relational either to have these verbs explicitly or to be able to give the same effect with a fairly brief combination of other commands. The difficulty in reading any significance into the differences in the table is in knowing how complex the formulation is in cases where the direct verb is not used.

If the product provides a user language, which data definition and re-structuring commands are included?

The more orthodox RDBMSs will include the commands in the table in the same user language, but some have separate facilities—and possibly provide just as adequate functionality.

```
                    CREATE TABLE
                    | ALTER TABLE
                    |  | ADD attribute
                    |  |  | DROP attribute
                    |  |  |  | DROP TABLE
                    |  |  |  |  | CREATE VIEW
                    |  |  |  |  |  | DROP VIEW
                    |  |  |  |  |  |  | NULL VALUE of attribute
                    |  |  |  |  |  |  | |
ADABAS:             x  x  x  x  x  x  x  x
BL700:              x  x  -  -  x  x  x  -
CA-UNIVERSE:        x  x  x  x  x  x  x  -
CRESTA/DB:          x  x  x  x  x  x  x  x
DATACOM/DB:         x  x  x  x  x  x  x  x
DB2:                x  x* x  -  x  x  x  x
FOCUS:              x  x  x  x  x  -  -  -
IDMS/R:             x  x  x  x  x  x  x  -
Model 204:          x  x  x  x  x  x  x  x
ORACLE:             x  x  x  x  x  x  x  x
SQL/DS:             x  x  x  -  x  x  x  x
SUPRA:              x  x  x  x  x  x  x  x
Sybase:             x  x  x  -  x  x  x  x
```

* The SQL ALTER statement allows changes to be made to indexes, tables, storagegroups, and tablespaces. Not all properties may be changed using the ALTER statement; some changes may require objects to be dropped and recreated.

The following is involved in modifying the data definition for each of the systems:

ADABAS	Use of PREDICT online data dictionary.
BL700	Copying table over. This requires one command.
CA-UNIVERSE	Change made to activate data dictionary using ALTER command or through the data modeling facility—the rest is automatic.
CRESTA/DB	Not difficult.
DATACOM/DB	Execution of the command which is processed by DATACOM/DB and recorded in DATADICTIONARY automatically.

DB2	Some modifications can be done via the ALTER statement; others might require DROP and RECREATE.
FOCUS	Changes are made to a key word-driven data definition file. Changes are actively reflected in applications.
IDMS/R	-
Model 204	-
ORACLE	The data definition held in the data dictionary is updated automatically whenever a data definition statement is executed.
SQL/DS	Fully interactive and dynamically executed. However, for performance reasons tables may need to be unloaded or reloaded.
SUPRA	Alter statement, either interactively or in batch. No table reload necessary. All views adjusted automatically.
Sybase	Issuing new command.

Does the user language (if provided) include the following options on the JOIN function?

- Nested JOIN syntax (e.g., SQL's IN)

- Symmetric linking condition (e.g., WHERE C. CUSTNUM = O.CUSTNUM)

- Recursive join (i.e., on two attributes in the same relation)

- Outer join

- Greater-than, less-than joins

- Full cartesian product

The second option of JOIN is generally regarded as more elegant than the first, although, especially where SQL is an option, both may be provided. Recursive JOIN is very desirable. The more complex types can be used to avoid what might otherwise be very long-winded circumlocutions. The trend is for more RDBMSs to offer them or to be working toward their early implementation.

```
                    Nested join syntax
                    |  Symmetric linking condition
                    |  |  Recursive join
                    |  |  |  Outer join
                    |  |  |  |  Greater-than and less-than joins
                    |  |  |  |  |  Full cartesian product
                    |  |  |  |  |  |
ADABAS:             x  x  x  x  x  x
BL700:              x  x  x  x  x  x
CA-UNIVERSE:        x  x  x  x  x  x
CRESTA/DB:          x  -  x  x  -  -
DATACOM/DB:         x  x  x  x  x  -
DB2:                x  x  x -* x  x
FOCUS:              x  x  x  x  -  -
IDMS/R:             -  x  x  x  x  -
Model 204:          x  x  x  x  x  x
ORACLE:             x  x  x  x  x  x
SQL/DS:             x  x  x  -  x  x
SUPRA:              x  x  x  x  x  x
Sybase:             x  x  x  x  x  x
```

*   No, except by program offering DB2 outer join.

Does the user language (if provided) include facilities to support the following requirements?

- Save a result relation into a temporary name
- Derived attributes within a row
- Aggregation (over all rows by attribute/column)
- Transaction control (e.g., LOCK, FREE)
- Update transaction control (e.g., COMMIT, ROLLBACK)

These facilities are not classic RDBMS language features but are desirable for practical purposes. For any multiuser situation, the last two can be regarded as essential—although in some packages they are provided in the embedded forms rather than in the user language.

```
                    Save a result relation
                      │ Derived attributes within a row
                      │  │ Aggregation
                      │  │  │ Transaction control
                      │  │  │  │ Update transaction control
                      │  │  │  │  │
ADABAS:              x  x  x  x  x
BL700:               x  x  x  -  x
CA-UNIVERSE:         x  x  x  x  x
CRESTA/DB:           x  -  x  -  -
DATACOM/DB:          x  x  x  x  x
DB2:                -*  x  x  x! x
FOCUS:               x  x  x  x  x
IDMS/R:              x  x  x  x  x
Model 204:           x  x  x  x  x
ORACLE:              x  x  x  x  x
SQL/DS:             x+  x  x  x^ x
SUPRA:               x  x  x  x@ x@
Sybase:              x  x  x  x  x
```

* Not within SQL, but QMF provides this function.
! At tablespace level.
+ Format 2 insert or QMF only.
^ Automatically handled except locktable.
@ Automatic.

Does the user language (if provided) support access to data in a different DBMS by allowing relational views to be defined on top of a possibly nonrelational structure? If so, what DBMSs/files can be handled?

ADABAS	Yes, ADABAS, DB2, DL/I, VSAM, OS data sets
BL700	No
CA-UNIVERSE	No
CRESTA/DB	Not yet
DATACOM/DB	No
DB2	Yes, VSAM through DB/2 VSAM Transparency Program Offering
FOCUS	Yes, SQL/DS, DB2 (Read/Write), SQL/DS, DB2, IMS, ADABAS, IDMS/R, TOTAL/TIS/SUPRA, DATACOM DB, Model 204 (read only)
IDMS/R	Yes, VSAM
Model 204	Yes, through Imagine/204: DB2, VSAM, DL/I, and others
ORACLE	Yes, DB2, SQL/DS, others planned
SQL/DS	Yes, VSAM through SQL/DS Application Interface for VSAM Feature under CICS/VM
SUPRA	VSAM, RMS, DB2, DL/I, and Rdb planned
Sybase	Oracle, RDB, IMS, Ingres, DB2, flat files; provides an open server environment which gives the user the tools to set up links with any DBMS or flat file system

The need for bridges to existing data held in other DBMSs is obvious when one considers that the relational product is often acquired by an organization as a "second" DBMS.

Does the RDBMS include an embedded language which can be used within a host programming language?

	COBOL	FORTRAN	PL/I	Ada	C	Pascal	BASIC	Other
ADABAS:	x	x	x	-	-	-	-	-
BL700:	x	x	-	-	x	-	-	-
CA-UNIVERSE:	x	x	x	-	-	-	-	x*
CRESTA/DB:	x	x	x	-	x	x	-	-
DATACOM/DB:	x	x	x	-	-	-	-	x!
DB2:	x	x	x	-	x	-	x	x@
FOCUS:	x	x	x	-	-	-	-	+
IDMS/R:	x	x	x	-	-	-	-	-
Model 204:	x	x	x	x	-	-	-	-
ORACLE:	x	x	x	x	x	x	-	x^
SQL/DS:	x	x	x	-	x	-	x	x$
SUPRA:	x	x	x	-	x	x	-	-
Sybase:	x	x	x	x	x	x	-	-

```
*  BAL.
!  RPGII, BAL.
@  Assembler, APL2.
+  BAL
^  Assembler.
$  Assembler, APL2, REXX.
```

It is generally a requirement that there are some cases of application logic that will be better written using a 3GL host programming language, and one would expect an RDBMS to support such a facility.

What facilities does the embedded language offer?

```
                    All facilities provided in user language
                    |  LOCK, COMMIT, ROLLBACK, etc
                    |  |  CURSOR functions (i.e. individual row
                    |  |  |                          functions)
ADABAS:             x  x  x
BL700:              x  x  -
CA-UNIVERSE:        x  x  x
CRESTA/DB:          x  -  x
DATACOM/DB:         x  x  x
DB2:                x  x  x
FOCUS:              -  -  x
IDMS/R:             x  x  x
Model 204:          x  x  x
ORACLE:             x  x  x
SQL/DS:             x  x  x
SUPRA:              x  x  x
Sybase:             x  x  x
```

Again the answers reveal different approaches, with some of the prerelational DBMSs offering concurrency and cursor functions through their old-style DML or HLI.

The embedded language should be functionally equivalent to the user language. It may also be the means by which applications involving concurrency control are implemented. Another frequent reason for using an embedded language is for record-by-record processing, where a row cursor is appropriate.

Which access control facilities are provided?

- DBA granting of access permissions
- Granting of access permissions can be delegated by authorized users
- Separate read and write access control
- Access control by table
- Access control by view
- Access control by specified columns
- Access control by rows (specified instances)
- Revoking of access permissions

Access control is clearly vital in any DBMS, since by definition it is concerned with the sharing of data. Therefore, most, if not all, of the above facilities are essential. Access control by views is a particularly valuable feature, since it provides an easy mechanism to introduce controls by both rows and columns.

	Access permissions granted by DBA	Access permissions granted by users	Separate read and write	By table	By view	By specified columns	By rows	Revoking of permissions
ADABAS:	x	x	x	x	x	x	x	x
BL700:	x	-	x	x	x	x	x	x
CA-UNIVERSE:	x	-	x	x	-	x	x	x
CRESTA/DB:	-	-	-	x	x	-	-	-
DATACOM/DB:	x	x	x	x	x	x	x	x
DB2:	x	x	x	x	x	x!	x!	x
FOCUS:	x	-	x	x	x	x	x	x
IDMS/R:	x	x	x	x	x	x	x	x
Model 204:	x	x	x	x	x	x	x	x
ORACLE:	x	x	x	x	x	x@	x!	x
SQL/DS:	x	x	x	x	x	x!	x!	x
SUPRA:	x	x	x	x	x	x	x*	x
Sybase:	x	x	x	x	x	x	x	x

! Using VIEWS.
@ Update access by column, rest by view.

What integrity checks may be defined for the data?

ADABAS	Domain integrity via PREDICT Dictionary (including unique values).
BL700	Macros can be created to test for existence of valid data ranges.
CA-UNIVERSE	Full referential and entity integrity is supported.
CRESTA/DB	Input validation. Check Reports defined by user.
DATACOM/DB	Full entity and referential integrity checking.
DB2	Checks utility, checks index integrity (DB2 V2 includes Check Data utility to check referential integrity). The CHECK utility can check the integrity of an index against the table it is defined for. Three data exits are provided which may be invoked to perform various functions against the data, including checking validity, etc. DB2 V2 includes referential integrity. All the existing DB2 utilities have been modified, as appropriate, to handle referential integrity. There is a new utility, CHECK DATA, which will check that no referential constraints are violated by data in the tables.
FOCUS	Range and existence checks plus referential integrity checks.
IDMS/R	Edit tables, referential integrity, value lists.

Model 204	-
ORACLE	Views may be created with check option such that any updates or insertions must satisfy the WHERE criterion specified.
SQL/DS	Referential integrity. Data must match data type. No domain integrity.
SUPRA	Entity, referential, domain validation.
Sybase	Full referential and domain integrity plus user-defined checks.

Because of their use as end-user as well as production tools, relational databases have a greater requirement for good integrity checking than do traditional databases. Few relational databases are well-endowed in this respect.

Of the following criteria for a fully relational DBMS (which are due to Dr. E. F. Codd), which does your RDBMS satisfy?

- Every value can be accessed via a combination of table name, primary key, and column name.

- The database description can be represented at the logical level in the same way as ordinary data.

- The RDBMS must support at least one language that includes data definition, view definition, data manipulation, integrity constraints, authorization and transaction begin, commit, and rollback.

- It must be possible to update all views that can be updated in theory.

- Applications and terminal activity must have physical independence from the data.

- Applications and terminal activity must have logical independence from the data.

- The integrity constraints must be definable in the relational sublanguage and stored in the catalogue, not in the application programs.

- It must not be possible to use any low-level language supported by the DBMS to subvert or bypass the integrity rules and constraints expressed in the high-level relational language.

Ted Codd is widely recognized as the man who created the relational database market. He has drawn up the above list of criteria which can be used to specify the degree of adherence to the relational model. Some of Codd's criteria may be considered to be of academic interest only; the above list shows the criteria which will be of interest to practical users.

```
                 Access by combination
                 │ Database description at logical level
                 │ │ Language support
                 │ │ │ Update of all views
                 │ │ │ │ Physical independence
                 │ │ │ │ │ Logical independence
                 │ │ │ │ │ │ Definable integrity constraints
                 │ │ │ │ │ │ │ Prevention of subversion
                 │ │ │ │ │ │ │ │
```

	Access by combination	Database description at logical level	Language support	Update of all views	Physical independence	Logical independence	Definable integrity constraints	Prevention of subversion
ADABAS:	x	x	x	x	x	-	x	-
BL700:	x	x	x	-*	x	x	-	-
CA-UNIVERSE:	x	x	x	x	x	x	x	x
CRESTA/DB:	x	-	-	x	x	x	x	-
DATACOM/DB:	x	x	x	x	x	x	x	x
DB2:	x	x!	x	-@	x	x	x	x
FOCUS:	x	x	x	-	x	x	x	x
IDMS/R:	x	x	x	x	x	-	x	-
Model 204:	x	x	x	x	x	x	-	x
ORACLE:	x	x	x	-	x	x	-	x
SQL/DS:	x	x+	x	x^	x	x	x	x
SUPRA:	x	x	x	x	x	x	x	x
Sybase:	x	x	x	x	x	x	x	x

* Most but not all.
! Information about all DB2 objects is stored within DB2 tables (the Catalog).
@ Some but not all.
+ System catalogs are tables themselves.
^ Only views derived from a single table.

DB2 Version 2, Release 2

Since its launch in 1983, DB2 has experienced a growing recognition in the marketplace. It was originally intended as an ad hoc query database management system (DBMS) for use by decision support systems (DSS) with IMS providing the performance necessary for the online transaction processing environment. This dual database strategy has now disappeared and DB2 has become the accepted standard by many customers as the online database system of choice. This chapter reviews the highlights of previous DB2 releases before examining the latest offering, Version 2, Release 2.

Basic research into relational databases continued throughout the 1970s and the 1980s. System R research between 1974 and 1979 culminated in the introduction of Structured Query Language/Data System (SQL/DS) into the VM environment. The announcement of Release 1.1 was made in February 1981. It was not until June 1983 that DB2 Version 1, Release 1 was announced for the MVS environment.

This release was intended for the ad hoc environment using the Query Management Facility (QMF) to assist users in formatting their queries. Also at this time the dual DBMS strategy was essential since DB2 was capable of less than 50 benchmark transactions per second. (TP1 benchmarks were used at this time; they tested the limits of the software but told us little about the performance of the relational model because the workload on which TP1 is based used virtually no relational facilities.

In 1986 DB2 Release 1.2 was announced. It introduced two new features: Sequential Prefetch and the EXPLAIN utility. Sequential Prefetch meant that when a table space scan was being performed, the I/Os would be processed asynchronously, reading in 16 pages at a time. There is one I/O for each of the first 16 pages; at this point DB2 decides that sequential processing is occurring and reads in the next

16 pages with one I/O. From then on, only one I/O is required for each group of 16 pages read.

The EXPLAIN utility enables the application programmer to see how an SQL statement will perform by listing the access paths chosen by the optimizer. For example, in the case of a join, the explain utility will identify which table forms the outer table of the join and which forms the inner; which type of join will be performed (nested loop or merge scan); which indexes, if any, will be used; and whether any sorts will be performed. The Sequential Prefetch feature and a restructuring of the DB2 catalog managed to provide a 25 percent performance gain for this release. However, 25 percent of not much was still not a lot.

In 1987 DB2 Release 1.3 added further functionality. The essential features of this release were the added SQL functions for date and time (including timestamps), increased buffer pool usage, and the use for the first time of linear datasets.

B.1   DB2 2.1: THE END OF THE DUAL DBMS STRATEGY

DB2 Version 2, Release 1 was announced in 1988 with a flurry of claims for vast performance improvements, especially in the ESA world. However, these initial claims have been refined and a performance boost of 25 percent would seem to be much more realistic. It is worth noting that for specific workloads, performance improvements of up to 100 percent have been recorded.

With the announcement of Release 2.1, it was no longer considered necessary to have a dual DBMS strategy: DB2 had come of age and was capable of executing in the order of 200 transactions per second on large processors. So what were the features introduced in 2.1? These fall into the three broad categories of integrity, security, and performance.

Until this release of DB2, all referential integrity constraints had to be coded in the application logic by the programmer. It was now possible to specify the constraints to DB2 and let the system enforce the integrity rules for you. The security features introduced in this release made life easier for the database administrator, who could now grant the appropriate access privileges to a resource access control facility (RACF) group identifier as a secondary ID. Each individual member of the group would then obtain access privileges from the RACF group. There is a security exit which maps the user's identifier (the primary ID) to the RACF group (the secondary ID).

An audit facility was also introduced in this release to allow the auditing of access to DB2 users. There are eight classes that can be invoked but the usual ones for a production system would be tracking access denials, grant and revoke statements, and authorization ID changes via the SET CURRENT SQLID statement.

The performance improvements were essentially brought about by reducing the path lengths involved. For example, the authorization check performed at every transaction execution was reduced from thousands of instructions to just a few hundred, resulting in a marked improvement in performance. A new feature that indirectly affected performance was the resource limit facility. This allowed the database administrator to restrict the number of CPU service units available for a particular dynamic SQL user. In this way it was theoretically possible to allow ad hoc queries to process the same data as the online environment at the same time.

One other feature of 2.1 was the introduction of the segmented table space. This overcame the problems that were associated with having more than one table in a table space. Prior to this release, if a table space scan was performed, the pages for all the tables in the table space were read, even though you only wanted to process one table. Furthermore, empty pages had to be read to discover that they were empty and not required. As you can imagine, this was not a very efficient process.

With segmented table spaces, a segment can be defined to hold the pages for a single table and therefore only the segments for the required table would be read during a table span. What's more, the bit map is referenced so that empty pages are no longer read in order to discover that they are empty.

B.2   DB2.2

So what does 2.2 have to offer us? Announced in October 1988, it became available for general use at the end of September 1989. This release introduced a limited form of distributed data processing to DB2 users for the first time. It is limited in the sense that online transaction processing systems can only read data from a remote location. However, both batch programs and TSO users can update data both locally and at remote destinations.

This release provides a step forward in the sense that data sharing is now possible, but it is a step backward in the sense that a programmer needs to know where the data resides. One of the major driving forces behind the implementation of relational database systems was that in an hierarchical database such as IMS the programmer needed to be able to navigate around the hierarchy in order to retrieve the required data. The introduction of SQL in a relational data system removed this requirement: the programmer simply told the database manager which data was required and it was presented to the program I/O area. It was the job of the database manager to determine the optimal access path required to retrieve the data.

To some extent, DB2 Version 2.2 has introduced a retrograde step in that a single SQL statement can access data from only one DB2 location. Therefore the programmer cannot simply code the SQL without giving some thought to where the data resides. For example, to join data from two or more tables, the programmer must be able to guarantee that these tables physically reside in the same DB2 system. Fine, no problem, the tables are not going to move, or are they? One of the advantages of a distributed system is that it does not matter where the data actually resides; it is freely available to all the systems authorized to access it.

Returning to the origins of the relational database concept for a moment, one of the essential 12 rules defined by Codd was that there should be physical data independence. It should not be necessary to modify an application program if the physical placement of the data changes. However, if in DB2 2.2, you decide to move a table from one location to another (to balance CPU loads, for example), it will be necessary to modify all the application programs that access the moved table if they also access, in the same SQL statement, another table that has not been moved.

"No problem," I hear you say, "We can simply move all the tables involved to the new location and avoid program maintenance overhead." A good solution, or is it? Who actually decides what tables to move to which location? Is it the application programmers who have coded the SQL? Unlikely. It is probably the performance analysts or technical support team who will make the recommendations about what to move and where, based upon performance considerations. Do these people have regular contact with the application programmers? Do they know what programs may be affected by this move? Probably not. Therefore, a system to control all programs used in the distributed environment needs to be established. Alternatively, you could disallow joins, but this is a very restrictive and not very practical approach to take.

B.3   LOCAL VERSUS REMOTE

Having highlighted a potential problem with single-site access from an SQL statement, it is perhaps a good time to clarify the concept of local and remote in the distributed environment. Figure B.1 illustrates three DB2 systems, two in London and one in Bristol. If user 1 signs on to the TDBB DB2 system in London, he will see this as his local DB2 system. Any other DB2 system that he can potentially ac-

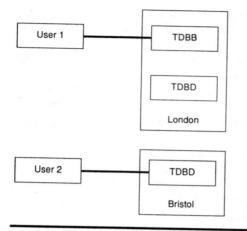

Figure B.1   Local and remote DB2 systems.

cess (TDBC and TDBD in this example), even if it resides in the same MVS system on the same processor, is a remote DB2 system. For user 2 in Bristol, the concept of local and remote is easier. She only has one DB2 system on her processor; the other two potentially accessible DB2 systems both reside in London and are obviously remote.

B.4 DISTRIBUTED DB2

Perhaps now is a good time to examine the way in which the distributed processing is actually accomplished. There are two new system components in this release of DB2, the Distributed Data Facility (DDF) address space and the Communications Database. The DDF is a new address space which enables the separation of any remote DB2 processing from the local DB2 system. This means that the DDF address space can be operated (i.e., initialized and terminated) independently of any local DB2 processing.

By means of database threads, the DDF controls communication between two DB2 systems using VTAM LU 6.2 support. These database threads process requests for remote DB2 data by sending the request to the specified remote system and returning the response to the user's application and, in addition, receive requests from other DDFs and send responses back to them.

The communications database consists of five tables and forms part of the DB2 Catalog. This database is used in conjunction with the DDF to map a DB2 system to VTAM. Before distributed data processing can commence, the communications database must be defined and populated. Data about the local and remote DB2 systems and, optionally, data about users and plans is stored in the database. This information allows users and plans to be stored in the database. It also allows DB2 and VTAM to use the correct modes for conversations.

A conversation is an LU 6.2 notion that marks the beginning and end of a dialogue between two programs over a session with a given mode. A session is the link between the two programs (in this case, the two DB2 systems), and a mode defines the characteristics of that session (e.g., the route through the network and the transmission priority).

We will not go into any great technical detail about the way the LU 6.2 links are established or the contents of the new tables in the communications database. However, we will cover the following aspects: changes to the boot-strap dataset, the types of conversation used, location transparency, block fetch, deadlocks, and finally a brief look at the nondistributed features of DB2 2.2.

B.4.1   Boot-Strap Datasets (BSDS)

There are three new data items which have to be inserted into the BSDS: the VTAM LU name for the local DB2 system (the name that VTAM can identify this system by, for example, DB2LO1), a password, and a location name (a name that the users can identify the DB2 system by, for example, London). The change log utility is used to insert these values into the BSDS. When DB2 wishes to establish a connection to a remote DB2 system for the first time, the password and LU name specified in the BSDS are passed to VTAM for identification and to verify that the password received from the BSDS match was that defined in the VTAM APPL macro.

B.4.2   Types of Conversation

Conversations in DB2 Version 2 consist of two types: a system conversation and a user conversation. When a DB2 system detects that an SQL call requires data from a remote location with which it is not currently connected, it requests a conversation with it. The remote system in turn requests a conversation back to the originating DB2, thereby establishing a full-duplex communication path between them. This is known as a system conversation and is used for unsolicited status information, for example, error detection. Once the system conversation is established, at least one user conversation will be requested for each location referenced in the SQL statement. It is the user conversation that is used to process the SQL requests, including commit and roll back processing.

B.4.3   Location Transparency

Bearing in mind our earlier comments about the programmer knowing the location of the data, DB2 provides a mechanism to make the location transparent to the user and application program. This transparency allows for migration from a single DB2 system to a network of systems. A three-part naming convention has been introduced which enables the end user or application program to point directly to a specific location. In order to simplify proceedings, it is also possible to define an alias for those tables and views that frequently move between locations.

This three-part name consists of the location, the authorization ID, and the object name. Local objects can be defined using either the existing two-part name or the new three-part naming convention. The DB2 catalog table SYSIBM.SYSTABLES has been modified to contain information about objects defined using an alias. For example, the TYPE column has until now contained a T for table or V for view. Now it can also contain an A for alias.

B.4.4   Block Fetch

When retrieving data from a remote DB2 system, it is obviously better from a performance point of view to return data from the remote location in blocks containing several rows than to return it one row at a time. This will reduce the overall transmission overheads and avoid delays between each SQL fetch statement issued by the program. Once the block of data has been returned to a buffer on the local system, the individual rows are fetched for this local buffer, providing the same response as a local SQL request.

In order not to affect processing in the local DB2 system, the data returned from the remote system is not held in any of the local buffer pools (i.e., BP0, BP1, BP2, or BP32K) but instead is held in a separate buffer allocated in the database services address space.

Block fetch is only used when the data retrieved will not be updated. There are several methods that DB2 can use to determine whether the data is required for read-only processing. However, the simplest way to convince DB2 of your read-only intent is by modification to the declare cursor statement in the application program. A new option, for fetch only, should be specified so that DB2 knows that the data will not be updated and will make use of the block fetch mechanism.

Even though you have obtained your data via block fetch, it is still possible to update it. But you cannot specify the update where current of or delete where current of cursor statements. It should be remembered that this only applies to TSO programs or those using the call attach facility since CICS and IMS cannot perform updates at a remote location.

To illustrate this block fetch mechanism, imagine an SQL query sent to a remote system at Bristol which retrieves 500 rows from a table with 1 million rows. These 500 rows will be returned to the requesting DB2 system in London in blocks. The size of these blocks will depend upon the number of rows to be transmitted and the row size but will not exceed 32K.

If you attempt to update data that you have retrieved via the block fetch mechanism, you should bear in mind a potential integrity exposure. Where the cursor stability isolation level has been specified during the bind process, there is a chance that the rows returned to the requesting DB2 system could be updated or deleted on the remote system before the application program fetches them into its I/O area. This is because more rows are read from the remote system than are required at a given instant because of the use of block fetch. If the repeatable read isolation level is specified for the bind process, this situation cannot arise because the pages containing the rows that were transmitted to the requesting program will be locked. No other program can therefore update or delete them until the first program releases the page locks. This affects data concurrency because the rows are returned one at a time.

B.4.5 Deadlocks

In a nondistributed deadlock situation, DB2 chooses the victim of the deadlock on the basis of the smallest number of log records written. With distributed deadlocks, resolution is through a time out at the local site (i.e., one program will time out and the other will continue processing).

B.5 HOW IT ALL WORKS

Having introduced the components of the distributed system, now is the time to describe how the system works. When an application program executes an SQL statement, the SQL request is passed to the database services address space (DBAS). The data manager component in the DBSAS is responsible for accessing the DB2 Catalog, directory, and user data with assistance from the buffer manager. The use of a three-part name (or an alias defined on one) in the SQL statement means that the data manager will know that this could be a request for data from a remote DB2 system. It will examine the communications database and identify the remote system to connect to. The request is then routed to the distributed data facility address space

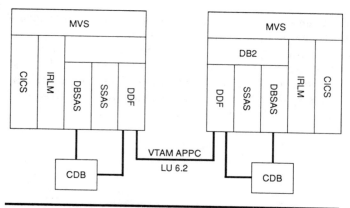

Figure B.2   Distributed database processing.

(DDF) from where a dynamic SQL request is sent to the DDF on the appropriate remote system via a VTAM LU 6.2 conversation.

The request is then routed from this DDF to the DBSAS where it is processed and the data accessed. The qualifying rows are now returned one at a time, or in blocks using the block fetch mechanism via the two DDFS, to the DBSAS on the originating DB2 system. To avoid contention with the local DB2 processing, the usual buffer pools are not used; instead the buffers are allocated from a separate storage area in the DBSAS itself.

Finally, when the application program (in the CICS, IMS, or TSO address space) issues a fetch instruction, one row of data is presented to the program's I/O area. This process is illustrated in Fig. B.2.

B.6   CONCLUSION

In conclusion, we point out that the introduction of distributed processing is not the only new feature in Version 2.2. There are two other aspects that make this release beneficial to users even if they have no intention of using distributed processing or have no requirement to implement some form of data sharing. These aspects are improved index usage and performance.

It is now possible for multiple indexes to be used during query processing. For example, if you were to issue a select statement specifying three predicates which each had an index, the three indexes would be processed asynchronously to produce three subjects of data. The qualifying rows would then be obtained from these subsets. The improvement is obtained by the capability to issue I/Os against all three indexes at the same time. General improvements in performance for this release have been estimated at 11 percent, providing a transaction throughput of 3000 simple transactions per second.

This appendix has highlighted the significant features of previous DB2 releases and, we hope, given you an insight into the world of distributed data processing in the DB2 environment. Despite the limitations discussed earlier, DB2 Version 2.2 offers a practical first step along the road toward distributed processing.

Bibliography

Atre, S., *Data Base: Structured Techniques for Design, Performance, and Management,* J. Wiley, New York, 1988.

Brathwaite, K. S., *Analysis Design and Implementation of Data Dictionaries,* McGraw-Hill, New York, 1988.

———, *Data Administration,* J. Wiley, New York, 1985.

———, "Management Involvement in Data Security, Integrity, and Privacy," *AGT Tech. Memo,* No. 15, 1980.

———, "A Study of Data Base Security, Integrity and Privacy in a Large Public Utility," *AGT Tech. Memo,* No. 20, 1980.

Brown, D., "RACF—A Program to Enhance Security and Control," *EDPACS,* vol. 6, no. 12, Institute of Internal Auditors, June 1979.

Brown, P. S., "Computer Security—A Survey," *NCC,* 1976, AFIPS Press.

———, *Security: Checklist for Computer Center Self-Audits,* AFIPS Press, Arlington, VA, 1979.

Chen, P. P. (ed.), *Proceedings of the International Conference of Entity-Relationship Approach to Systems Analysis and Design,* North-Holland Publishing, 1979.

———, *Proceedings of the International Conference on Entity-Relationship Approach to Information Modelling and Analysis,* North-Holland Publishing, 1981.

Courtney, R. H., "Security Risk Assessment in Electronic Data Processing Systems," *AFIPS Conf. Proc. 46,* 1979, NCC 97–104, AFIPS Press, Arlington, VA, 1977.

Davenport, R. A., "Data Analysis for Database Design," *The Australian Computer Journal,* vol. 10, no. 4, 1979, pp. 122–137.

Dinardo, C. T., *Computers and Security,* AFIPS Press, Arlington, VA, 1978.

Durell, W. R., *Data Administration,* McGraw-Hill, New York, 1985.

Engelman, C., "Audit and Surveillance of Multi-level Computing Systems," *MTR-3207,* The Mitre Corporation, June 1975.

Fernandez, E. B., *Database Security and Integrity,* Addison-Wesley, Reading, MA, 1981.

Fisher, A. S., *CASE Using Software Development Tools,* J. Wiley, New York, 1988.

Fosdick, H., *Using IBM's ISPF Dialog Manager,* Van Nostrand Reinhold, New York, 1987.

Gillenson, M., *Database: Step-by-Step,* J. Wiley, New York, 1985.

———, and Goldberg, R., *Strategic Planning Systems Analysis and Data Base Design,* J. Wiley, New York, 1984.

Grady, R., *Software Metrics,* Prentice-Hall, Englewood Cliffs, NJ, 1987.

Hoffman, L. J., "The Formulary Model for Access Control and Privacy in Computer Systems," *SCAC Report No. 119,* May 1970.

Hsiao, D. K., *Computer Security,* Academic Press, New York, 1979.

Hubbard, G., *Computer-Assisted Data Base Design,* Van Nostrand Reinhold, New York, 1981.

Kahn, B. K., "A Method for Describing the Information Required by the Data Base Design Process," *Proc. Int. ACM/Sigmod Conf. Management of Data,* 1976.

Katzan, H., *Computer Data Security,* Van Nostrand Reinhold, New York, 1973.

Korth, H. F., and Silbersehatz, R., *Database System Concepts,* McGraw-Hill, New York, 1986.

Larson, B., *The Database Experts Guide to DB2,* McGraw-Hill, New York, 1988.

Lusardi, F., *The Database Experts Guide to SQL,* McGraw-Hill, New York, 1988.

Lusk, E. L., "A Practical Design Methodology for the Implementation of IMS Databases Using the E-R Model," *ACM,* vol. 4, 1980.

Martin, J., *Information Engineering,* Prentice-Hall, Englewood Cliffs, NJ, 1989.

———, and McClure, C., *Structured Techniques: The Basis for CASE,* Prentice-Hall, Englewood Cliffs, NJ, 1988.

McClure, C., *CASE Is Software Automation,* Prentice-Hall, Englewood Cliffs, NJ, 1989.

Novak, D., and Fry, J., "The State of the Art of Logical Database Design," *Proc. 5th Texas Conf. Computing Systems (IEEE),* Long Beach, CA, 1976.

Statland, N., "Data Security and Its Impact on EDP Auditing," *EDPACS,* vol. 3, no. 4, Institute of Internal Auditors, October 1979.

Weldon, J. L., *Database Administration,* Plenum Press, New York, 1981.

Whitmore, J. C., "Design for Multics Security Enhancements," *ESD-TR-74-176,* Honeywell Info. Systems, 1974.

Whitten, N., *Managing Software Projects,* J. Wiley, New York, 1990.

Yao, S. B., "An Integrated Approach to Logical Database Design," NYU Symposium on Database Design, May 18–19, 1978.

Index

Index note: Entries in capital letters are commands.

ABOUT THE AUTHOR

Kenmore S. Brathwaite has been an author, lecturer, and consultant to the computer industry for more than 20 years. He is president of AKI Group, Inc., a company that specializes in consulting and publishing in database design and development.